Central America Urbanization Review

DIRECTIONS IN DEVELOPMENT
Countries and Regions

Central America Urbanization Review

Making Cities Work for Central America

Augustin Maria, Jose Luis Acero, Ana I. Aguilera, and Marisa Garcia Lozano, Editors

WORLD BANK GROUP

Contents

Boxes

Figures

Foreword

Central America is today the second-fastest urbanizing region in the world. Urbanization is progressing at unprecedented rates and cities are becoming the place where challenges and opportunities are increasingly concentrated. Within the next generation, 7 out of 10 Central Americans will live in cities, adding 700,000 new urban residents every year in the next three decades. At current rates of urbanization, the region's urban population will double in size by 2050, welcoming over 25 million new urban dwellers. Underestimating this transition could increase the creation of informal settlements and the concentration of population and economic activity in risk-prone areas, undermining productivity and reducing the capacity of countries and cities to withstand shocks. Unplanned and uncontrolled urbanization undermines social inclusion, exacerbating crime and violence, which is today one of the most pressing challenges in the region. Moving forward, cities in Central America need to prepare and adapt to provide more and better services, improve infrastructure, expand access to affordable housing, and enable the private sector to create quality jobs for all.

The ongoing decentralization process in Central America has extended the responsibilities of local governments across the region, enabling them to contribute more directly to tackling their countries' most pressing development challenges. This increased responsibility relies on their institutional and financial capacity and on their ability to plan and coordinate with different levels of government where functional roles intersect. Strengthening local governments' capacity is key to improving service delivery and reducing bottlenecks to expand access to affordable housing for low-income families. Meanwhile, understanding the social and economic losses inflicted by natural disasters will be essential as local governments work on preventing future risk, reducing vulnerability, and building resilient cities. In addition, local economic development strategies will help governments support economic growth and job creation, promoting city competitiveness based on the comparative advantages exhibited by urban agglomerations and the region's strategic location near U.S. and South American markets.

Understanding the causes and potential impacts of urbanization is essential to shaping a more sustainable future and to ensuring that all citizens enjoy the benefits of this transition. *Central America Urbanization Review: Making Cities Work for Central America* provides evidence on urbanization trends and the implications for central and local governments. This information will enrich their policy dialogue and foster more sustainable, resilient, and competitive cities. The book focuses on four policy areas: (i) city management and institutions, (ii) access to housing, (iii) city resilience, and (iv) city competitiveness. Taking a closer look at these policy areas is vital for the long-term development of the region as rapid urbanization puts pressure on municipal finances and on the provision of basic urban infrastructure.

I am sure that this book will stimulate an open and constructive dialogue on the challenges and opportunities of urbanization for Central America and will help frame policies and investments, so citizens can have a higher quality of life and enjoy the benefits of more equitable and productive cities.

J. Humberto Lopez
Director, Central America
Latin America and the Caribbean Region
World Bank

Acknowledgments

Central America Urbanization Review was prepared by a core team led by Augustin Maria (Senior Urban Specialist—Task Team Leader) and consisting of Jose Luis Acero (Urban Development Specialist), Ana I. Aguilera (Urban Development Specialist), and Marisa Garcia Lozano (Urban Development Analyst, Consultant). The team acknowledges the main authors of the report's chapters: Ana I. Aguilera [Chapter 1]; Mats Andersson (Municipal Management Expert, Consultant) [Chapter 2]; Jonas Ingemann Parby (Urban Development Specialist) and David Ryan Mason (Urban Development Specialist) [Chapter 3]; Oscar A. Ishizawa (Senior Disaster Risk Management Specialist) and Haris Sanahuja (Disaster Risk Management Expert, Consultant) [Chapter 4]; and Albert Solé (Senior Economist) [Chapter 5].

The team gives special recognition to Catalina Marulanda (Lead Urban Specialist) for her guidance and support throughout several rounds of revision.

The book was enriched thanks to peer review input by Alexandra Ortiz (Program Leader), Nancy Lozano Gracia (Senior Economist), and Austin Kilroy (Senior Economist).

The team also appreciates the important contributions made by J. Humberto Lopez (Country Director); Anna Wellenstein (Practice Manager); Christian Peter (Program Leader); Ana Campos (Senior Disaster Risk Management Specialist); Angelica Nuñez (Senior Urban Specialist); Lizardo Narvaez (Disaster Risk Management Specialist); Luis Aviles (Operations Analyst); Luis Triveño (Urban Development Specialist); Tatiana Peralta Quirós (Urban Mobility and Technology Specialist); and Rafael Van der Borght; and Federico Ortega, Kshitij Batra, Leonardo Espinosa, Rocio Calidonio, Dmitry Sivaev, Benjamin Stewart, and Christoph Aubrecht (Consultants). Bruce Ross-Larsson at Communications Development Incorporated provided editorial support.

This book reflects several rounds of discussions with the governments of the six Central American countries: Costa Rica, El Salvador, Guatemala, Honduras, Nicaragua, and Panama. The continued support and guidance of each government was critical for this analysis.

The study would not have been possible without the generous financial contribution of the Korean Green Growth Partnership Trust Fund (KGGPTF) and the Multi-Donor Trust Fund for Sustainable Urbanization of Switzerland's State Secretariat for Economic Affairs (SECO), the United Kingdom's Department for International Development (DFID), and the Norwegian Ministry of Foreign Affairs.

About the Editors and Contributors

Editors

Augustin Maria is a Senior Urban Specialist in the Social, Urban, Rural, and Resilience Global Practice at the World Bank. He currently works on municipal management, urban revitalization, housing, and urban resilience in Central America and Argentina. Since joining the Bank in 2008, he has worked in Latin America and the Caribbean, the Middle East and North Africa, and South Asia on issues related to urban development, disaster risk management, and water supply and sanitation. He graduated as an engineer from the École des Mines in Paris and holds a PhD in economics from Paris-Dauphine.

Jose Luis Acero is an Urban Development Specialist at the World Bank. Since joining the Bank in 2013, he has provided operational and analytical support to projects in Argentina, Bolivia, Central America, Colombia, Mexico, and Morocco, including work on urbanization assessments, urban policy, access to housing finance for low-income segments, land value capture, and local economic development. While earning his MPA at Columbia University, he had the opportunity to be a member of a team led by Prof. Jeffrey Sachs to provide advice to the government of Paraguay on industrial and economic development. He also worked as an Operations Coordinator at the United Nations Center for Regional Development (UNCRD), promoting regional integration initiatives in Colombia's main metropolitan areas. Jose Luis holds a master's in public administration in development practice from Columbia University, a master's in economics, and a BSc in industrial engineering from Los Andes University in Colombia.

Ana I. Aguilera is an Urban Development Specialist at the World Bank. Her work focuses on improving city management with an emphasis on urban economics and spatial development. She has studied the relationships among urban morphology, productivity, and access to basic services in cities. Her work also comprises survey management and design to measure living standards and socioeconomic indicators in countries such as Jordan, Lebanon, Sierra Leone, South Africa, and Tanzania and in the Kurdistan region. Ana has contributed to various World Bank Urbanization Reviews, including for Ethiopia, Nigeria, Turkey, and Central America. In 2014 she was awarded the Youth Innovation Fund for her work using big data to understand mobility patterns in cities. Ana graduated as an economist from Universidad Católica Andrés Bello in Caracas and holds an MSc in public policy from the University of Chicago.

Marisa Garcia Lozano is an Analyst (Consultant) in the Latin America and Caribbean Urban and Disaster Risk Management unit at the World Bank. She provides analytical and operational support to projects on slum upgrading, urban renewal, and local economic development in Central America and Argentina. Before joining the Bank, Marisa was an Environmental Peacebuilding Intern at the Environmental Law Institute, where she conducted research on populations displaced by Hurricane Katrina and Superstorm Sandy and benefit-sharing natural resources trust funds. Between 2011 and 2013, she worked on a Caribbean cultural heritage project at the Organization of American States. She has also performed consulting work for Nathan Associates Inc. and RTI International. Marisa holds a master's degree in international development studies from The George Washington University and a bachelor's degree in international relations from Tecnológico de Monterrey.

Contributors
Chapter 1: Ana I. Aguilera, Urban Development Specialist

Chapter 2: Mats Andersson, Municipal Management Expert, Consultant

Chapter 3: Jonas Ingemann Parby, Urban Development Specialist, and David Ryan Mason, Urban Development Specialist

Chapter 4: Haris Sanahuja, Disaster Risk Management Expert, Consultant, and Oscar A. Ishizawa, Senior Disaster Risk Management Specialist

Chapter 5: Albert Solé, Senior Economist

Abbreviations

AAL	annual average loss
AAUD	Authority of Urban and Household Sanitation
AI	Agglomeration Index
AMG	Metropolitan Area of Guatemala
ANIP	National Authority for Public Income, Panama
BPO	business process outsourcing
CAPRA	Central American Probabilistic Risk Assessment
CDRP	Country Disaster Risk Profile
CEPAL	United Nations Economic Commission for Latin America and the Caribbean
CINDE	Costa Rican Investment Promotion Agency
COAMSS	Council of Mayors of the Metropolitan Area of San Salvador
CPF	Country Partnership Framework
CRCR	Constitution of the Republic of Costa Rica
CRES	Constitution of the Republic of El Salvador
CRG	Constitution of the Republic of Guatemala
CRH	Constitution of the Republic of Honduras
CRN	Constitution of the Republic of Nicaragua
CRP	Constitution of the Republic of Panama
DMSP	Defense Meteorological Satellite Program
DRFI	Disaster Risk Financing and Insurance Program
DRM	disaster risk management
EM-DAT	Emergency Events Database
EMPAGUA	Municipal Water Company, Guatemala City
ENSO	El Niño-Southern Oscillation
EPZ	export processing zone
EQ	earthquake
FDI	foreign direct investment
FODES	Social Development Fund, El Salvador

FUNDASAL	Salvadorian Foundation for Development and Low-Cost Housing
GDI	gross domestic investment
GDP	gross domestic product
GFDRR	Global Facility for Disaster Reduction and Recovery
GHSL	Global Human Settlements Layer
GLEAM	Global Economic Activity Map
GMA	greater metropolitan area
HU	hurricane
IDB	Inter-American Development Bank
IMF	International Monetary Fund
INIFOM	Nicaraguan Institute for Municipal Development
INVU	National Institute for Housing and Urbanism, Costa Rica
ISDEM	Salvadorian Institute for Municipal Development
LAC	Latin America and the Caribbean
LED	local economic development
MFI	microfinance institution
MIDES	integral management of solid waste
MIVIOT	Ministry of Housing and Territorial Planning
MNC	multinational corporation
NOAA	National Oceanic and Atmospheric Administration
NTL	nighttime lights
OECD	Organisation for Economic Co-operation and Development
OPAMSS	Planning Office of the Metropolitan Area of San Salvador
PCGIR	Policy for Disaster Risk Management
PPD	public-private dialogue
PPP	purchasing power parity
PSD	private sector development
SAT	Tax Administration Superintendence, Guatemala
SCD	Systematic Country Diagnostic
SEDLAC	Socio-Economic Data Base for Latin America and the Caribbean
SEGEPLAN	Planning and Programming Secretariat of the Office of the President, Guatemala
SEZ	special economic zones
SWM	solid waste management
TS	tropical storm
UN	United Nations
UNDP	United Nations Development Program

UNODC	United Nations Office on Drugs and Crime
US$	United States dollar
WB	World Bank
WDI	World Development Indicators
WSP	Water and Sanitation Program (of the World Bank)

Overview

Why Does Urbanization Matter for Central America?

Central America is undergoing an important transition, with urban populations increasing at accelerated speeds, bringing pressing challenges as well as opportunities to boost sustained, inclusive, and resilient growth. Today, 59 percent of Central America's population lives in urban areas, but it is expected that within the next generation 7 out of 10 people will live in cities, equivalent to adding 700,000 new urban residents every year. At current rates of urbanization, the region's urban population will double in size by 2050, welcoming over 25 million new urban dwellers, calling for better infrastructure, higher coverage and quality of urban services, and greater employment opportunities. As larger numbers of people concentrate in urban areas, Central American governments at the national and local levels face both opportunities and challenges to ensure the prosperity of their country's present and future generations.

The region's main development challenges are linked to the lack of social inclusion, vulnerability to natural disasters, and the lack of economic opportunities and competitiveness. A review of the World Bank's most recent Systematic Country Diagnostics (SCDs) (World Bank 2015b, 2015d, 2015e, 2015f, 2016) for Costa Rica, El Salvador, Guatemala, Honduras, Nicaragua,[1] and Panama highlights common development challenges across the region. The reports show that countries experience, at varying degrees, limitations to economic growth and competitiveness. Costa Rica and Panama are the two most advanced economies in the region, yet their education and training systems are not adequately responding to their pace of development, creating a mismatch of skills and jobs. Other causes of low growth and competitiveness relate to low productivity, low investment levels, and lack of export diversification. In terms of social inclusion, the region continues to witness income inequality, economic exclusion, low access to quality basic services, and high levels of crime and violence. Last, the SCDs underline the exposure and vulnerability of all six Central American countries to natural disasters, and identify resilience as an important policy priority. While improved urban policies alone cannot address all these issues, they are instrumental in conjunction with other sector-specific policies.

Due to rapid urbanization in the region, Central American cities increasingly concentrate these development challenges. Despite important gains in poverty reduction and increases in gross domestic product (GDP) per capita in the last decades, rapid urbanization in Central America has amplified the challenges concentrated in cities. Inadequate housing, vulnerability·to natural disasters, and low economic growth are common in urban centers. As cities in the region have expanded to accommodate migration and population growth, the quality of the housing stock, particularly in terms of infrastructure access, has not kept pace with demand. A significant portion of the region's recent territorial development has taken place in areas prone to disaster risk. Today, Central American cities contain 70–80 percent of assets at risk, or infrastructure exposed to the potential effects of adverse natural events. This concentration will further rise with increasing urbanization. If the earthquake that struck El Salvador in 2001 hit again today, the potential economic losses would amount to US$1,810 million, or 7 percent of the country's GDP. Despite concentrating the majority of economic activity, cities in Central America are not realizing their full potential. They need to accelerate job creation for the booming young demographic in order to increase growth and boost per capita incomes.

The region's development challenges can be addressed in cities by focusing on the economic opportunities they offer. By addressing the costs of urbanization, Central American countries have the opportunity to improve the region's prosperity and livability. The pace of urbanization in the region demands immediate policy action to realize the many benefits that cities can deliver and to avoid the costs of negative externalities. As in other regions in the world, urbanization in the region has gone hand in hand with economic growth. Cities can benefit from economies of agglomeration, by which the spatial concentration of people and firms leads to higher productivity. In 1994, when less than half of the region's population lived in urban areas, per capita GDP in Central American countries averaged US$5,318. Twenty years later, as the region became more urbanized, per capita incomes doubled to an average of US$11,531,[2] albeit with significant differences between the countries. But the benefits of urbanization are not automatic. Nor can urbanization alone determine countries' development trajectories. Despite the recent growth, most Central American countries would need per capita growth of real income of between 6 and 14 percent to close the gap with the most prosperous countries by 2030.

The *Central America Urbanization Review* provides a better understanding of the trends and implications of urbanization, and the actions that central and local governments can take to reap the intended benefits of this transformation. The report makes recommendations on how urban policies can contribute to addressing the main identified development challenges—lack of social inclusion, high vulnerability to natural disasters, and lack of economic opportunities and competitiveness. Specifically, the report focuses on four priority areas for Central American cities: institutions for city management, access to adequate and well-located housing, resilience to natural disasters, and competitiveness through local economic development (LED). This overview summarizes the main messages developed throughout the Urbanization Review, which includes one diagnostic chapter and four sectoral chapters:

Chapter 1, "How Urbanization is Transforming Central America," offers a diagnostic of present and future urbanization trends, including an overview on the speed and spread of urbanization, the characteristics of the system of Central American cities, and the concentration of economic activity in cities. It also introduces economic and social challenges faced by cities, which will be explored in more detail in the four remaining sectoral chapters.

Chapter 2, "Managing Cities and Agglomerations: Strengthening Institutions for Effective Planning and Service Delivery," highlights the key role of local governments in effective city management to ensure quality service delivery, as well as coordinated planning with the national government for a coherent and sustainable development of urban areas.

Chapter 3, "Making Cities Inclusive by Improving Access to Adequate and Well-Located Housing," discusses the constraints in the housing sector, which policy makers need to address in order to drive a more efficient, inclusive, and sustainable model of housing, integrated with urban development. It identifies priorities at the national and city levels to improve access to quality affordable housing.

Chapter 4, "Making Cities Resilient to Reduce Central America's Vulnerability to Natural Disasters," advocates building resilient cities to reduce the long-term impact of natural disasters on the population and economy. It characterizes the risks and exposure to risk in the region's urban areas, and describes mechanisms through which countries can strengthen disaster risk management (DRM) and increase urban resilience.

Chapter 5, "Making Cities Competitive to Create More and Better Jobs," discusses the potential for local economic development (LED) in raising local and country-level competitiveness, contributing to fostering macroeconomic stability, and strengthening private sector development. It applies the World Bank's global framework on competitive cities (World Bank 2015a) to the Central American context.

How Urbanization Is Transforming Central America (Chapter 1)

Central America is the second-fastest urbanizing region in the world, second only to Africa. When plotted against the global average of urbanization and countries at similar stages of urbanization, Central American countries exhibit high urban population growth rates. Figure O.1 shows that Costa Rica has the highest urban population share (75 percent) in the region, and at the same time one of fastest annual growth rates in the world for countries at similar urbanization levels (2.5 percent in 2014). By contrast, Guatemala and Honduras are at lower urbanization levels with more than half of their population living in cities, but they experience two of the highest urban population growth rates in the region (at an annual rate of 3.4 percent and 3.2 percent, respectively, in 2015).

Figure O.1   Urban Population Growth of Central American Countries Is High When Compared with Countries at Similar Levels of Urbanization

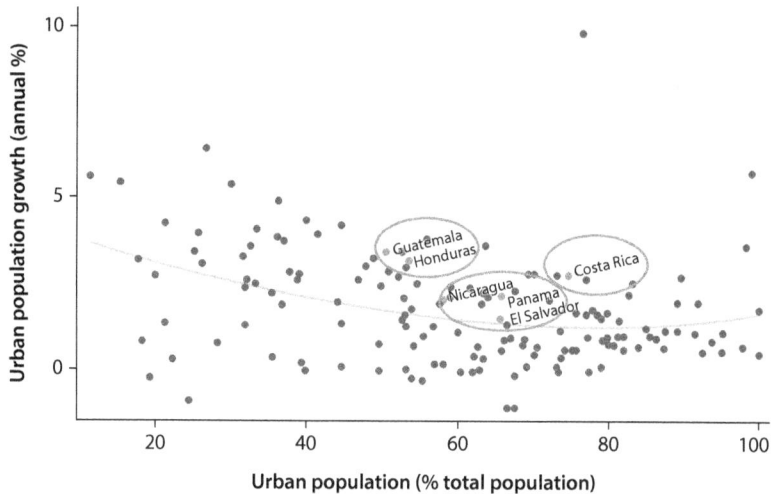

Source: United Nations 2014.

Panama, El Salvador, and Nicaragua have intermediate urbanization levels, around 60 percent, with urbanization rates exceeding the world average and comparable to the growth rates of South Africa or Morocco.

Urban areas are growing faster than the urban population, contributing to rising levels of low-density sprawl. Using data from the Global Human Settlements Layer (GHSL), this report looked at the territorial impact of the urbanization process in Central America between 1975 and 2014. The data shows that total built-up area[3] in the region has tripled over the past 40 years. While the increases in built-up area and population followed similar trends until 2000, the recent trend shows that developed land has been increasing much faster than population. This expansion of built-up area translates into larger sprawling urban areas, increasing the cost of providing basic services and connecting infrastructure. More compact urban development and higher population densities would lower not only infrastructure costs but also maintenance costs. Within the region, El Salvador has seen the greatest transformation, quadrupling its built-up land since 1975. Improved land use planning is needed to manage this expansion in a more sustainable way.

Many urban areas are extending far beyond municipal boundaries. This report presents the results of analysis conducted to identify the largest urban areas in the six countries using various spatial databases. The analysis identified 167 urban agglomerations with a population over 15,000 people. Map O.1 locates the identified urban areas on a regional map. Many of the capital and secondary cities have outgrown their municipal boundaries. Of the 167 agglomerations in the region, 72 encompass three or more municipalities.

Map O.1 Identified Urban Agglomerations in Central America

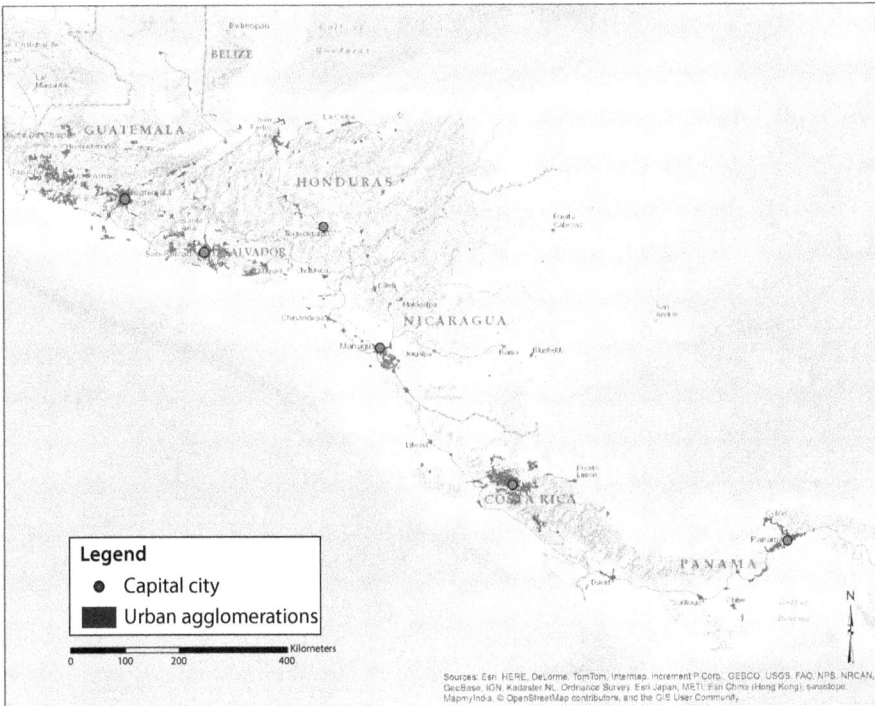

Legend
- Capital city
- Urban agglomerations

Source: World Bank calculations using Country Disaster Risk Profile (CDRP) data and GHSL Alpha version.

The spatial extension of urban agglomerations beyond municipal boundaries poses a challenge to city management. Without the proper intermunicipal cooperation mechanisms, it is difficult to ensure adequate and coordinated urban planning and service delivery at the scale of the agglomeration, particularly in larger cities. With the exception of Tegucigalpa, all the capital cities extend beyond numerous municipal boundaries (map O.2). While all countries in the region have official metropolitan delimitations for their capital cities—depicted in light blue—some of these need to be updated to reflect changing urban dynamics and ensure proper management of agglomerations. San Salvador is a striking example, with the urban agglomeration surpassing the official metropolitan area by twice the size of the official metropolitan boundaries.

Capital cities concentrate a larger share of the urban population than those reported by official figures. In official statistics, about a third of the urban population of Central America lives in one of the six capital cities, and these cities are expected to contribute less than 15 percent of the projected increase in urban population over the next decade. However, with urban agglomerations extending beyond official boundaries, the demographic and economic weight of the capital agglomeration in the country is larger, sometimes dramatically larger, as in San José. More than two-thirds of the urban population in Honduras is distributed between the two largest metropolitan areas (San Pedro Sula and Tegucigalpa). Likewise,

Map O.2 Official Municipal and Metropolitan Boundaries Compared with Urban Agglomerations

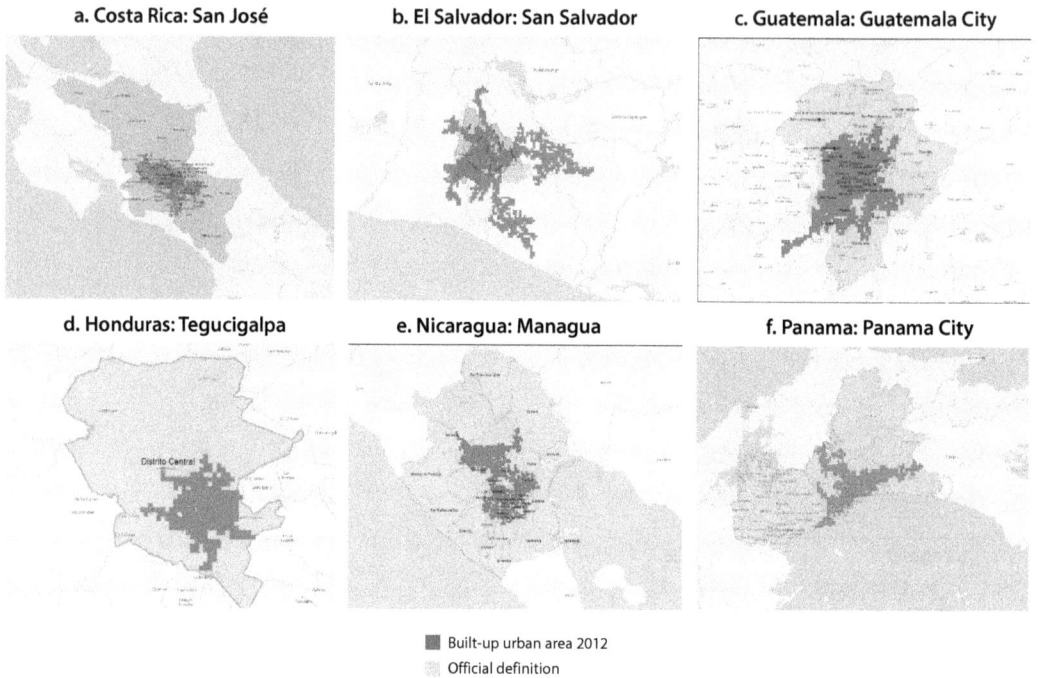

a. Costa Rica: San José	b. El Salvador: San Salvador	c. Guatemala: Guatemala City

d. Honduras: Tegucigalpa	e. Nicaragua: Managua	f. Panama: Panama City

■ Built-up urban area 2012
▨ Official definition

Source: World Bank calculations using GHSL data and census data.

metropolitan Managua concentrates 55 percent of the urban population in Nicaragua, while San José and its satellite cities account for nearly 85 percent of the urban population in Costa Rica. This highlights the imperatives of managing these large agglomerations, due to their current and future roles in their countries.

Secondary cities have grown significantly over the last decade and represent between 15 and 65 percent of the national urban systems. According to official census figures, secondary cities contributed nearly two-thirds of the urban population growth in Nicaragua and Guatemala over the last decade. Cities with a population size between 15,000 and 100,000 inhabitants accounted for 20–30 percent of the population growth in urban areas, escalating their role in the national urban systems. While large metropolitan areas accounted for at least 40 percent of the demographic boom in urban areas, secondary cities and towns are growing fast. In Guatemala and El Salvador, for example, migrant remittances contribute to the growth and expansion of secondary cities. These secondary cities represent a very significant share of the population, and even in small countries, well-functioning secondary cities and small towns play an important role. This report calls for policies that can support the management of secondary and small cities. While most of the existing literature focuses on managing large and capital cities—which requires greater metropolitan coordination to ensure connectivity of services such as transport, sewage, and waste collection—improving the provision of basic services and connecting infrastructure in small and medium-sized cities can enhance their role as trade and logistic centers connecting farmers in rural areas to industrial markets.

Cities Are Where Central America's Most Pressing Development Challenges Need to Be Addressed

Cities increasingly concentrate the region's main development challenges—lack of social inclusion, vulnerability to natural disasters, and lack of economic opportunities and competitiveness—as well as the opportunities to address them. Based on the World Bank's SCDs[4] (Country Partnership Framework in the case of Nicaragua), table O.1 summarizes the key development challenges for each of the region's countries. Due to the clustering of people and economic activity, cities concentrate not only these challenges but also the opportunities to address them. If managed well, urbanization is an opportunity to improve prosperity and livability, but the benefits of urbanization are not automatic. The speed and spread of urbanization in the region demand immediate policy action to realize the many benefits that cities can deliver and to avoid the unnecessary costs of negative externalities. The benefits of cities come from the economies of agglomeration through which the spatial concentration of people and firms leads to higher productivity. However, agglomeration is also associated with increasing challenges, "diseconomies of agglomeration," or "congestion effects" such as traffic congestion, unaffordable housing, and environmental degradation, which can reduce the quality of life and the productivity of cities.

Table O.1 Key Development Challenges in Central America

	Lack of economic opportunities and low competitiveness	Lack of social inclusion	Vulnerability to natural disasters
Costa Rica	• Fiscal pressures threatening the Social Compact and Green Trademark. • Mismatch of skills and jobs.	• Stagnant poverty reduction and rising inequality. • Low access to sewage treatment and solid waste management.	• High exposure to hazards, especially hydrometeorological and geophysical.
El Salvador	• Lack of opportunities and low economic competitiveness. • Limited mobility of the middle class.	• Lack of social and financial inclusion.	• High vulnerability to natural disasters.
Guatemala	• Low economic growth. • Low investment levels and low agricultural productivity. • Weak institutions (low taxation, weak investment climate, frail rule of law).	• Fragmented social contract. • Widespread inequality and economic exclusion. • Malnutrition. • Lack of quality education.	• Vulnerability to natural disasters which disproportionly affect the poor.

table continues next page

Table O.1 Key Development Challenges in Central America *(continued)*

	Lack of economic opportunities and low competitiveness	*Lack of social inclusion*	*Vulnerability to natural disasters*
Honduras	• Regulatory frictions affecting the labor and products markets. • Continued fiscal instability. • Inadequate infrastructure and low access to capital. • Shortage of skills.	• Low access and quality of basic services. • Unequal distribution of access to services harming the poor. • High levels of crime and violence. • Limited access to education.	• Low resilience to natural hazards.
Nicaragua	• External vulnerability due to low economic diversification. • Vulnerability to food price increases.	• High crime rates. • Unequal access to services between income groups. • Limited access to primary education.	• High vulnerability to hazards, especially hitting basic infrastructure, roads, and housing.
Panama	• Limited effectiveness of public institutions and regulatory framework. • Weaknesses in coverage and quality of secondary and tertiary education.	• Increasing crime and violence. • Weak protection of land rights • Increasing concentration of the extremely poor in the indigenous territories.	• Climate change and increased variability in rainfall.

Source: Synthesis of Systematic Country Diagnostics (SCDs); except for Nicaragua, which is based on the Country Partnership Strategy for the period FY13–FY17.

Cities Concentrate a Large Share of Economic Activity and Can Become Engines of Growth

Job opportunities and economic activity are concentrated in cities, especially the largest ones. Research worldwide suggests that more than 80 percent of global economic activity is concentrated in urban areas. Cities also drive the large majority of economic activity in Central American countries. The overlay of urban areas defined in this study with a new spatial GDP disaggregation model applied to Central America shows that cities contribute more than 78 percent to the regional economy. Cities in Costa Rica and Panama represent more than 84 percent of each country's GDP, while urban areas in other countries in the region contribute between 72 percent and 78 percent of their national economies. Within each country, more than two-thirds of the economic activity is clustered in the largest cities (six capital cities and San Pedro Sula).

Cities can contribute to reducing poverty and increasing prosperity. International evidence suggests that urbanization and economic growth are closely correlated. In Central America, urbanization has gone hand in hand with higher per capita incomes and diminished poverty. But the benefits are not automatic nor directly causal for economic development. For instance, Costa Rica and Panama are the two most urbanized countries in the region, and have also experienced better development trajectories in terms of reducing poverty and increasing per capita incomes. However, other factors such as economic and political endowments have facilitated this growth. Despite intraregional disparities, Central American countries made progress in reducing poverty during this period of increased share of urban population, dropping from approximately 48 percent of urban residents living in poverty in 1994 to 33 percent in 2013. Urban areas offer better jobs, higher wages, better access to safe drinking water, and shorter distances to health care facilities. At the same time, cities can sustain economic growth if they transform their economies into higher-value-added economic portfolios.

However, growth in most of the economies in the region builds on weak competitive foundations. Despite the more predominant role of services and industry in recent years, most economies in the region are characterized by the production and trade of commodities with little value added, except in Costa Rica and Panama. These commodities are generally sold through international marketing and distribution channels controlled by large foreign multinational corporations (MNCs) and are subject to both price volatility and the emergence of new entrants in global supply chains. Investment as a percentage of GDP in the Northern Triangle[5] is well below the average of middle- and low-income countries,[6] and, since it tends to target low-skill sectors, productivity gains have remained low, and even flat in some cases, over the last decade.

High Poverty and Crime Rates in Urban Areas Are a Challenge for Social Inclusion

Urbanization has been accompanied by a decrease in poverty levels, but the number of poor living in cities keeps increasing. Despite intraregional disparities, countries made progress in reducing poverty. However, as more people move to cities in search of better living conditions, the number of urban poor has increased in absolute terms, reaching more than 8.3 million urban poor by 2011.

Crime and victimization rates tend to be higher in urban areas. All six capital cities have higher homicide rates per 100,000 population than the national average, with the largest gap observed in Guatemala City (116.6 versus 41.6 in 2010) and Panama City (53.1 versus 17.2 in 2012). Reports by the World Bank and the United Nations Office of Drugs and Crime[7] acknowledge a link between urbanization and higher levels of crime and violence in the region, given the inherent characteristics of urban areas and urban development unfolding in Central America. Poor urban planning, residential crowding, deterioration or lack of public recreational spaces, and insufficient basic public services, compounded with limited access to educational and job opportunities, are well-documented risk factors for crime and violence.

The Growth and Expansion of Informal Settlements Are Linked to Dysfunctional Housing Markets in Cities

Housing, a key driver of economic growth, is an important foundation for inclusive urbanization. The quality and location of housing in cities have long-term consequences for households and governments. Well-located housing provides additional benefits to households by its proximity to jobs, amenities, infrastructure, and services such as schools and health clinics. Housing with immediate access to these services can reduce travel time and expenditures and provide better education and health outcomes. Proximity to basic services such as improved water and sanitation facilities and solid waste collection has direct impacts on mortality rates and economic productivity. As each of these factors influence urban competitiveness, livability, and resilience, broad access to quality urban housing is essential.

However, countries in the region face substantial housing deficits, which contribute to the formation of slums and informal settlements that house about 29 percent of urban residents. The share of urban residents in the region living in these informal and precarious conditions approaches the global average of 32 percent. Between 3 and 10 percent of houses are located in high-risk, disaster-prone areas. The available data suggest the situation is more prevalent in Nicaragua and Guatemala, with approximately 45 and 39 percent of the population living in slums, respectively. In 2009 there were an estimated 11.3 million households in Central America, 37 percent of which faced some type of qualitative deficit. For example, recent data suggest that between 30 and 66 percent of urban dwellers across the region lack sewer systems. Alternatives such as septic systems are more common, but still in most countries more than 25 percent (more than 50 percent in the case of Nicaragua) do not have even these facilities. Additionally, an estimated 290,000 new households are established annually in the region, exerting further pressure on the demand for quality housing.

Countries in the region face similar challenges in access to affordable housing. Cities in the region have been expanding to accommodate migration and population growth, but the quality of the housing stock, particularly infrastructure access, has not kept pace with the need. Housing units with infrastructure connections and in proximity to urban services are scarce—and unaffordable for the poor. Existing mortgage subsidy programs aimed to improve affordability require documented incomes and a prior banking history, which many low-income groups do not have. As an alternative, the urban poor often live in self-built, self-financed housing of varying levels of infrastructure connection and dwelling quality, or in informal rental arrangements. The lack of urban planning and enforcement has also enabled low-density expansion of informal settlements to areas where land and housing costs are lower, including areas at risk of flooding, landslides, or earthquakes. The low-density urban form increases the cost of providing services to these housing developments and contributes to increased congestion and exposure to environmental and natural hazards.

In a Region Prone to Natural Disasters, Cities Concentrate People and Assets at Risk

Central America's geographic location makes it remarkably prone to disasters from adverse natural events, including hurricanes, droughts, floods, earthquakes, and El Niño-Southern Oscillations. In the past 50 years, the number of recorded natural events has increased substantially, affecting all countries. This has resulted in strong adverse impacts on GDP per capita, income, and poverty, hindering the capacity to foster sustainable growth. Earthquakes, hurricanes, and large floods drive the majority of economic losses in the region, especially in urban areas. Meteorological disasters have caused the largest economic losses, while earthquakes, despite their lower frequency, have registered the highest death tolls in the region.

The increasing concentration of population and economic activity in high-risk areas has increased the vulnerability to natural catastrophic events. In Central America, disasters generated from natural events have had devastating and disruptive effects on the foundations of economies, reversing development gains. Between 1970 and 2010, major disasters—including earthquakes, hurricanes, and large floods—caused damages and losses of more than US$80 billion. Annual average losses from natural catastrophic events account for between 0.7 and 2.6 percent of national GDP in El Salvador, Honduras, and Nicaragua. Adding all countries, the regional building stock exposed to risk totals US$232 billion, of which more than 75 percent is concentrated in cities.

Policy Priorities: How to Leverage Cities to Unlock Central America's Development Potential

Improved public policies can address some of the region's most pressing challenges by making cities more inclusive, resilient and competitive. The previous section presented a diagnostic of the ongoing urbanization process in Central America and the common development challenges countries are facing. This section moves on to identify four public policy priorities aimed at tackling these challenges at the city level. The priorities and their accompanying messages, developed in detail in each of the four sectoral chapters, are presented here in that same order.

Managing Cities and Agglomerations: Strengthening Institutions for Effective Planning and Service Delivery (Chapter 2)

Message 1: Empowering local governments, both institutionally and financially, is critical in order to enhance their performance in delivering key services and financing necessary investments for a growing urban population.

Improving local government capacities is key to making cities more competitive, more livable, and more resilient. To tackle urbanization's negative impacts and reap its intended benefits, effective city management is contingent upon strengthened municipalities. Municipalities are the predominant form of local government in Central America, and the ongoing decentralization process in the region has extended their responsibilities. However, their ability to fulfill these increasing responsibilities is constrained by their limited institutional and financial capacity. Today, municipalities' weight in national finances varies substantially throughout the region. In countries like Guatemala or Nicaragua (where local governments' income represents nearly 20 percent of government revenues), municipalities play a critical role. In countries like El Salvador and Honduras, this contribution is relatively moderate (10.2 and 12.1 percent, respectively), and in Costa Rica and Panama it is much lower (7.6 and 2 percent, respectively).

Strengthening the institutional capacity of municipalities is required for them to assume increasing responsibilities in terms of service delivery, and to effectively play their role in terms of territorial planning. Decentralization puts a strain on the capacity of many municipalities in the region, which are expanding their role from one mainly focused on local administrative functions to the delivery of local infrastructure and services. In addition, municipal governments have a central role to play in territorial planning. Although many municipalities do not have the technical capacity to prepare territorial development plans, they play a key role in their implementation as the responsibility of issuing building permits lies with them (except in Costa Rica). Given the magnitude of the challenge, Central American countries should develop a clear roadmap to improve the institutional performance of municipalities, and align their local government capacity-building programs with these objectives.

Although the financial weight of municipalities in Central America is comparable to other countries in Latin America—with local government revenue varying between 0.5 and 4 percent of GDP—resources remain limited in absolute terms. Figure O.2 shows the differences in local government income as percent of GDP. Given that all countries in the region have relatively low levels of public spending as percentage of GDP, the revenues per capita of the municipalities are uniformly low. In 2012, average local government revenues per capita ranged from US$90 in Panama to US$185 in Guatemala. The financial autonomy of municipalities in Central America has decreased, while the dependence on transfers from national governments has increased. As the scope of the functions performed by municipalities has grown over time, the devolution of spending responsibilities has not been matched. In the absence of adequate sources of revenues, the increase in responsibilities has given rise to unfunded mandates. Municipal expenditure has not been increasing in parallel with own-source revenues, deepening the vertical imbalance.

Central American countries can build on existing transfer mechanisms to increase the municipalities' capacity to finance required investments while strengthening administrative and technical capacity as well as accountability. Most Central American countries are using formula-based transfers as the main source of financial support for their municipalities. These types of transparent and predictable intergovernmental fiscal transfer mechanisms are an important component of a sound municipal finance framework. International experience offers examples of how national governments can build on these foundations to develop programs that integrate financial support to municipal investment, capacity building, and incentives for improved institutional performance at the municipal level.

Figure O.2 Financial Weight of Municipalities in Central American Countries

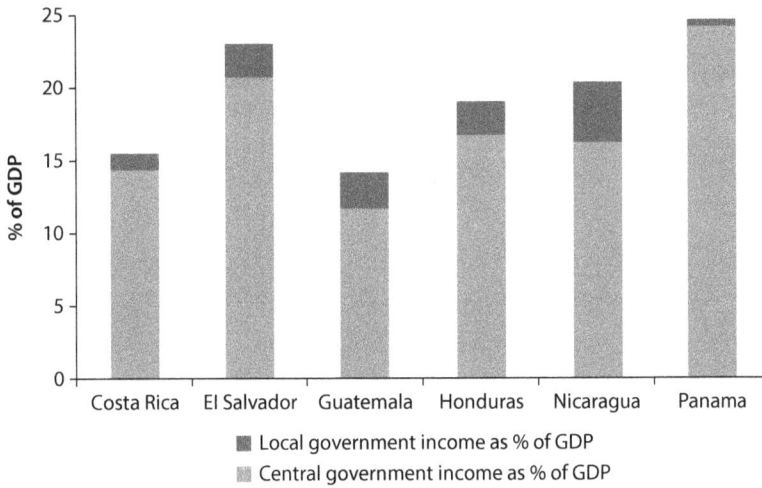

Source: Based on data from the countries' central banks and ministries of finance.

Message 2: Intermunicipal cooperation mechanisms can be strengthened to offer adequate service delivery and territorial planning within agglomerations covering various local government jurisdictions.

The growth of capital cities and other secondary cities is extending beyond municipal boundaries, calling for stronger intermunicipal cooperation. The urgency of developing effective mechanisms and instruments for metropolitan planning and management is especially pressing for the main cities. Many of these metropolitan areas are struggling with fragmentation, underscoring the need for greater coordination among municipalities. Only a few agglomerations have supramunicipal and intermunicipal coordinating mechanisms in place; the strongest example is the Council of Mayors of the Metropolitan Area of San Salvador (COAMSS). Other forms of coordination and cooperation among municipalities that are increasingly developing are Mancomunidades and associations of local governments based on legal agreements known as Convenios. Local governments must work collaboratively to ensure effective planning and equity in service delivery. Provision of some public services, such as drainage, waste disposal, and sewage collection, is often fragmented, resulting in higher costs and financing challenges for local governments. The lack of any formal or informal metropolitan arrangement tends to reflect missed opportunities in cost savings, which can be achieved through fair monetary contributions from all municipal governments sharing common issues. The essence of a metropolitan approach is for local governments to cooperate on some but not all initiatives or services.

Ensuring a basic legal framework and clarifying roles and responsibilities are keys to establishing a metropolitan arrangement. In all six countries, basic legal provisions exist for local governments to form intermunicipal cooperation arrangements. In any metropolitan governance arrangement, there needs to be clarity about functions and responsibilities among the involved parties, particularly if any new authority is introduced, including both the expenditure responsibilities and the revenue sources of the new entity. This needs to be effectively communicated to the constituencies in the area, so they know whom to hold accountable for what. If a metropolitan agency is not given *any* independent authority (and has only an advisory function), the risk of limited effectiveness would be high.

Message 3: Central and local governments can enhance coordination in areas where functional responsibilities intersect, particularly in spatial development and service delivery.

Central–local government coordination is critical, but the scope and emphasis depend on the local context. Municipalities and central government agencies work together on a multitude of subjects, ranging from spatial planning and municipal finance to shared local service provision and emergency response. In some sectors, municipalities may have an executing function within a national regulatory framework, with oversight by a central agency (such as housing, education, and health). Dialogue and coordination between both levels of government are important as more responsibilities are transferred to municipalities, especially when the central government is operating in municipal jurisdictions. The transfer of responsibilities is a gradual process that can be done in stages so that there is a clear distinction of "who does what," and there are no gaps or overlaps in service provision and land use planning.

The scope of functional responsibilities devolved from the central government to the local governments varies quite significantly among Central American countries, as do the need for and approaches to coordination. Depending on the sector and country, the context for coordination is usually one of the following: service provision at the local level is shared between the local and central governments; central government agencies are carrying out their responsibilities within municipal jurisdictions; and municipalities have an executing function within a national regulatory framework. In Costa Rica and Panama, where the central government delivers most local public services, coordinated spatial (land use) planning is critical, particularly for transport and housing development. In Guatemala and Nicaragua, where the municipalities deliver most local services, emphasis needs to be on finance in the vertical relationship (effective tax regimes and intergovernmental fiscal transfer system, ideally with built-in incentives for good local revenue collection and expenditure management).

Making Cities Inclusive by Improving Access to Adequate and Well-Located Housing (Chapter 3)

Message 4: Housing policies need to strengthen the overall system of housing delivery to improve housing quality and affordability for all, across all income groups.

Ensuring the availability of quality housing will help Central America maximize the social and economic benefits of urbanization. Where people live in a city is directly linked to the availability and access they have to jobs, schools, health care facilities, and other public services and amenities that cities provide. However, the current trend of urban expansion has placed new housing farther from employment centers and has raised the cost to government of providing infrastructure connections to these developments. Without improvements to housing quality and affordability, residents will miss out on the economic and human development as well as on the social benefits that cities can provide. The housing sector is a natural "aggregator" of most sector-specific investments in urban settings (such as transport, water, sanitation, and energy). Housing is a determinant of urban form and thus a driver of infrastructure provision and maintenance, and it has direct impacts on the quality of life of the poor and most vulnerable. Improving access and quality of affordable urban housing will have direct impacts on the living conditions and economic opportunities of the poorest and most vulnerable urban dwellers.

Policy interventions should focus on simultaneously increasing the accessibility of housing finance and improving the quality of the informal housing stock. Rather than favoring specific interventions, policy should focus on strengthening the entire housing sector to improve the affordability and availability of housing across income groups. While each country in the region has different housing needs and priorities, housing policies need to address three overlapping themes summarized in figure O.3 below.

- **Cross cutting areas:** These refer to interventions that would improve the overall function of housing markets across income groups. They can include improvements in municipal land administration as well as reforms to planning and building standards to allow formalization through incremental housing improvements and reducing the time and steps required to comply with registration and permitting regulations. This type of intervention would encourage investment for higher density and urban infill developments. Formalizing rentals would provide a flexible low-cost housing option across incomes and age groups.

- **Housing for growth:** Housing interventions should seek to reduce the cost of purchasing a formal house. Housing finance can be strengthened by reforms to the banking sector to encourage competition in mortgage lending and identify screening and qualification criteria for low-income borrowers, including additional support for microfinance lenders and savings groups. This would improve borrowing options for home purchase or self-construction. These policies would also increase demand for materials and labor for formal housing construction.

- **Reducing informality:** Housing stock in informal settlements does not meet standards and often lacks access to basic services. Targeted infrastructure investments in informal settlements can improve the quality of housing through in situ upgrading. This can be further complemented with finance and technical assistance for self-built, incremental housing improvement, and expansion.

Figure O.3 Reforming Housing for Growth and Inclusion

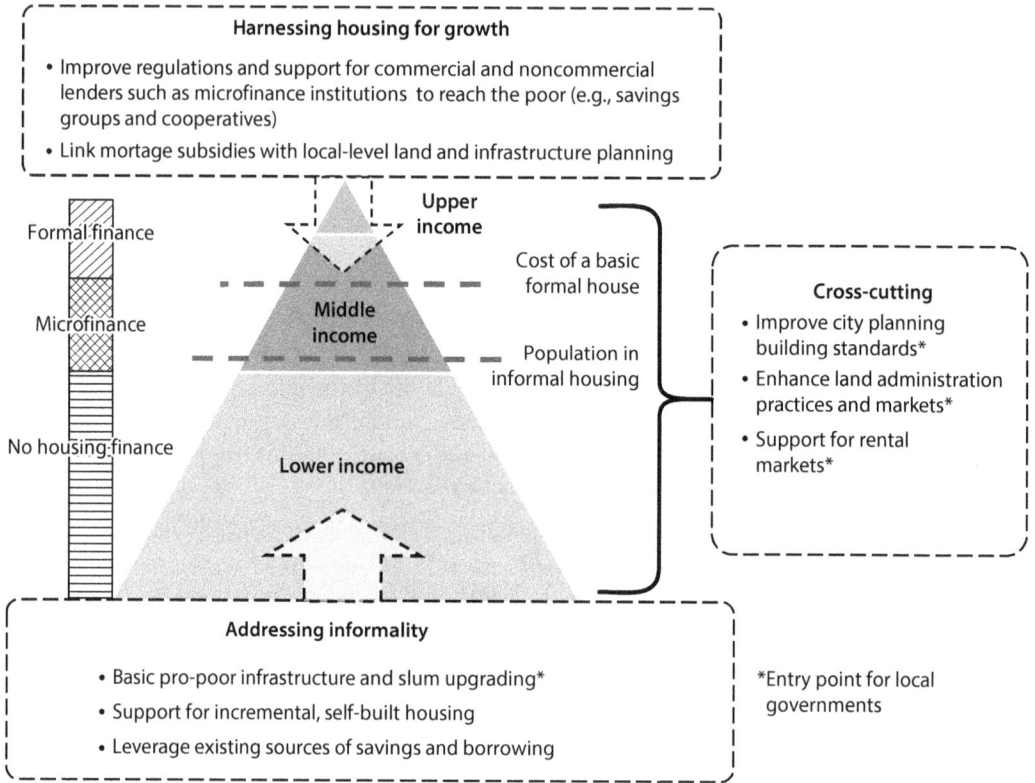

Current policies tend to focus on supporting homeownership while overlooking alternative solutions that could address the broader segment of the market. Homeownership is supported through mortgage subsidies for the purchase of a new, complete house. While these subsidies have expanded homeownership among formally employed middle- and upper-income groups, they do not address other areas of housing need. For example, governments have recognized the importance of upgrading and improving informal settlements to improve the quality of existing stock, but the need remains far greater than what has been delivered. Community organizations and nonprofits in partnership with local governments have also piloted neighborhood upgrading, but these projects have not achieved the necessary scale. Furthermore, renters constitute a significant proportion of urban residents. Renting provides labor mobility and flexibility to new migrants and young professionals, especially those who cannot afford a mortgage. But there is little support for increasing the quality and availability of formal rental housing or for improving the regulatory framework for rental housing to protect landlords and tenants. In order to promote a truly inclusive housing policy based on the actual housing market and stock, these gaps in existing housing policies need to be addressed and targeted on the basis of careful assessment of the national and local circumstances.

Message 5: Housing policies need to be better aligned and coordinated with national and local development planning, spatial planning, and management in order to promote sustainable and inclusive cities.

Cities can have a key role in developing an inclusive housing system, in coordination with national governments. The differing sizes and forms of primary and secondary cities should inform the policy options for supporting housing delivery. For primary and capital cities, a diversity of housing types close to existing job centers and services is needed. Growing secondary cities will need to improve planning and coordination to ensure that new urban growth provides residents access to services and reduces the incidence of new informal settlements. For example, the coordination of local land use and housing development plans with national housing subsidy programs would help align subsidies to improve housing affordability with local planning needs and housing market conditions.

Existing mortgage subsidy programs encourage new housing development outside urban areas, which present additional costs to beneficiaries and local governments. In order to ensure that the prices of eligible units meet subsidy requirements, developers seek to reduce costs by acquiring less valuable land, as has occurred in Managua in Nicaragua. Similarly, in Costa Rica, which awards large upfront subsidies, beneficiaries acquire vacant rural plots and then build housing units through savings or commercial mortgages. Such subsidies encourage the consumption of low-cost land for housing that is located far from employment centers and urban services, which increases the time and monetary cost of commuting to central cities. For local governments and utility providers, this form of development raises capital investment and maintenance costs for trunk infrastructure and public services that these new developments require. National-level housing subsidies programs should include locational criteria to encourage housing consumption through infill development and densification, rather than peripheral developments that contribute to urban sprawl.

Housing policies need to incorporate and strengthen links between national programs and subsidies and the tools and capacities of local governments. Housing policies should promote coordination between subnational governments and relevant ministries—including housing, transportation, finance, and infrastructure—with the purpose of improving low-income neighborhoods. This will reduce overlapping or redundant public investments and will contribute to making direct housing subsidies to urban areas more environmentally and economically sustainable. Similarly, housing policies should support a plurality of housing and tenure options (apart from privileging single-family detached houses) in line with local and regional needs. Local governments would benefit from obtaining tools and capacities to develop local plans that would enable better coordination of long-term infrastructure investment and housing planning with neighboring jurisdictions.

Making Cities Resilient to Reduce Central America's Vulnerability to Natural Disasters (Chapter 4)

Message 6: To prevent future risk, municipalities need to be provided with adequate information capacity and incentives to incorporate disaster risk management criteria into local territorial development plans, investment plans, and building regulations.

In a context of rapid urbanization, with Central American cities expected to host more than 50 million people by 2050, land use planning, building regulations, and disaster-risk-sensitive investments are key to building future urban resilience. Initial location on safe sites is inherently more economical than relocation of existing settlements. Therefore, making Central American cities more resilient is critical to reducing the long-term impact of natural disasters on people and economies. Natural disasters not only have a significant negative impact on the lives of the urban residents in the region—especially the poor—but they also hinder the national growth trajectory. Cities presently contain between 70 and 80 percent of the assets at risk in the different countries, and this concentration will further increase along with increasing urbanization, rising population, and faster economic growth. Poorly managed urbanization leads to increased vulnerability to natural disasters because precarious settlements usually develop in risk-prone areas, inadequate building standards increase vulnerability to earthquakes, and sprawling urban areas with inadequate infrastructure increase flood risks.

Urban and local development planning are under the domain of local governments and offer an important entry point to influence DRM and urban resilience. Infrastructure that is now being damaged by disasters was once the result of public or private investment decisions, so including disaster risk analysis as part of the planning and project investment cycle is a key aspect toward building resilient investment strategies. Additional funding, staffing, and enforcing capacity are needed to implement building regulation at the local level. While most of the countries have national building codes that include disaster risk criteria, permit-related and inspection services are usually expensive and overly complex, acting as a deterrent to complying with code requirements. This encourages informal building, increasing the vulnerability of urban populations to seismic risk. For example, obtaining a construction permit in Nicaragua took 189 days in 2005, but "municipal simplification projects" in pilot municipalities reduced the compliance costs of operating and construction permits by 30 percent on average, and increased business formalization seven-fold.

Message 7: Reducing existing risk will require investments that will need the financial support of the central governments. However, cities will need to lead the prioritization of investments in new risk-mitigation infrastructure and in retrofitting existing critical infrastructure and buildings.

Reducing existing risk requires addressing the vulnerability of built structures. This could be achieved by developing effective systems to prioritize infrastructure retrofitting and, in extreme cases, promoting preventive resettlement.

In a context of limited resources available to local governments, major corrective disaster risk reduction measures prioritized in DRM municipal plans need to be negotiated and supported by central governments. New construction with appropriate designs can be made disaster-resistant for a small percentage of the construction cost (on the order of 5–10 percent), while retrofitting existing vulnerable structures may require 10–50 percent of the building value.

In addition to local government commitment, engagement by the central government remains critical to support financing disaster reduction plans, as part of broader disaster risk reduction strategies. The lack of clear mandates pertaining to DRM responsibilities in the countries' sectoral regulatory frameworks (water, electricity, transport, housing, and so on), compounded by the slow decentralization of public services, have hindered the capacity of local governments to efficiently deliver disaster-resilient public services. In this context, there is work to be done within line ministries and central entities providing public services to update their sectoral regulatory frameworks to include explicit responsibilities to identify and reduce disaster risks.

Reducing the vulnerability of the existing built infrastructure is critical. Most of the major urban agglomerations in Central America are in seismic-prone areas and have been affected by destructive earthquakes at different times in history. Removing, replacing, and retrofitting existing unregulated and unsafe buildings require an incremental approach that can reduce disaster risk over a reasonable period at a feasible cost. Prioritizing critical infrastructures—such as schools, hospitals, potable water treatment plants, bridges, and drainage systems—can facilitate the engagement of local and national governments and increase the efficiency of public spending.

Message 8: To enhance the understanding of disaster risk, national governments need to improve the knowledge base of vulnerability exposure and hazard profiles at the city level and make them available to local actors.

Improving the knowledge base of vulnerability exposure and hazard profiles is a basic condition to identify and implement policies to reduce disaster risk and improve urban resilience. Understanding disaster risk implies, first, comprehensive knowledge of the natural events that could have a negative impact on peoples and assets in the territory, including attributes such as frequency, returning periods, probabilities, and intensities (understanding the hazard). Second, it is necessary to identify people and the type of assets (including construction materials and values) that are exposed to those hazards (understanding the exposure), which is a dynamic aspect in a context of rapid urbanization processes. Third, once the exposed segments of the population and assets are identified, the assessment of their specific vulnerability to specific hazards needs be determined (understanding the vulnerability), to finally assess the likelihood of a negative impact (understanding the disaster risk).

Sound local hazard information needs to be developed for the effective inclusion of disaster risk criteria in local land use planning. Currently, hazard maps in the region are mostly available at low-resolution national scales (especially for small and medium-size cities), and therefore inadequate to inform the

Map O.3 CDRP Building Exposure Model for Panama City, Panama

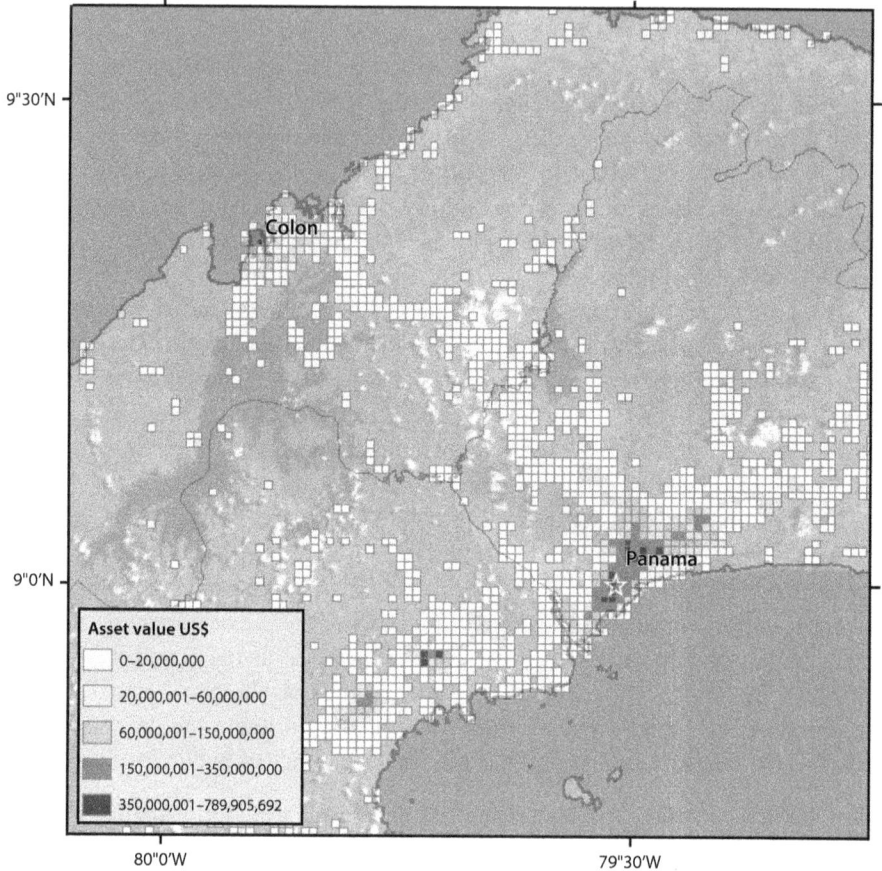

Source: World Bank 2015c.

diagnostic stages of local land use plans. Comprehensive risk identification methodologies such as risk maps (based on historical impacts) or probabilistic risk assessments can inform local actors and be easily incorporated in land use planning and spatial zoning. The Central America Country Disaster Risk Profile project, led by the World Bank, had the objective of contributing to this goal by assessing potential direct economic losses from adverse natural events and by assisting governments in long-term planning and preparedness. Map O.3 shows the building exposure model for Panama City, where most of the value of building stock is concentrated in the downtown area.

Making Cities Competitive to Create More and Better Jobs (Chapter 5)

As urbanization concentrates economic activity in cities, improving their competitiveness becomes more important. International experience shows that a subnational lens to economic development can provide Central American countries with new avenues for policy making to support their economic transition. Competitive cities can sustain economic success by adopting LED policies to support the growth of existing firms, attract outside investors, and stimulate the creation of new businesses. In Central America, measures to boost competitiveness have traditionally been led mostly by national governments and geared to improving the investment climate. Complementary policies geared toward LED should be promoted more broadly—to help local governments implement job creation initiatives that incorporate and leverage local comparative advantages.

Message 9: Through effective LED policies, Central American cities can improve their competitiveness and facilitate economic growth and job creation.

International experience shows that competitive cities focus their interventions across four broad policy levers to influence local determinants of competitiveness. First are institutions and regulations that improve the business environment. Second is the provision of adequate infrastructure and land for economic activities. Third are programs and policies aimed at developing skills and innovation. And fourth is enterprise support and finance. A recent World Bank global analysis on competitive analysis shows that cities that are performing well in terms of economic growth and job creation build effective local partnerships between public and private actors—"growth coalitions"—to devise and implement strategies that combine actions across the four policy levers.

Local governments with the support of national or regional bodies can learn from each other to further improve the local business environment, promoting convergence toward best practices in the region. Today, there are substantial variations in business regulations (starting a business, obtaining a construction permit, registering a property) and their implementation across countries, and among cities in the same country. A comparison of general rankings of the *Subnational Doing Business Report 2015* shows that Panama City and San José de Costa Rica are ranked in the top positions followed by Guatemala City. However, differences across cities within those countries and between the other cities from El Salvador, Honduras, and Nicaragua are substantial. An effective way to correct and improve public policy is through peer-to-peer learning, which makes reform easier to implement and share with the citizens and prevents duplications of effort.

To bridge the skills gap, cities are well positioned to match supply and demand of human capital. Improving human capital is imperative to address the jobs challenge, considering the region's gap in educational development indicators. An unskilled workforce hinders economic development and ties an economy to low-wage industries, making it more difficult to break the vicious circle of inequality, youth unemployment, and migration. Broad government efforts to overhaul the educational system must be coupled with pragmatic policies to bring these skills closer to firms, through a demand-driven approach to secondary and higher education, to improve the rates of graduates entering the labor market.

Central American countries can develop a more strategic approach to investment promotion through better understanding the opportunities at the local level. They can build on their success in attracting investment in special economic zones (SEZs) to accelerate the transformation of their economies. Central American countries have been early adopters of export processing zones, *zonas francas*, and SEZs along with Colombia, the Dominican Republic, and Mexico. SEZs account for a large share of light manufacturing jobs in El Salvador, Guatemala, Honduras, and Nicaragua. However, international evidence suggests that attracting cost-based production without capitalizing on local spillovers limits the sustainability of the economic gains. LED agencies can leverage their understanding of their territory's assets and productive specialization to encourage technology and know-how spillovers from existing SEZs and inform the planning of new ones.

Strengthened capacity for LED can facilitate the access of local firms to business support mechanisms, which tend to be scattered across multiple tiers and departments of national government. Efforts to streamline and consolidate national support for competitiveness are ongoing. The rationalization of the national provision of business services should be accompanied by the development of similar integrated windows at the local level. Doing so would simplify the interaction with firms and business environment—and allow public officials to gain a more complete understanding of the competitive challenges of cities.

Message 10: Critical success factors for LED are a clear understanding of local economic advantages, a strong public-private dialogue (PPD) at the local level, and local capacity at the appropriate geographical scale.

Local authorities must capture the distinct nature of their local economies to understand potential sources of comparative and competitive advantage. Initiatives such as the *Municipal Competitiveness Index* in El Salvador and similar attempts to assess subnational investment climates are important steps toward gathering accurate benchmarking economic indicators in local settings. In this context, firm-level surveys and investment climate indicators are important sources of information about the perceived constraints to private sector development in each country and the region. LED policies should be based on a comprehensive view of local economic actors, including local microenterprises as well as large and medium firms.

Promoting an effective local PPD is the key element to translate LED strategies into action. Involving the private sector in "growth coalitions" is key to understanding the local economy, defining economic and investment plans, and implementing LED strategies. In Central America, LED success stories have built on the influence of public and private leaders, such as mayors, local businesspeople, or industry experts. Local growth coalitions can help cities not only identify and pursue key priorities but also leverage investments from the national government.

Identifying the right geographical scale to develop LED policies is critical. A local approach to economic development allows for a closer understanding of the local economic conditions, and a closer relation between public and private stakeholders. However, it is important to seek the economies of scale required to make the provision of LED services economically sustainable at the local level, and to take into account the economic linkages between neighboring territories. In Central America's larger cities, where urban agglomerations extend beyond municipalities, LED capacity should be developed at the metropolitan or intermunicipal level. For cities with a less developed entrepreneurial fabric, the regional scale is probably the best to reach critical mass.

Who Does What? The Role of the National and Local Governments in Addressing the Policy Priorities

Each of the four policy priorities identified here calls for the active and continuous engagement of both the national and local governments. In realizing these priorities, each level of government has a distinctive and complementary role to play. Table O.2 presents concrete actions that can be taken to improve planning and service delivery, offer adequate urban housing, improve resilience to natural disasters and attain higher levels of competitiveness. It distinguishes what the national and local governments can each do to achieve sector-specific objectives.

Table O.2 What National and Local Governments Can Do to Make Cities More Inclusive, Resilient, and Competitive

	National	*Local*
Strengthening institutions for effective planning and service delivery	• Invest in building the technical capacity of municipal governments. • Align financial resources with functional responsibilities. • Provide legal frameworks, incentives, and technical assistance for intermunicipal cooperation.	• Integrate planning for land use and infrastructure investment at local level. • Improve mechanisms to generate own-source revenues. • Coordinate planning and service delivery across municipalities and agglomerations.
Providing access to adequate and well-located housing	• Develop a comprehensive housing policy. • Improve subsidy targeting. • Strengthen land administration systems. • Provide resources and incentives for municipalities to align territorial development and capital investment plans to national housing goals. • Improve information systems at national levels.	• Integrate housing programs with local development plans. • Prioritize the generation of serviced land in accessible locations. • Implement targeted neighborhood improvement investments to extend access to basic services in poor neighborhoods.
Building resilience by reducing disaster risk	• Improve the quality and accessibility of disaster risk information with a focus on urban areas. • Incorporate disaster risk information in public investment decisions. • Allocate financial resources to fund critical risk reduction investments.	• Develop and enforce risk-informed land use plans and building regulations. • Identify and prioritize critical investments needed to reduce risk at the city level.

table continues next page

Table O.2 **What National and Local Governments Can Do to Make Cities More Inclusive, Resilient, and Competitive** *(continued)*

Increasing competitiveness through local economic development	• Improve the quality and availability of economic data for decision making. • Build subnational capacity for business support services for local firms. • Adopt a more strategic approach to investment promotion in order to maximize spatial and sectoral comparative advantages.	• Improve the business environment at the local level. • Incorporate economic development considerations into local development plans. • Strengthen public-private dialogue (PPD) at the local level.

In conjunction with the ongoing decentralization process in the region, countries have made progress on some of these policy priorities in recent years, but implementation challenges remain.

The overview of the policy priorities highlights the importance of integrating policies at the city level. Local integration clearly appears as a key transversal element of the policy priorities identified. Integration of territorial planning with capital investment planning can lead to more effective local service delivery. Articulating the housing programs with local territorial development plans is critical in ensuring that the associated investments do not translate into costly urban sprawl. The report notes that incorporating disaster risk information in territorial planning is a very cost-effective way to prevent the creation of future risk. Finally, incorporating economic development into local development plans is an important element contributing to increasing competiveness at the local level. While some countries in the region have advanced on these agendas, strengthening these efforts at the city level will be needed in the future.

Municipalities are at the forefront of integrating policies at the local level, but they need to be empowered to play this role. Because they are the predominant form of local government in all Central American countries, municipalities have a central role to play in achieving the local articulation of policies mentioned above. It is important to note that this responsibility adds to the service delivery functions already assigned to them, and for which they often lack the financial and technical capacity. The policy priorities identified to make cities more inclusive, resilient, and competitive therefore strengthen the case to empower local governments both institutionally and financially. This means aligning financial resources with functional responsibilities in terms of service delivery and infrastructure provision, developing the municipalities' administrative capacity to adequately plan for and execute the required investment, and strengthening their technical capacity to effectively plan and manage rapidly growing cities.

Support from the national government is critical and should be focused on addressing key challenges and being results-oriented. National governments in Central America are well aware of the need to support municipalities in fulfilling their increasing functions, and the challenges and opportunities identified in this report only reinforce this priority. A challenge that national governments face when developing policies and programs aimed at providing municipalities with the resources and tools they require to make cities work is to provide them with a consistent legal and policy framework and a clear set of priorities in terms of performance improvement. This requires both a dialogue between the national and local governments and internal coordination between the national government agencies which interact with local governments in the many areas involved in local development.

Approaching issues at the metropolitan or intermunicipal scale presents the opportunity to address these at the relevant territorial scale, and harness economies of scale. One of the key elements of the urbanization diagnostic presented in this report is the emergence of agglomerations extending beyond municipal boundaries. This phenomenon is taking place not only in the main metropolitan areas but also in secondary cities and smaller towns. This represents yet an additional challenge for municipalities by requiring them to coordinate investments and service delivery at the agglomeration level; however, it also represents an opportunity to develop policies at the relevant territorial scale. For example, by working together, municipalities can adopt an integrated approach to water management and think about water supply, sanitation, and drainage at the scale of a watershed. They can approach LED at the level of employment catchment areas. And, perhaps more important, they can pool scarce human and financial resources to address the many challenges they face in a more efficient manner.

Notes

1. No SCD has been recently prepared for Nicaragua; the Country Partnership Strategy FY13–FY17 was used in lieu of it.
2. Per capita income equals GDP per capita average (2011 constant prices), weighted by the country's total population.
3. Built-up area is defined as areas characterized by developed land due to human intervention such as buildings, concrete, asphalt, and suburban gardens (that is, any land or buildings and non-building structures which are present as part of a larger developed environment, such as an illuminated section of a road) (USGS 2012).
4. Between 2012 and 2016, the World Bank prepared a series of Systematic Country Diagnostics (SCDs) for countries in the Central American region. These reports— which are produced in close consultation with national authorities and key stakeholders— provide an overview of a country's strategic development goals. These diagnostics identify the key goals and activities that have a high impact and are aligned with the global goals of ending absolute poverty and boosting shared prosperity in a sustainable manner.
5. The subregion formed by the countries of El Salvador, Guatemala, and Honduras.
6. The countries average 18 percent of GDP compared with the 31 percent of countries in the low-income category according to the Plan of the Alliance for Prosperity, a road map to advance regional integration signed by El Salvador, Guatemala, and Honduras in 2014.
7. World Bank 2010.

Bibliography

United Nations. 2014. *World Urbanization Prospects 2014*. United Nations Publications.

USGS (U.S. Geological Survey Land Cover Institute). 2012. Washington, DC. US Department of Interior. http://landcover.usgs.gov/urban/umap/htmls/defs.php.

World Bank. 2009. *World Development Report 2009: Reshaping Economic Geography*. Washington, DC: World Bank.

———. 2010. "Crime and Violence in Central America." Vol II. Report No. 56781-LAC. Poverty Reduction and Economic Management Unit, World Bank, Washington, DC.

———. 2015a. "Competitive Cities for Jobs and Growth: What, Who, and How." World Bank, Washington, DC.

———. 2015b. "Costa Rica—Systematic Country Diagnostic." World Bank, Washington, DC.

———. 2015c. "Country Disaster Risk Profiles for Costa Rica, El Salvador, Guatemala, Honduras, Nicaragua and Panama." World Bank, Washington, DC.

———. 2015d. "El Salvador: Building on Strengths for a New Generation—Systematic Country Diagnostic." World Bank, Washington, DC.

———. 2015e. "Honduras: Unlocking Economic Potential for Greater Opportunities—Systematic Country Diagnostic." World Bank, Washington, DC.

———. 2015f. "Panama: Locking in Success—Systematic Country Diagnostic." World Bank, Washington, DC.

CHAPTER 1

How Urbanization Is Transforming Central America

Ana I. Aguilera

Overview

Central America is the second-fastest urbanizing region in the world, and its urban population is expected to double by 2050. This demographic transition opens a unique opportunity to tackle some of the region's most pressing challenges. Due to the high concentration of people, economic activity, and risks in urban areas, cities are increasingly the place where Central America must invest to tackle some of the region's key development bottlenecks: lack of opportunities, lack of social inclusion, and increased vulnerability to disasters. Understanding the way urbanization is unfolding in the region is key for policy makers to better identify the challenges and opportunities that this transition can bring to their countries.

This chapter outlines the main patterns of the urbanization process and sheds light on how it shapes the key challenges and opportunities for the region. Section 2 provides a description of the trends observed in the region over the last decades and describes the methodology that constitutes the basis of the analysis. Section 3 goes more deeply into the elements that link urbanization and economic prosperity. Last, section 4 delves into the challenges that a growing urban population brings for building sustainable and livable cities.

Key Messages
- Central America is in the midst of a rapid urban transformation. Urban population is growing at fast speeds, even when compared with countries at similar stages of urbanization. Within one generation, 7 out of 10 people will live in cities, adding 700,000 new urban residents every year.
- Built-up areas are expanding at a faster rate than urban population, leading to the development of urban agglomerations extending beyond municipal boundaries. The report identified 167 urban agglomerations in the region, 72 of which extend over three or more municipalities.

- While most of the urban population is concentrated in large agglomerations, secondary cities accounted for 20–30 percent of the population growth in urban areas in recent years, escalating their role in the national urban systems.
- Cities in the region concentrate economic opportunities. Urbanization in Central America, as in other regions of the world, has gone hand in hand with higher per capita incomes and diminished poverty. Cities drive the large majority of jobs and economic activity in Central America, with more than 78 percent of the region's gross domestic product (GDP) concentrated in urban areas.
- Cities increasingly concentrate social challenges and vulnerability to disasters. Today, one out of four urban residents lives in informal settlements lacking access to improved sanitation, while homicides rate are above 53 per 100,000 people in most countries. At the same time, the increasing concentration of people and economic activity in high risk areas has resulted in rising vulnerability to catastrophic events, with cities concentrating 70–80 percent of the assets at risk in the region.

Toward an Urban Central America: Why Does Urbanization Matter for the Region?

Within the next generation, 7 out of 10 people in Central America will be living in cities. Today, 59 percent of the region's population resides in urban areas, but rapid urbanization is changing the region's demographic landscape. By 2050, the region will double its urban population within one generation's lifespan. "Pull" factors attracting rural workers and their families to urban areas have the potential to move large numbers of poor people to places with better economic opportunities and access to basic services. However, the large influx of urban residents presents significant challenges for cities in providing adequate urban infrastructure and reliable basic services. At the same time, it opens up an opportunity to create an enabling environment for job creation and higher productivity in cities that can contribute to reduce poverty and boost livability.

More than 78 percent of GDP is concentrated in the largest cities of Central America, although the transition to high-productivity sectors is ongoing.[1] Research worldwide suggests that over 80 percent of global economic activity is concentrated in cities. Globally, 72 percent of the 750 largest cities in the world outperform their own national economies in terms of economic growth. Competitive cities sustain economic success by engaging in proactive policies across three channels of firm-level growth: the growth of existing firms, the attraction of outside investors, and the creation of new businesses. Cities, too, drive the large majority of economic activity in Central American countries. Urban areas offer better jobs, higher wages, better access to safe drinking water, and shorter distances to health care facilities. However, despite concentrating most of the economic activity, cities are not as productive as they can be. Most of the region's manufacturing sector is distinguished by low-technology products, and little of the services sector is knowledge intensive.

And, while both sectors have shown important growth in recent years, employment growth continues to take place mostly in low-skill occupations (Bashir, Gindling, and Oviedo 2012).

Cities can help sustain Central America's growth while improving living conditions for the poor. Driven primarily by China's growing demand for commodities, the recovery in the United States, and continued weakness in international energy prices, the region has benefited from a "virtuous cycle" of stronger demand, lower inflation, and better external position that boosted job creation, improved salaries, and reduced poverty incidence across countries. GDP growth in 2015 averaged 4.25 percent, slightly below that of 2014 (4.5 percent), due to a cooling of remittances in countries like El Salvador and country-specific drags to growth including Intel's withdrawal from Costa Rica (IMF 2015). Despite good economic performance in recent years, some of the hoped-for gains are still tentative, while stronger policies are essential to reap durable benefits. As the region explores ways to sustain this growth and continue to make progress on social outcomes, cities can become engines of growth through supporting ongoing structural transformation and enhanced productivity in urban agglomerations.

City-level policies can help to effectively manage the benefits and negative outcomes of rapid urban growth. Addressing the need for urban services and infrastructure is becoming increasingly important in Central America given the accelerated pace of urbanization. With the rise of urban residents, local governments are faced with the need to respond to greater challenges and population demands, such as expanded provision of water and sanitation services, and resilient housing. To be able to provide solutions to these and other urgent problems, local governments can be empowered institutionally and financially. In doing so, they can work with the central government and in close collaboration with other municipalities, especially in large agglomerations where city and metropolitan boundary lines become blurry.

Understanding the Speed and Spread of Urbanization in Central America

Urban Population Is Growing at Challenging Speeds

Central America is the second-fastest urbanizing region in the world. After Africa, the region displays the highest urban growth rate globally. As shown in figure 1.1, until the late 1990s, the region's rate of urbanization followed closely the global trend and was much slower than the transformation experienced by its Latin American peers. Over the last two decades, its urban population has grown at an average rate of 3.8 percent per annum—1.7 times faster than the global average and twice as fast as the Latin American average.[2] The share of people living in cities increased from 48 percent in 1990 to about 59 percent today, although the region remains the least urbanized in Latin America. Official projections show that Central America will double its urban population within the next 35 years, welcoming 25 million new residents to cities as a result of both rural-to-urban migration and natural population growth. This is equivalent

Figure 1.1 Central America Is the Second-Fastest Urbanizing Region in the World

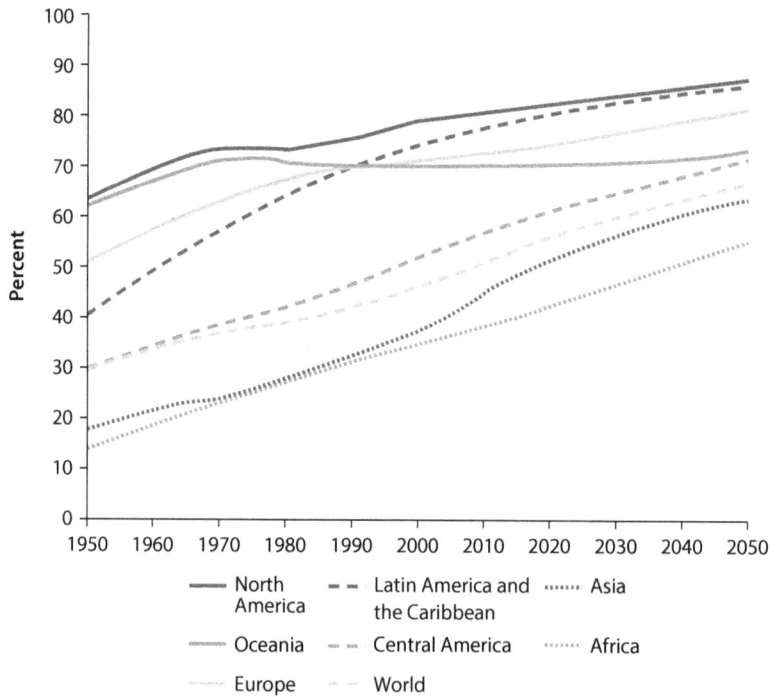

Source: United Nations 2014.
Note: Latin America and the Caribbean excludes Central American countries.

to adding today's combined populations of Guatemala and Honduras, the two most populous countries in the region.

Central American countries have experienced different growth trends over the past half century. As displayed in figure 1.2, not all countries experienced this demographic transformation at the same time. On the one hand, the shift from the countryside to urban areas took place earlier in Panama and Nicaragua, whose populations became predominantly urban in the late 1970s and beginning of the 1980s (that is, with over 50 percent of the population living in urban areas). By that time, only one out of three people was living in cities in the rest of the Central American countries. While Costa Rica and El Salvador followed a similar trend since 1960, with both becoming predominantly urban between 1990 and 1992, the two countries took divergent trends starting in the early 2000s. Last, Honduras and Guatemala achieved the 50 percent threshold at a later stage in 2008 and 2012, respectively, and can benefit from the lessons learned by their regional neighbors. By 2050 all countries are projected to exceed urbanization rates of 70 percent, with the exception of Guatemala (67.3 percent), with Costa Rica and Panama's urban populations projected to reach close to 90 percent of total.

The region's urban population is growing faster than other countries at similar stages of urbanization. Central American countries exhibit high urban population growth rates when compared to the global average and countries at similar stages of urbanization, although there are variations across the group of countries. On the one hand, figure 1.3 shows that Costa Rica has the highest urban population share (75 percent) in the region, and at the same time one of fastest annual growth rates in the world for countries at similar urbanization levels (averaging 2.5 percent in 2014). On the other hand, Guatemala and Honduras are at a lower

Figure 1.2 Urbanization Has Come at Different Moments in Time for Countries in the Region

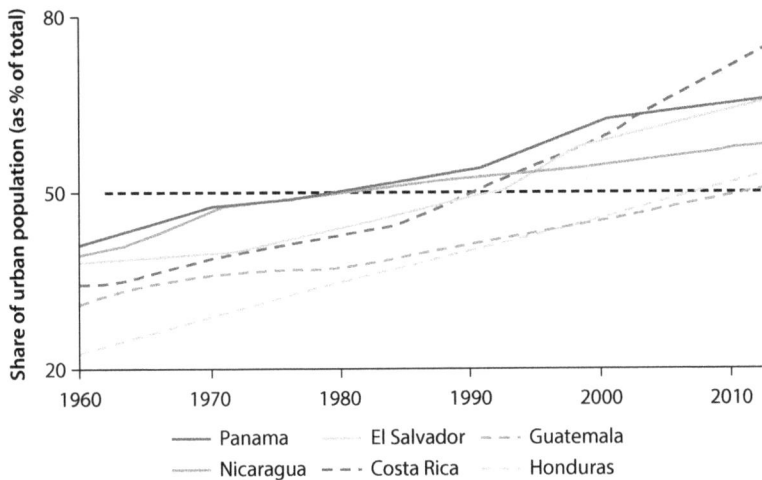

Source: World Development Indicators 2016.

Figure 1.3 Urban Population Growth Is Above Average Compared with Countries at Similar Levels of Urbanization

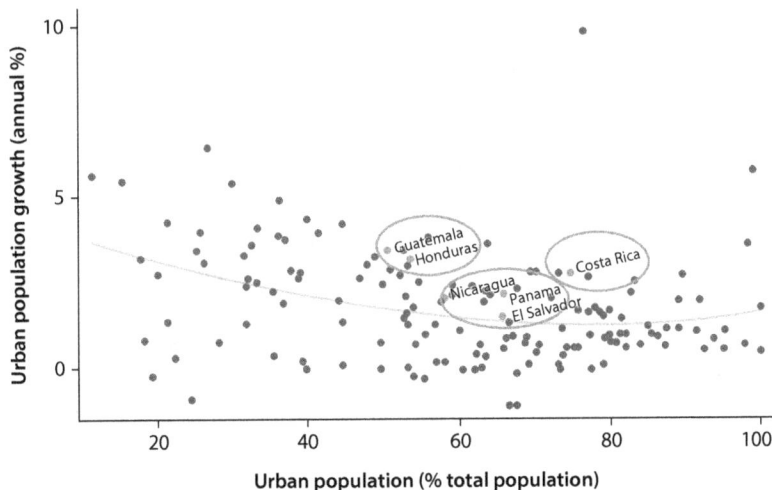

Source: United Nations 2014.

urbanization level, with over half of their population living in cities, but experience two of the highest urban population growth rates in the region (at an annual rate of 3.4 percent and 3.2 percent, respectively, in 2015). Last, El Salvador, Nicaragua, and Panama have intermediate urbanization levels, around 60 percent, with urbanization rates exceeding the world average and comparable to the growth rates exhibited by Morocco, South Africa, and Tunisia.

Research points to rural-to-urban migration as an important driver of urbanization in Central America. Rural populations are migrating to cities in search of better employment and educational opportunities and quality of life. Push factors such as declining agricultural prices, environmental degradation, and natural disasters have urged rural households to move to cities, particularly in El Salvador, Guatemala, Honduras, and Nicaragua. The International Organization for Migration and the World Food Programme have identified food insecurity, vulnerability to shocks, and economic instability as dominant forces affecting migration in the countries of the Northern Triangle, resulting in relocations either to other countries or to urban areas (WFP and IOM 2015). This study identified a significantly positive correlation between food security and migration in the three countries. It calculated between 5 and 12 percent of households having one or more of its members migrating within one month prior to the survey as a responsive measure to a continuous dry spell (5, 10, and 12 percent in El Salvador, Honduras, and Guatemala, respectively).

How Urban Is Central America?

Differences in the official definitions of *urban* across countries make comparison between countries difficult. In Central America, as in the rest of the world, different countries have different definitions of what is considered urban. For instance, Guatemala and Honduras classify as urban any human settlement with a population greater than 2,000 residents that has access to basic infrastructure such as piped water and electricity. In Nicaragua and Panama, this threshold goes down to 1,500 and 1,000 inhabitants, respectively. In contrast, Costa Rica and El Salvador define urban areas as those in which residents are living within municipal boundaries (*cantones o cabeceras municipales*), regardless of population size. Table 1.1 below summarizes the definition of urban areas in the six Central American countries.

Previous work has addressed some of these variations by providing a standard measure of urbanization. When using an alternative measure of urbanization in Central America, the level of urbanization in most countries is lower than the official level. The Agglomeration Index (AI) is a comparable measure of urbanization developed by the World Bank as a means to provide a globally consistent definition of urban concentration to conduct cross-country comparative and aggregated analyses. The AI calculates urbanization rates in the region to be between 3 and 10 percent lower than those reported by official urbanization figures. This also holds true for the rest of Latin America and the Caribbean region (LAC), where Central America continues to be the least urbanizing region within LAC. The exception is El Salvador, where the AI is above the official figure, given the country's high population density. Table 1.2 below shows the differences in values as calculated by the AI and the World Development Indicators (WDI) in two points of time. In both periods, the AI in El Salvador was higher than the official urban share by at least 10 percentage points. Similarly, the weighted-average difference in urbanization at the regional level between the AI and official figures was 3.2 percent in 2000 and 8.1 percent in 2010.

This report takes a step forward in providing comparable measures of urbanization that are consistent with official census figures in Central America. This work presents a new analysis of the evolution of urban areas in Central America. In order to provide a better understanding of the dynamics of urban areas in the region, this report uses comparable urban definitions that are based on the study of satellite imagery to provide a harmonized perspective of urbanization in the region and allow for cross-country comparisons. The definition of an urban

Table 1.1 The Definition of "Urban" Varies across Countries

Country	Official urban definition
Costa Rica	Population living in municipalities (*cantones*), including parts of the primary district and surrounding areas. These areas are delineated a priori considering physical and functional criteria, such as street coverage, electricity, and urban services.
El Salvador	Residents living in municipal areas (*cabeceras municipales*), regardless of population size or structural characteristics.
Guatemala	Cities, villas, and towns with more than 2,000 residents and with at least 51 percent of households with access to electricity and piped water inside dwelling.
Honduras	Population living in settlements with a population size over 2,000 residents and with access to: (i) piped water; (ii) roads, railroads, or air/maritime connectivity; (iii) provision of complete primary school (6 grades); (iv) mail or telegraph, and at least one of the following services: electricity, sewerage system, and health facilities.
Nicaragua	Localities within the set of municipal areas with a population over 1,000 inhabitants and with access to planned roads and streets, electricity, commercial and industrial establishments, and so on.
Panama	Localities with a population over 1,500 inhabitants and access to electricity, piped water, sewerage system, paved roads, commercial establishments, communication facilities, secondary schools, and so on.

Table 1.2 Urbanization Level
Share of urban population as % of total

	Agglomeration index		WDI urban population	
	2000	*2010*	*2000*	*2010*
Costa Rica	55.40	53.0	59.05	71.73
El Salvador	73.70	73.8	58.91	64.29
Guatemala	36.60	39.5	45.13	49.32
Honduras	41.60	42.9	45.46	51.70
Nicaragua	48.40	43.0	54.74	57.26
Panama	52.60	55.2	62.20	65.11
Weighted Average	**48.60**	**48.8**	**51.80**	**56.88**

Sources: World Bank 2009, 2016.

Map 1.1 Looking at Urban Agglomerations beyond Administrative Boundaries in Central America

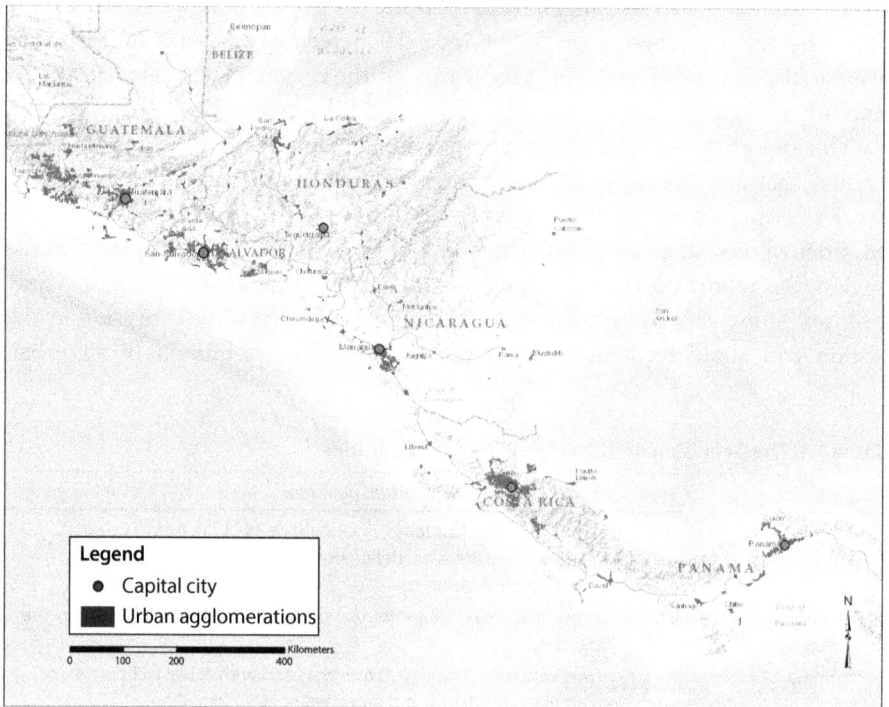

Source: World Bank calculations using CDRP data and GHSL Alpha version.

agglomeration refers to the geographical space where people work and live in the city, and is not limited to the municipal or metropolitan administrative boundaries of a city.

In order to achieve a balance between cross-country comparability and consistency with official urban statistics, these urban definitions combine the use of satellite imagery with census data. On the one hand, these urban definitions are derived from processed satellite imagery, the National Oceanic and Atmospheric Administration's Defense Meteorological Satellite Program (DMSP) nighttime lights, as well as gridded population layers derived from census data such as Worldpop. This analysis takes into account the physical extent in which residents of an urban center interact for delineating urban boundaries within the contiguous built-up area of a city. However, the extent of these urban boundaries also considers census data as the main source of demographic information in order to provide urban headcounts that are consistent with official statistics at the national level.

Looking at urban agglomerations provides a better understanding of the national urban systems today. Along with urbanization trends based on official national census data, this report uses the notion of urban agglomerations to better understand the composition of the urban system across the region. The new analysis described above is used to examine the distribution of

Table 1.3 Number of Agglomerations by Size

	>1M	100K–1M	15K–100K
Costa Rica	1	2	14
El Salvador	1	5	13
Guatemala	1	10	45
Honduras	2	5	22
Nicaragua	1	5	27
Panama	1	2	10
Total	7	29	131

urban population and land across the national territories. However, since this analysis is only available for one period in time, the study of regional historical trends relies mostly on publicly available data from official and international sources.

Using this definition, this analysis shows that the region's system of cities is comprised of 167 urban agglomerations with a population greater than 15,000 inhabitants. Map 1.1 shows the geographic extension of the 167 urban agglomerations identified for the purposes of this report. Out of these, seven metropolitan areas have a population that surpassed 1 million people in 2012, namely the six capital cities and San Pedro Sula in Honduras. A total of 29 cities have a population between 100,000 and 1 million inhabitants, while at least 131 urban agglomerations were reported to have a population between 15,000 and 100,000 people. In most cases, the majority of these urban agglomerations are concentrated in surrounding territory of the capital city. Table 1.3 provides the disaggregated distribution of cities by country and population size. Guatemala stands out by having the highest number of cities both between 100,000 and 1 million people and between 15,000 and 100,000.

Urban Population Is Growing at Challenging Speeds, with Secondary Cities Growing Relatively Faster

While capital cities account for most of the population, urbanization in recent years has mainly been driven by growth in secondary cities. Contrary to what is observed in some countries in South America, urbanization in the region is not only driven by the largest urban agglomerations. According to official figures, most of the urban population growth in Guatemala and Costa Rica, for example, is taking place outside the capital regions. As shown in figure 1.4, the contribution of secondary cities to urbanization in these two countries has been rising steadily since 1973 and 1984, respectively, with intermediate cities now accounting for over 65 percent of the total urban population in their countries. In countries like Panama and Honduras, however, the contribution of secondary cities to national urban growth has remained stagnant since 1960, as shown by the flat lines depicted in the figure below, which represent the share of urban population (as a percentage of the total) that is living outside the country's largest agglomeration. In these two

Figure 1.4 Urbanization in the Region Is Not Driven Only by the Main Urban Agglomerations

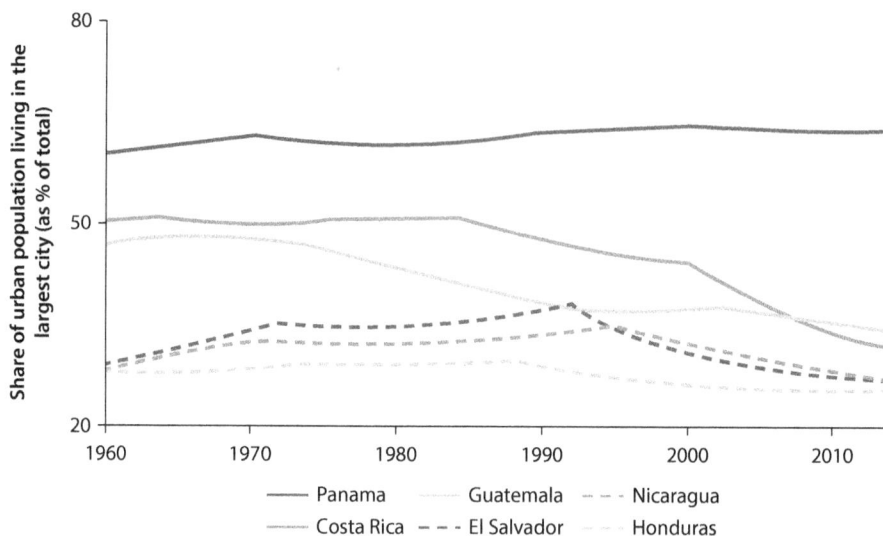

Source: World Development Indicators 2015.
Note: In the case of Costa Rica, the share of population living in the largest city only includes the residents of the San José municipality (not greater metropolitan region).

countries, Panama City and Tegucigalpa continue to account for the vast majority of urban growth.

When treated as urban agglomerations, cities concentrate a larger share of the urban population than those reported by official figures. Independent analysis using satellite data and official population figures carried out for this study finds that over two-thirds of the urban population in Honduras is distributed between the two largest metropolitan areas in the country (San Pedro Sula and Tegucigalpa). Figure 1.5 shows the differences in the estimated urban population concentrated in the largest city, comparing the official figures compiled in the World Bank's WDI with the custom analysis carried out for this study. Following this analysis, metropolitan Managua concentrates 55 percent of the total urban population in Nicaragua, while official figures report 27 percent. Likewise, while independent estimates show that San José and its satellite cities account for nearly 85 percent of the national urban population in Costa Rica, the official census reports that only one out of three urban residents in the country resides in San José. This major discrepancy is due to the fact that the official definition considers only the central San José municipality and not its neighboring cities.[3]

As in other parts of the world, while urban population is clustered in large agglomerations, secondary cities are growing at relatively higher speeds. Map 1.2 depicts the population sizes and annual growth rates for 74 cities in four Central American countries for which official census data were available at a comparable scale. The size of each circle is proportional to the number of inhabitants registered in each agglomeration in the last census year. The color scheme represents the

Figure 1.5 Population in Largest Cities, Urban Agglomerations vs. Official Urban Boundaries

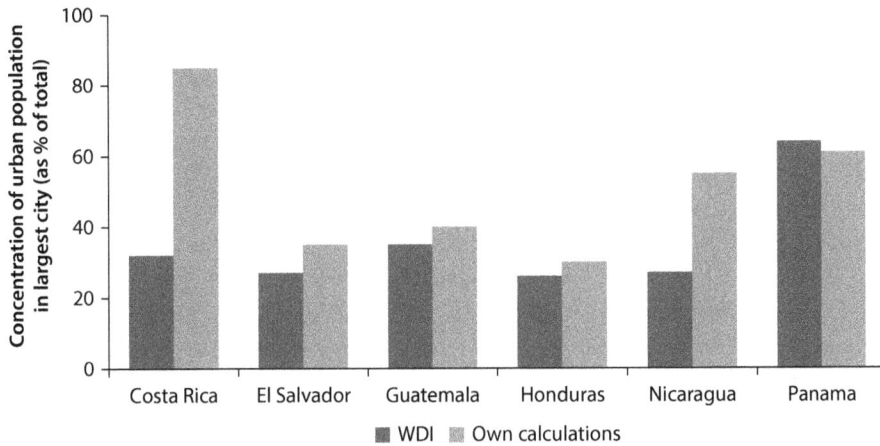

Source: Calculations using WDI 2015 and WB's CDRP data.

Map 1.2 Intermediate Cities Are Growing at High Speeds, but Large Agglomerations' Growth Rates Are below National Averages

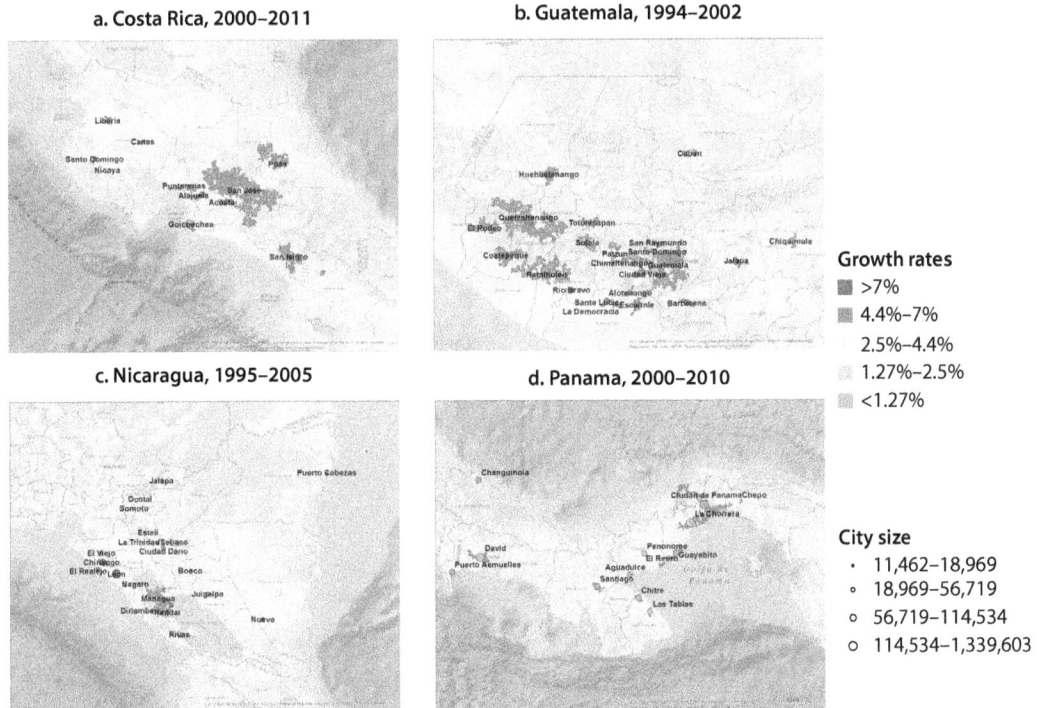

a. Costa Rica, 2000–2011

b. Guatemala, 1994–2002

Growth rates
- >7%
- 4.4%–7%
- 2.5%–4.4%
- 1.27%–2.5%
- <1.27%

c. Nicaragua, 1995–2005

d. Panama, 2000–2010

City size
- · 11,462–18,969
- ○ 18,969–56,719
- ○ 56,719–114,534
- ○ 114,534–1,339,603

Source: World Bank calculations using CDRP estimates and official census figures.

speed of the annual urban population growth rate—where dark red indicates a fast growth rate (7 percent per annum or above), and dark green corresponds to a relatively slow growth rate (1.3 percent or below). The Guatemalan capital region experienced rapid growth between 1994 and 2002, with cities such as Chimaltenango, Retalhuleu, and Quetzaltenango growing at a faster pace than the national average. In Nicaragua, the Jinotega-Matagalpa triangle experienced high urban population growth between 1995 and 2005, while larger cities in the West corridor underwent a slower growth. In Costa Rica, San José is growing more slowly than San Isidro and Punta Arenas, but faster than other secondary cities in the country, such as Guápiles and Acosta. Last, Panama experienced a period of relatively slow urban population growth rates during the 2000s throughout the country, with Penonomé and the western suburbs of Panama City among the fastest growing urban areas in the country.

Secondary cities have grown significantly over the last decade and represent up to 65 percent of the national urban systems. According to official census figures, intermediate cities contributed nearly two-thirds of the urban population growth in Nicaragua and Guatemala over the last decade. As shown in figure 1.6 below, agglomerations with a population size between 15,000 and 100,000 inhabitants accounted for 20–30 percent of the population growth in urban areas, escalating their role in the national urban systems. While large metropolitan areas accounted for at least 40 percent of the demographic boom in urban areas, secondary cities and towns are growing fast. In Guatemala and El Salvador, for example, a factor contributing to the growth and expansion of secondary cities is migrant remittances. A 2010 study exploring the urbanization sprawl of the intermediate cities of Quetzaltenango (Guatemala) and San Miguel (El Salvador)—where over

Figure 1.6 Distribution of the Urban Population by Size of Agglomeration, 2012

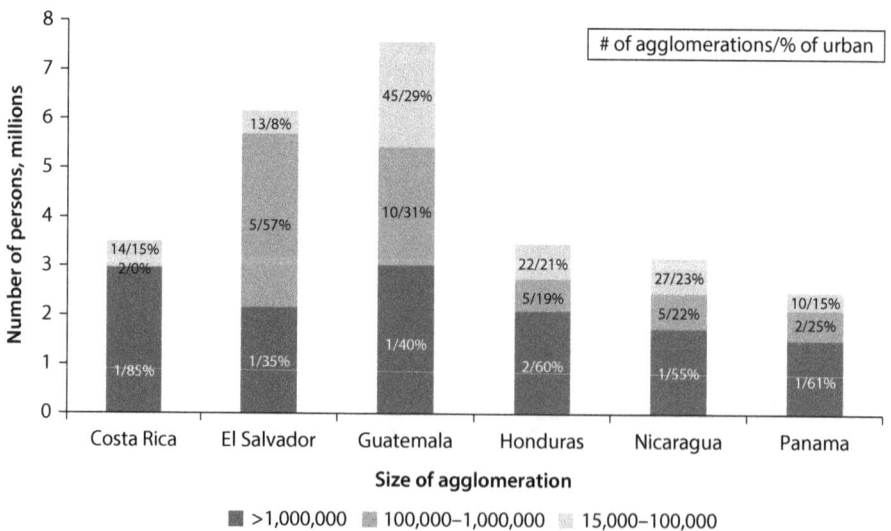

Source: Calculations using official census data and satellite imagery.

40 and 30 percent of the population receives remittances, respectively—found that real estate and residential projects targeting the middle class have unfolded rapidly in areas with a significant share of remittance-receiving populations. Many of these developments are characterized by gated communities and expensive homes, a share of which remains unused (Klaufus 2010).

Land Is Urbanizing Faster than Population

Despite rapid demographic growth, built-up areas[4] are expanding at a faster rate than population. In 1990, countries in the region built on average 91 m^2 of land per capita.[5] Today, this figure has grown by a third, with an average 120 m^2 of built-up land per capita. As shown in figure 1.7, using built-up land per capita as a comparable measure of sprawl across the region, El Salvador and Honduras have seen the greatest increases in this indicator mostly driven by the resurgence of the construction industry in the 1990s. Meanwhile, this ratio has followed a much more moderate increase in Guatemala and Nicaragua, while in Costa Rica urban sprawling accelerated during the last decade.[6] Last, Panama has experienced a contrary process, with greater densification driven by the mass developing of high-density buildings funded with foreign investments that helped fuel Panama's real estate market over the past 14 years. However, a parallel process is occurring in Panama's urban periphery as new semi-gated housing developments are accommodating the growing middle-class urban population.

Total built-up area in the region has tripled over the past 40 years. Expanding at an average rate of 7.5 percent per year, built-up area in Central America has grown twice as fast as other cities in the region. For example, in Mexico, Tijuana and Guadalajara expanded their built-up coverage at an average rate of 4.9 percent, 2.8 percent per annum, while Montevideo, in Uruguay, and Valledupar, in Colombia, grew 2.9 percent and 2.8, respectively (Angel et al. 2010).

Figure 1.7 Built-Up Areas Are Expanding at a Faster Rate Than the Population

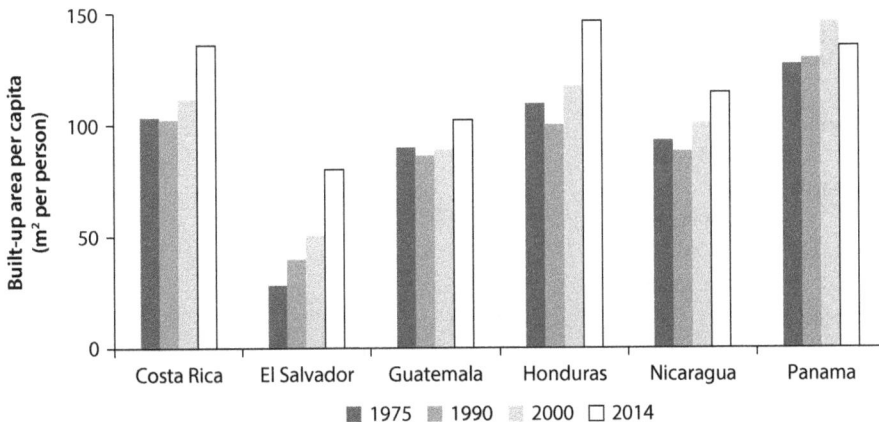

Source: World Bank calculations using CDRP urban agglomeration polygons and UN World Urbanization Prospects.

Table 1.4 summarizes the evolution of the built-up coverage for four periods of time using information derived from satellite imagery calculations. Developed land in the region has expanded substantially throughout the territory at an exponential trend. By 2000, most countries in the region had doubled their built-up extension from that in 1975. Today, total developed land is three times larger than four decades ago. Within the region, El Salvador has seen the greatest transformation, quadrupling its built-up land since 1975.

In 72 urban agglomerations across the region, urban expansion has grown beyond the official administrative boundaries. Map 1.3 below shows how cities, when defined as urban agglomerations, extend beyond one or more municipal boundaries. While all countries in the region have official metropolitan delimitations for their capital cities—depicted in light blue–some of these may need to be updated to reflect changing urban dynamics. In this sense, the case of San Salvador is strikingly notorious, with the urban agglomeration surpassing the official metropolitan area by twice the size of the official metropolitan boundaries. The same is true for non-capital cities. Analysis carried out for this study found that 72 out of the 167 urban agglomerations in the region encompass three or more municipalities, stressing the need to strengthen intramunicipal coordination for better urban planning and service delivery.

Low-density sprawl is concentrated in the urban periphery or outside large cities in the region. Most of the urban expansion that the region has experienced in recent years has taken place primarily along three areas: (i) at the periphery of capital cities, (ii) in secondary cities, or (iii) in the vicinity of road corridors connecting urban centers. Map 1.4 shows the period in which recent land development has taken place across the Quetzaltenango-Guatemala City corridor. As shown in map 1.3, most of the developments in recent years have taken place outside metropolitan Guatemala City. Built-up growth between 2000 and 2014 occurred predominantly in the outskirts of Quetzaltenango and along the

Table 1.4 Total Built-Up Area Has Tripled in the Past 40 Years

Country		1975	1990	2000	2014
Costa Rica	Km²	211.77	315.2	439.14	669.25
	Relative growth	1	1.49	2.07	3.16
El Salvador	Km²	118	212.36	299.71	511.46
	Relative growth	1	1.8	2.54	4.33
Guatemala	Km²	555.68	765.24	997.01	1,631.01
	Relative growth	1	1.38	1.79	2.94
Honduras	Km²	340.03	491.5	730.66	1,212.85
	Relative growth	1	1.45	2.15	3.57
Nicaragua	Km²	259.92	363.82	514.87	708.16
	Relative growth	1	1.4	1.98	2.72
Panama	Km²	223.06	323.31	446.31	530.79
	Relative growth	1	1.45	2	2.38

Source: GHSL Landsat Alpha Version, European Commission JRC 2015.

Map 1.3 Official Municipal and Metropolitan Boundaries Compared with Urban Agglomerations

a. Costa Rica: San José

b. El Salvador: San Salvador

c. Guatemala: Guatemala City

d. Honduras: Tegucigalpa

e. Nicaragua: Managua

f. Panama: Panama City

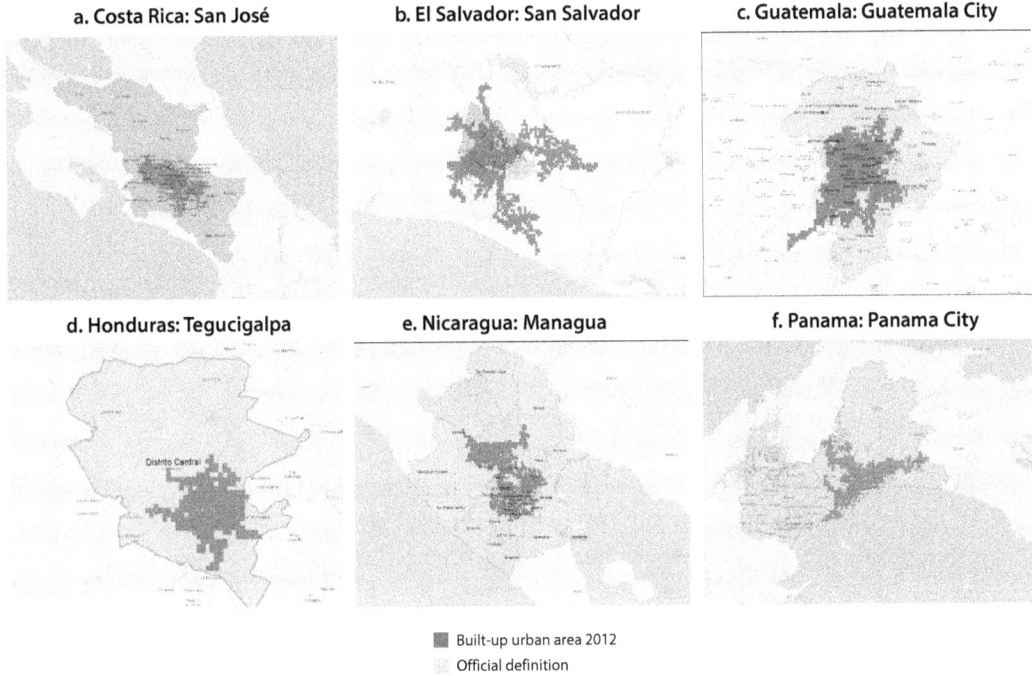

■ Built-up urban area 2012
▨ Official definition

Source: World Bank calculations using GHSL data (from CDRP project) and census data.

Map 1.4 In Situ Urbanization Has Taken Place in Guatemala over the Past 15 Years

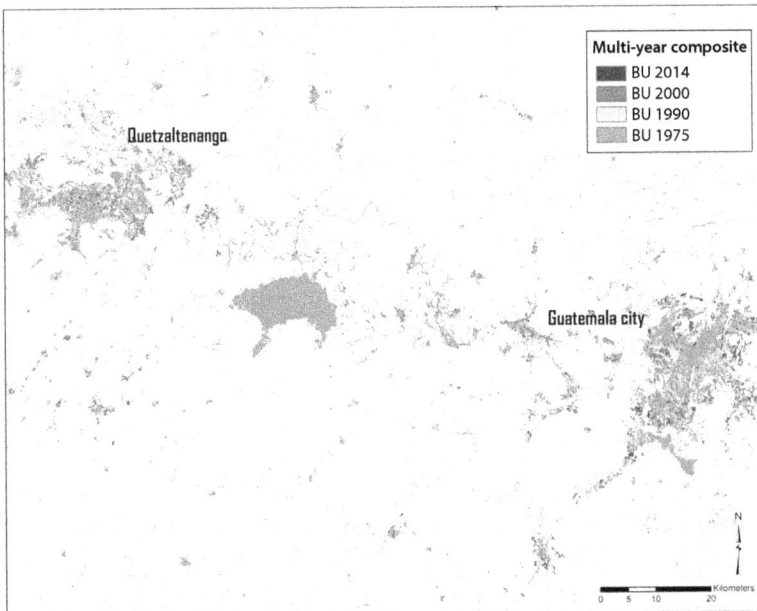

Multi-year composite
■ BU 2014
■ BU 2000
□ BU 1990
■ BU 1975

Source: Calculations using GHSL Landsat Alpha Version, European Commission JRC 2015.
Note: BU=Built-up area.

road network connecting these two urban centers. In fact, the large majority of these new developments seemed to have happened spontaneously in the form of in situ urbanization[7] or low-density settlements taking place in rural areas or far from exiting urban agglomerations.

Due to Rapid Urbanization, Cities Are Increasingly Concentrating the Region's Most Pressing Challenges—But Also the Opportunities for Development

A review of the World Bank's strategic diagnostic reports shows that countries in the region face common challenges and opportunities. Between 2012 and 2016, the World Bank prepared a series of Systematic Country Diagnostics (SCDs) for Central American countries.[8] These reports—which are produced in close consultation with national authorities and key stakeholders—provide an overview of a country's strategic development goals. These diagnostics identify the key goals and activities that have a high impact and are aligned with the global goals of ending absolute poverty and boosting shared prosperity in a sustainable manner. The reports show that countries experience, at varying degrees, limitations to economic growth and competitiveness. Last, the SCDs underline the exposure and vulnerability of all six Central American countries to natural disasters, and identify strengthened resilience as an important policy priority.

The region's main development challenges are linked to lack of social inclusion, vulnerability to natural disasters, and lack of economic opportunities and competitiveness. While Costa Rica and Panama are the two most advanced economies in the region, their education and training systems are not adequately responding to their pace of development, creating a mismatch of skills and jobs. Other causes of low growth and competitiveness relate to low productivity, low investment levels, and lack of export diversification. In terms of social inclusion, the region continues to witness income inequality, economic exclusion, low access to quality basic services, and high levels of crime and violence. Table 1.5 below offers a summary of the key development challenges in each country as identified in the World Bank's SCDs and Country Partnership Framework (CPF).

Cities Can Contribute to Increased Prosperity by Transitioning toward Sustained Economic Growth

Cities provide the needed space for firms to benefit from locating close to each other (localization economies) through labor market pooling and the creation of knowledge spillovers. The mushrooming of technology companies concentrated in Silicon Valley is a perfect example of this type of scale economy. While labor costs are high, firms continue to locate there because of the advantages of gaining access to a highly specialized labor force. Within Central America, Guatemala is a good regional example. In Guatemala, call center operations have grown substantially. The country accommodates 75 of the 103 call centers located throughout Central America (Prensa Libre 2015). The industry employs 35,000 workers, up

Table 1.5 Key Development Challenges in Central America

	Lack of economic opportunities and low competitiveness	Lack of social inclusion	Vulnerability to natural disasters
Costa Rica	• Fiscal pressures threatening the Social Compact and Green Trademark. • Mismatch of skills and jobs.	• Stagnant poverty reduction and rising inequality. • Low access to sewage treatment and solid waste management.	• High exposure to hazards, especially hydro-meteorological and geophysical.
El Salvador	• Lack of opportunities and low economic competitiveness. • Limited mobility of the middle class.	• Lack of social and financial inclusion.	• High vulnerability to natural disasters.
Guatemala	• Low economic growth. • Low investment levels and low agricultural productivity. • Weak institutions (low taxation, weak investment climate, frail rule of law).	• Fragmented social contract. • Widespread inequality and economic exclusion. • Malnutrition. • Lack of quality education.	• Vulnerability to natural disasters which disproportionally affect the poor.
Honduras	• Regulatory frictions affecting the labor and products markets. • Continued fiscal instability. • Inadequate infrastructure and low access to capital. • Shortage of skills.	• Low access and quality of basic services. • Unequal distribution of access to services, harming the poor. • High levels of crime and violence. • Limited access to education.	• Low resilience to natural hazards.
Nicaragua	• External vulnerability due to low economic diversification. • Vulnerability to food price increases.	• High crime rates. • Unequal access to services between income groups. • Limited access to primary education.	• High vulnerability to hazards, especially hitting basic infrastructure, roads, and housing.
Panama	• Limited effectiveness of public institutions and regulatory framework. • Weaknesses in coverage and quality of secondary and tertiary education.	• Increasing crime and violence. • Weak protection of land rights. • Increasing concentration of the extremely poor in the indigenous territories.	• Climate change and increased variability in rainfall.

Source: Synthesis of Systematic Country Diagnostics (SCDs); except for Nicaragua, which is based on the Country Partnership Strategy for the period FY13–FY17.

from 9,000 in 2008, and adds close to US$160 million to the local economy in employment generation. Likewise, growing population allows the fixed cost of new infrastructure—such as utilities, transport, and urban amenities—to be spread over a larger number of people and firms.

Due to the proximity of various economic activities, cities facilitate the exchange of ideas, knowledge, and technology. The economies of scale in cities promote a higher level of specialization and productivity. The proximity of firms, workers, and markets in large metropolitan areas enables agglomeration economies that can become global platforms for the exchange of knowledge, goods, and services. Intermediate cities can benefit from policies that promote sectoral clusters and enable access to large markets, while smaller cities and towns can take advantage of the provision of basic urban infrastructure and services that enable their insertion in the national productive chains.

International evidence suggests that urbanization and economic growth are closely related. Through higher densities, cities enable more frequent social and economic interactions than nonurban settings (World Bank 2013, 2015a). These interactions create a vibrant place for entrepreneurs and investors to translate ideas into innovative products and services. As shown in figure 1.8, countries around the world experience higher per capita incomes as they become more urbanized. This trend also holds for the Central American context. Costa Rica and Panama, the two most urbanized countries in the region, have the highest per capita incomes. On the contrary, Guatemala and Honduras, which exhibit the lowest urbanization levels (at nearly 55 percent), rank lower in per capita incomes among the group of six countries considered in this report.

As in other regions of the world, urbanization in Central America has gone hand in hand with higher per capita incomes and diminished poverty. In 1994, when less than half of the region's total population was considered urban, per capita GDP in Central American countries averaged US$5,318. Twenty years later, as the region became more urbanized, incomes per capita have doubled to an average of US$11,531,[9] albeit with significant differences (for example, Panama's GDP per capita in 2013 was US$19,082, while in Honduras and Nicaragua it amounted to less than US$5,000). Despite intraregional disparities, countries made progress in reducing poverty during this period, dropping from approximately 48 percent

Figure 1.8 Countries with Higher Levels of Urbanization Experience a Higher Income per Capita

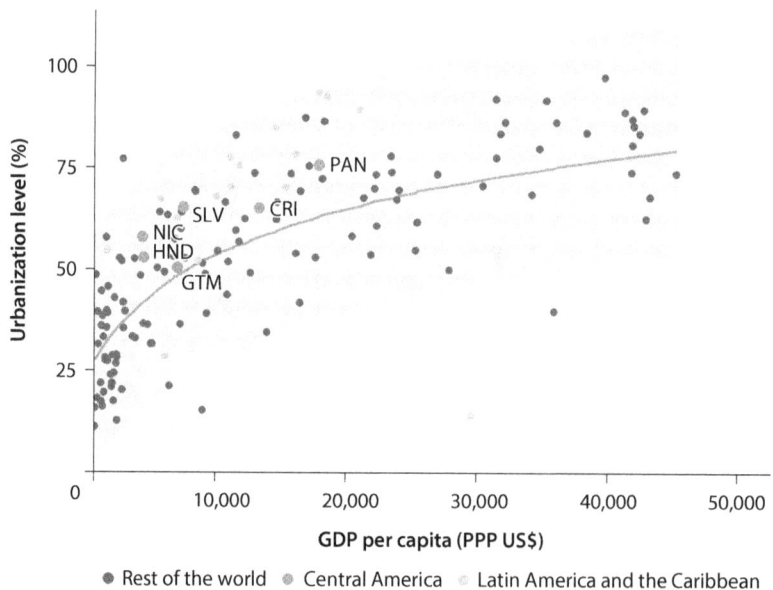

Source: Calculations using WDI 2015.
Note: CRI = Costa Rica; GDP = gross domestic product; GTM = Guatemala; HND = Honduras; NIC = Nicaragua; PAN = Panama; PPP = purchasing power parity; SLV = El Salvador.

of urban residents living in poverty in 1994 to 33 percent in 2013. However, the region still faces important challenges in improving the living conditions of more than 8.3 million urban poor, while at the same time lifting out of poverty nearly 11 million rural residents living under the national poverty lines.

Along with being the most urbanized countries in the region, Costa Rica and Panama have economic and political endowments that have facilitated different development trajectories. For instance, Panama's exceptional growth performance over the past decade stems from a number of factors, from which the transfer of the Canal to Panama in 2000 stands out. This allowed the country to benefit from the growth of world trade and to leverage its geographical position to transform itself into a well-connected logistics and trade hub and a financial center. Moreover, Panama has managed to attract increasing foreign direct investment (FDI) flows and private investment while undertaking important public investment projects. Overall, this has enabled the country to increase its capacity to invest in and manage urban development. In the case of Costa Rica, political stability, significant investment in education, a highly educated and bilingual workforce, and trade openness are among the factors that have defined its economic success. Most important, productivity has risen rapidly thanks to shifts in investments from low-tech sectors, such as textiles, to high-tech and high-value-added sectors, such as electronics and advanced manufacturing. This has allowed Costa Rica to produce high-tech manufacturing products and services for export.

Cities play an important role in the economy, contributing 80.5 percent of the regional GDP while hosting 56.9 percent of the population. In order to provide estimates on the contribution of cities to national GDP, this report builds on the methodology designed by the World Bank's Country Disaster Risk Profile team that divides the countries in 1 Km^2 grid and calculates GDP in each cell (see box 1.1). Throughout the region, the share of overall product clustered in urban areas is larger than the share of population concentrated in cities. Take Nicaragua as an example, where over half of the population (57.7 percent) is living in cities, yet urban areas contribute more than 72.6 percent to the national economy. Guatemala and Honduras experience a similar ratio, with urbanization levels reaching nearly 50 percent while urban GDP is over 76 percent in each country. As shown in table 1.6, even in more urbanized countries such as Costa Rica and Panama, the concentration of economic activity in cities and urban areas is higher than the share of population living in cities. Through enabling higher productivity, cities can become catalysts to promote sustained economic growth, create jobs, and achieve prosperity for Central American residents.

Similar to population dynamics, economic activity in Central America is also highly concentrated in the largest agglomerations. In the absence of abundant economic data disaggregated at the subnational level, this report builds on the work of Henderson, Storeygard, and Weil (2012) and uses the amount of lights at night and brightness as a proxy to measure economic activity[10] (see box 1.1). With the exception of Honduras, over two thirds of the total brightness is concentrated in the countries' capital cities. In the case of San José, Costa Rica, this

Box 1.1 Measuring Economic Activity from Outer Space

When official data are not available, this report relies on ancillary data to calculate subnational estimates of economic activity. This analysis uses the best data available to describe the observed trends as precisely as possible. However, as in many developing economies, there are data limitations in some of the countries in the region, which means that some estimates, projections, and figures might be discounted or overestimated. Therefore, calculations in this report should be interpreted more as indications of overall trends rather than precise figures. Additionally, although this report relies on primary data from official sources—mainly reported by the national statistical agencies in each country—for most of the analysis, complementary data were used in cases where disaggregated information were unavailable.

For instance, GDP growth is rarely measured in cities or subnational regions. But recent innovations based on the use of satellite imagery have developed methods to estimate growth

Map B1.1.1 Extent of Lights at Night and Brightness of Central American Agglomerations

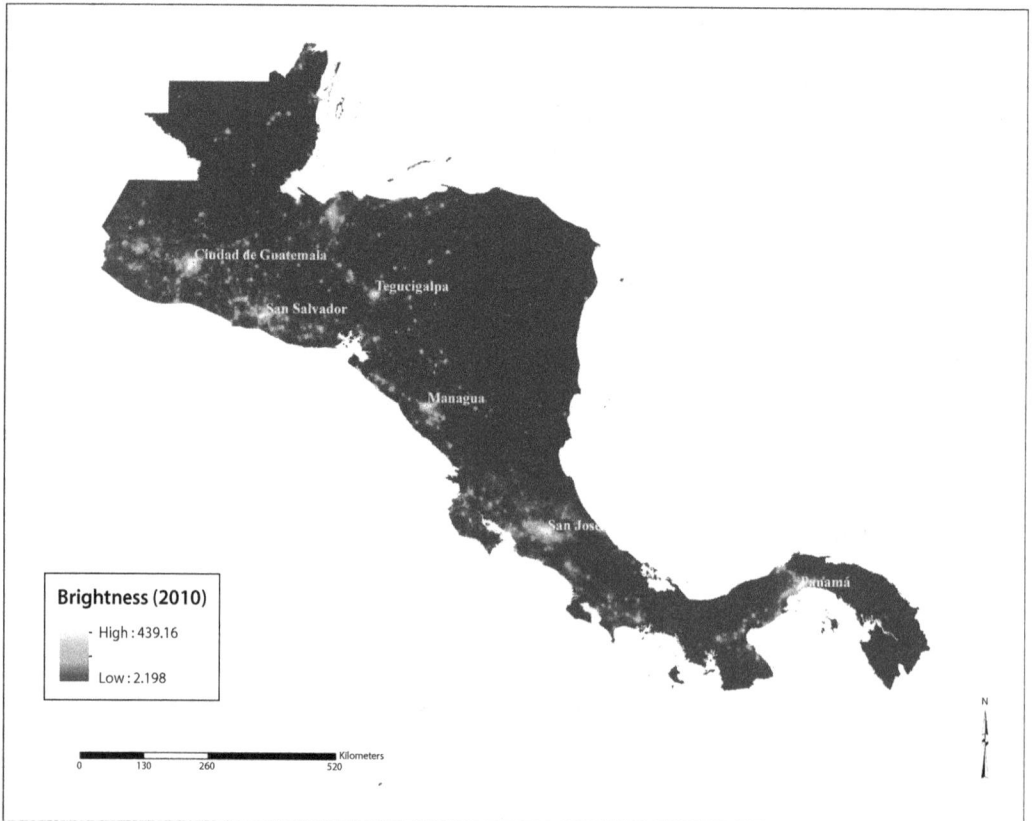

Brightness (2010)

High : 439.16

Low : 2.198

Source: World Bank LCR Probabilistic Risk Assessment Program, CAPRA (P144982) and funded by the World Bank through a Global Facility for Disaster Reduction and Recovery (GFDRR) grant (TF014499) from the Government of Australia (AusAid). The methodology will be available in a World Bank Working Paper in preparation: "Gross Domestic Product Disaggregation Methodology and applications in Disaster Risk Management" by P. Blanchard, B. Blankespoor, J. Rivera-Fuentes, R. Gunasekera, O. Ishizawa, and L.F. Jiménez-Salazar. Contact: oishizawa@worldbank.org.

box continues next page

Box 1.1 Measuring Economic Activity from Outer Space *(continued)*

in economic activity at the subnational level. By looking at the extent of the lights at night and the brightness (intensity) of these lights, Henderson, Storeygard, and Weil (2012) propose the use of satellite data on lights at night as a proxy to measure GDP growth (map B1.1.1). They develop a statistical framework that uses growth in lights to augment existing income growth measures, under the assumption that measurement error in using observed light as an indicator of income is uncorrelated with measurement error in national income accounts. For countries with poor data on national accounts, this new estimate of average annual growth differs as much as 3 percentage points from official data. Most important, lights data allow for measuring income growth in cities and subnational regions, as well as economic activity in the formal and informal sectors.

Exploratory analysis uses new computational methods to disaggregate national GDP at the subnational scale. This report builds on the methodology designed by the World Bank's Country Disaster Risk Profile team. The methodology was designed to estimate a spatial high-resolution map ($1 Km^2$) of subnational GDP improving the previous methodology developed by the Global Economic Activity Map (GLEAM). In particular, the new methodology maintains the distinction between agricultural and nonagricultural sectors considered in the former methodology, but the major improvement relies on the nonagricultural component estimation technique. The approach adopted for disaggregating the agricultural production only uses a Global Landcover grid that gives the percentage of land used for agricultural production by cell. On the other hand, the nonagricultural GDP disaggregation process uses population data from LandScan 2012 database3, 2010 Nighttime Lights (NTL), and a market access proxy5. In addition to this, subnational GDP data were collected from various sources including United Nations Development Programme reports, central banks, ministries of economy, and national bureaus of statistics of the countries considered. When available, the sectorial structure of the GDP at a subnational level was also compiled.

Source: World Bank LCR Probabilistic Risk Assessment Program, CAPRA (P144982) and funded by the World Bank through a Global Facility for Disaster Reduction and Recovery (GFDRR) grant (TF014499) from the Government of Australia (AusAid). The methodology will be available in a World Bank Working Paper in preparation: "Gross Domestic Product Disaggregation Methodology and applications in Disaster Risk Management" by P. Blanchard, B. Blankespoor, J. Rivera-Fuentes, R. Gunasekera, O. Ishizawa, and L.F. Jiménez-Salazar. Contact: oishizawa@worldbank.org.

Table 1.6 Cities Concentrate a Larger Share of Economic Activity Than Their Share of Population

	Urban GDP (as % of total)	Urban population (as % of total)
Costa Rica	84.82	72.87
El Salvador	78.11	64.79
Guatemala	78.10	49.77
Honduras	76.02	52.32
Nicaragua	72.62	57.54
Panama	86.17	65.40
Weighted average	**80.50**	**56.88**

Source: Calculation using World Bank gridded GDP project and Hsu et al. 2015.

figure reached 82 percent of the total amount of lights at night. In Honduras, the existence of a large economic pole outside the capital city—in San Pedro Sula—is reflected in the light distribution between the two largest urban centers in the country. Together, Tegucigalpa and San Pedro Sula account for 68 percent of the country's economic activity—with 38 percent and 29 percent, respectively. Additional exploratory analysis looking at the spatial disaggregation of GDP figures at the subnational level leads to similar results under the World Bank's Gridded GDP project. Based on information derived from satellite imagery in conjunction with official statistical reports, this report estimated the share of total GDP that is concentrated in each agglomeration, as shown in the last column in table 1.7. below.

The proximity of markets, firms, and labor in cities can enable economic transformation and growth. As countries become more urbanized, they transition from economies based on agricultural production toward more diversified economies where industry and high-value services play a larger role. Figure 1.9 depicts the sectoral composition of 170 economies ordered by their level of urbanization in 2014, where the diameter of each circle is proportional to the size of a country's overall economy, as measured by GDP per capita. The charts illustrate that, as countries become more urbanized, the contribution of agriculture to national GDP falls, while industry and services capture a larger share in the economy. Within the region, the service sector is the largest contributor to the national economies, and has become the leading sector faster than in other countries around the world. Nicaragua is the exception, where the share of agriculture in GDP is among the highest in the world when compared to countries at similar levels of income and urbanization.

However, most economies in the region are characterized by the production and trade of commodities with little value added. Despite a more predominant role of the service and industry sectors in recent years, most economic growth in Central America takes place in low-technology manufacturing and services that are not knowledge intensive. Only Costa Rica and Panama have significantly increased their exports based on knowledge-intensive and specialized

Table 1.7 Share of Total Brightness and GDP in the Main Central American Agglomerations

Country	Agglomeration	Share of total brightness (%) (DMSP 2010)		Share of GDP (%) (WB's gridded GDP project)
		1996	*2010*	*2011*
Costa Rica	San José	81	82	81
El Salvador	San Salvador	68	62	71
Guatemala	Guatemala City	52	57	63
Honduras	San Pedro Sula	37	29	34
Honduras	Tegucigalpa	33	38	36
Nicaragua	Managua	74	74	68
Panama	Panama City	71	69	65

Source: Calculations based on WDI 2014, World Bank Gridded GDP project and DMSP 2010.

Figure 1.9 As Countries Urbanize, the Sectoral Composition of the Economy Changes toward a Service-Based Economy

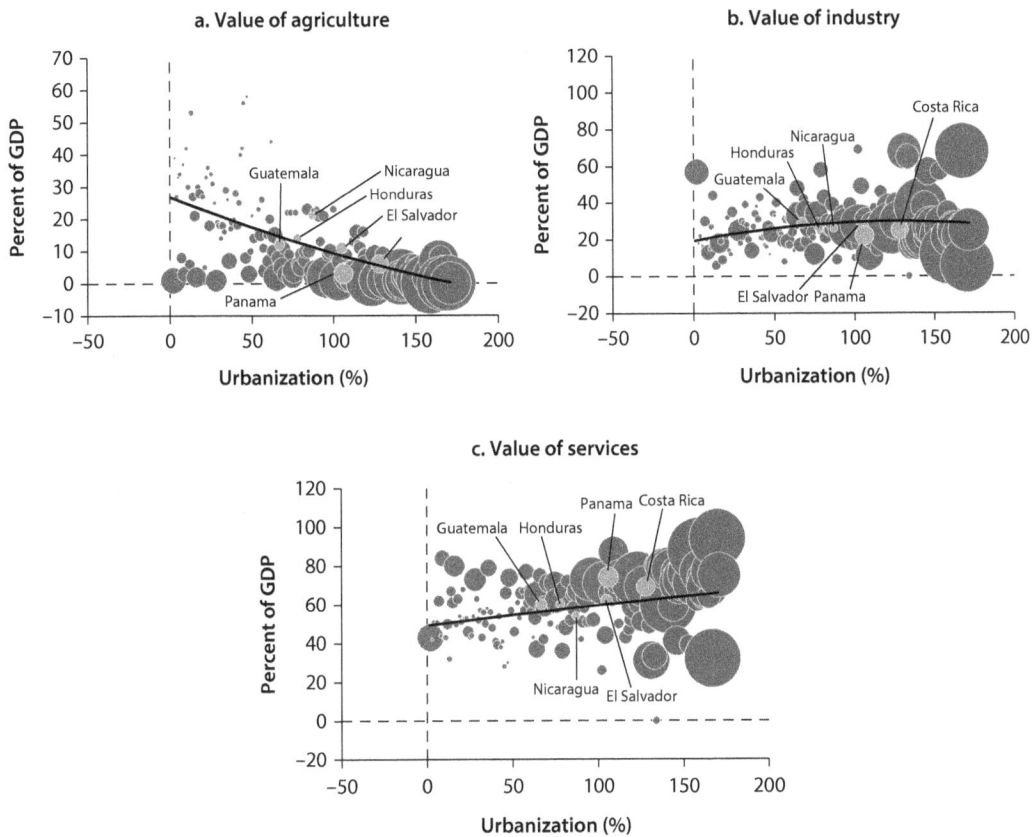

a. Value of agriculture

b. Value of industry

c. Value of services

Source: World Development Indicators 2015.

services, as shown in figure 1.10 below. Costa Rica shows the highest share of knowledge-intensive service exports in both absolute and relative terms, representing 35 percent of all service exports and worth US$1.4 billion. To contrast with a high-income country, knowledge-based service exports in the United States accounted for 64.6 percent of all service exports in 2011. Figure 1.11 shows that Costa Rica is the only country with a large proportion of high-technology manufacturing exports, while low-technology manufacturing exports constitute the majority in the other five countries, representing between 43 and 74 percent of all manufacturing exports.

Through Sustained Economic Growth, Cities Can Help Reduce Poverty

Despite economic growth in recent decades, Central America has underperformed in poverty reduction when compared to other countries in Latin America, and GDP per capita has increased below the average of middle-income economies. Central America's pace of decline in income inequality has been stagnant over the

Figure 1.10 Service Exports Are Not Driven by Knowledge-Intensive Services

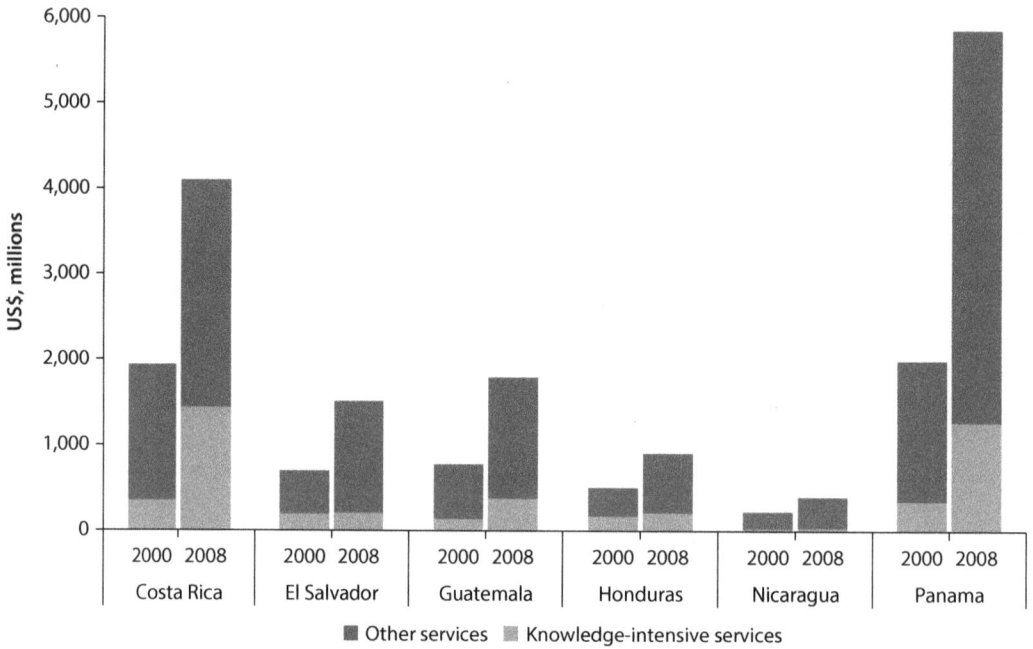

Source: Bashir, Gindling, and Oviedo 2012.

Figure 1.11 Manufacturing Exports Are Driven by Low-Technology Products, Except in Costa Rica

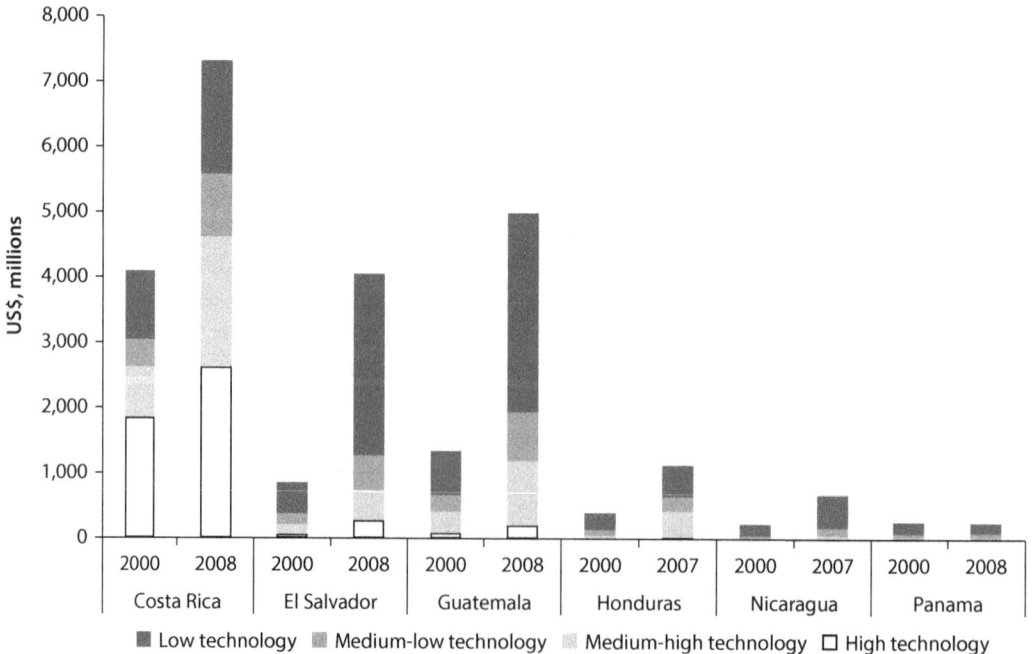

Source: Bashir, Gindling, and Oviedo 2012.

last decade, hindering the region's capacity to lift people out of vulnerability and into the middle class. Although unemployment rates are low for Latin American standards, data may ignore important factors such as outbound migration and the prominent role of the informal economy. Central American countries are within the 4–6 percent band (see table 1.8), except in Costa Rica where unemployment hit 8 percent in 2014. However, underemployment is high across the board, reaching 30–40 percent in the Northern Triangle.[11] Lack of opportunity has translated into social pressures that hinder sustainable development. By the mid-2000s, countries in the Northern Triangle—namely El Salvador, Guatemala, and Honduras—suffered mounting migration while crime and violence presented the width of the social drama. Out of the 3 million Central American immigrants living in the United States, 90 percent arrived from these countries. In 2012, four Central American countries ranked in the top five for highest homicide rates in the world.

Central American cities can become platforms for lifting people out of poverty. Through enabling agglomeration economies, empirical studies around the world show that urbanization is linked to poverty reduction. Within Latin America, some of the most urbanized countries have the lowest urban poverty and inequality levels. For example, Argentina, Chile, Peru, and Uruguay are among the ten countries with the highest urbanization rates in the region that show both declines in urban poverty and inequality—with Argentina, Peru, and Uruguay currently registering among the lowest Gini coefficients in the region (42.28, 44.73, and 41.87 in 2013, respectively), and Argentina and Chile having the two lowest urban poverty rates (4.7 percent and 12.4 percent in 2013, respectively). The evidence is mixed in Central America. On the one hand, Costa Rica and Panama, the two most urbanized countries in the region, show the two lowest urban poverty rates (19.5 percent in 2014 and 13.8 in 2013, respectively), although Costa Rica has registered slight increases in very

Table 1.8 Despite Growth, Central America Underperforms LAC in Poverty Reduction Outcomes

	Percent of population living in poverty ($4/day)	Percent in extreme poverty ($2 day)	World Bank Gini index 2016	Unemployment rate (% of labor force in 2013)
Costa Rica	12.2	4.6	49.2	7.6
El Salvador	31.8	12.7	43.5	6.3
Guatemala	62.4	40.5	52.4	2.8
Honduras	59.4	39.6	53.7	4.2
Nicaragua	52.2	29.3	45.7	7.2
Panama	20.4	9.9	51.7	4.1
Central America	**43.7**	**24.9**	**0.50**	**5.3**
LAC	**25**	**5.4**	**0.50**	**6.3**

Source: World Development Indicators 2016.
Note: LAC = Latin America and the Caribbean.

recent years. However Panama, being among the most urbanized has the third highest Gini coefficient (51.67 in 2013), just behind Honduras and Guatemala, which are the two least urbanized countries in the region and with the largest share of urban poor. Contrary to this case are Costa Rica and El Salvador, which rank among the three most urbanized countries and register the fourth- and sixth-lowest Gini coefficients, respectively.

While the share of urban dwellers living in poverty has been in decline, poverty incidence still remains high. The past ten years have been characterized by sustained growth in economic indicators and reduced poverty throughout Central America. However, as more people move into cities in search of better living conditions, the number of urban poor has increased in absolute terms (figure 1.12), reaching 8.3 million urban poor. Costa Rica, NIcaragua, and Panama have reduced the absolute number of poor living in cities. However, while the urban poverty rate in Costa Rica and Panama is below 20 percent, over half of the total urban population in Nicaragua lives under the poverty line. At the same time, El Salvador, Guatemala, and Honduras have shown progress in reducing urban poverty over the last 15 years, but poverty rate in cities is still over 40 percent and the total number of urban poor has increased to over 1.4 million residents in each country. In January 2016 alone, more than 30,000 people fell into poverty in Honduras as unemployment remains very high and families are unable to cover their living costs (Proceso Digital 2016).

Figure 1.12 Poverty Incidence Is Declining in Urban Areas, although the Number of Poor Is Growing with Urbanization

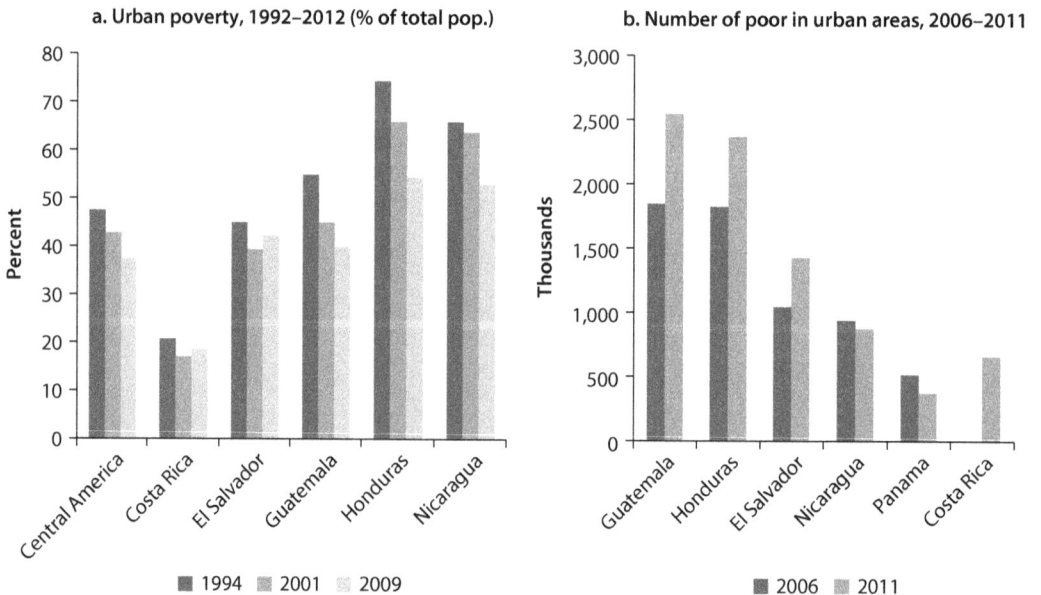

a. Urban poverty, 1992–2012 (% of total pop.)

■ 1994 ■ 2001 ■ 2009

b. Number of poor in urban areas, 2006–2011

■ 2006 ■ 2011

Source: Calculations using WDI 2015 and CEPAL 2014.

Cities Can Help to Boost Livability in Central America by Providing Solutions to the Region's Most Pressing Challenges

Despite progress in recent years, important challenges on livability remain, with cities often being associated with the growth and expansion of informal settlements. In 2005, over 30 percent of the urban population in the region lived in informal settlements with precarious living conditions—above the Latin American average of 26 percent. Between 2001 and 2010, 45 percent of the urban growth in San Salvador took place in informal human settlements, while secondary cities such as San Juan de Opico y Colón, Santa Ana, and San Miguel witnessed similar figures, at 38, 45, and 36 percent, respectively. Guatemala and Nicaragua had the highest rate of urban population living in slums, only below Belize, Bolivia, Jamaica, and Haiti when compared to the rest of Latin America. The spatial concentration of poverty in slums adds to the rising crime rates and vulnerability to risk, two of the most pressing challenges in the region's development agenda.

Fast and spreading urbanization puts pressure on municipal finances and provision of basic urban infrastructure. In Mexico, for instance, the current model of sprawled urban expansion increased the cost of infrastructure provision, which is then transferred on to firms through higher fees and taxes. Similarly, providing housing in the outskirts of Santiago de Chile is ten times more expensive than building housing units in the city core. Recent studies find that municipal spending on public works and infrastructure per capita was nearly 1.5 higher in the least dense municipalities in the country, when compared to cities with higher population densities. Moreover, scenario planning available for different urban growth trajectories showed that more compact urban development could save cities up to 70 percent of infrastructure and maintenance costs.

Addressing Priorities in Urban Housing Is Critical for Building Inclusive Cities

Through shortcomings in basic urban services, land, housing, and urban transport, residents and firms can prematurely experience the downside of urban concentration. Failing to provide adequate housing policies and programs needed to cope with rapid urbanization can translate into rising informality and slum proliferation, high land costs, social conflict over plot tenure, degraded public areas, threats to public health, and emerging crime (Kessides 2005). Further, the shortage of fiscal resources for providing the needed investments by national and local governments reduces the benefits of urbanization and raises the costs of major private and public investments that cities attract.

In Central America, a large segment of housing is produced and consumed informally. The quality and location of housing has important long-term consequences for both households and communities. Housing with immediate access to jobs, amenities, and services can reduce travel time and expenditures, and provide access to better education and health outcomes. Further, proximity to basic services such as improved water and sanitation facilities and solid waste collection has direct impact on mortality rates and economic productivity. However, vulnerable populations often tend to concentrate in areas where housing is most affordable, but may lack these key services. In Central America, slums and informal settlements are the biggest challenges to the provision of quality housing in cities, and unmanaged urbanization has driven income inequality and contributed to the concentration of poverty in slums and information settlements.

Today, one out of four urban residents in the region lives in slums and lacks access to improved sanitation. Access to improved sanitation is the most critical infrastructure deprivation for poor urban households in Central America. Despite substantial achievements in recent years in terms of increasing electricity and potable water access in the region, improved sanitation systems are absent from a substantial share of urban dwellings, even in wealthier countries such as Costa Rica. In nearly all countries, a third or more of urban households do not have access to improved toilet or are not connected to the sewage network. Improved sanitation systems, such as septic systems, are a more common alternative, but in most countries more than 25 percent of households do not even have these facilities. This figures reaches over 50 percent in Nicaragua.

There are significant levels of housing deficit in Central America, particularly qualitative deficit, as shown in table 1.9. In 2009 there were approximately 11.3 million households, and the total housing deficit reached 44 percent, out of which 7 percent represented quantitative deficit and 37 percent qualitative deficit. In 2005, approximately 31 percent of the urban population lived in slums; however, there were significant differences between countries as slum populations in Costa Rica and Panama reached 11 percent and 23 percent respectively, while in Guatemala and Nicaragua the populations were above 40 percent, reaching 41 percent and 46 percent, respectively.[12] Additionally, an estimated 290,000[13] new households are established annually in the region, which exert further pressure on the demand for housing.

Table 1.9 Urban Housing Deficit, 2009
% households

	Quantitative deficit	Qualitative deficit				
		Total	Materials	Overcrowding	Infrastructure	Lack of secure tenure
Central America	7.2	37.5	19.3	15.3	27.2	11.3
Costa Rica	2	10	5	1	1	6
El Salvador	8	41	21	16	30	17
Guatemala	11	46	32	27	32	10
Honduras	2	41	18	14	26	12
Nicaragua	12	58	33	28	52	10
Panama	8	29	7	6	22	13

Source: Inter-American Development Bank 2012.

Crime and Violence in Central American Cities Are Hampering the Benefits of Urbanization

Crime and violence are two of Central America's greatest challenges to its prosperity and development. Criminal violence and gang warfare are costing the region an estimated 8–9 percent of GDP each year (Negroponte, Caballero, and Amat 2012). Along with Southern Africa, the region suffers from the highest homicide rates in the world. The rate of intentional homicide per 100,000 population varies among Central American countries, from a high rate of 91 in El Salvador in 2012 to a visibly lower rate of 8.4 in Costa Rica in the same year (UNODC 2014). The Northern Triangle accounts for the steepest rates in the region, with the three ranking among the five countries with the highest homicide rates in the world.

Homicide is the defining crime of Central America. While other violent crimes such as robbery and assault prevail in the region, their magnitudes are lower, and are normally below the average of Latin America. However, El Salvador and Guatemala face extremely high rates of violent victimization, affecting almost 1 in 6 adults (World Bank 2010). Figure 1.13 shows the patterns of homicide rates over the period 2000–2012/13. Although homicide levels are significantly lower in Costa Rica, Nicaragua, and Panama, they have registered recent rises, most notably in Panama. Their proximity to the Northern Triangle countries and strategic position as an illegal drug trade corridor puts them at risk for greater crime and violence.

Crime and victimization rates tend to be higher in urban than rural areas. All six capital cities have higher homicide rates per 100,000 population than the national average, with the largest gap observed in Guatemala City (116.6 versus 41.6 in 2010) and Panama City (53.1 versus 17.2 in 2012). Reports by the World Bank and the United Nations Office of Drugs and Crime (UNODC) acknowledge a link between urbanization and higher levels of crime and violence in the region, given the inherent characteristics of urban areas, as well as the kind of urban development unfolding in Central America. International evidence shows that rapid and mismanaged urbanization can be linked to higher levels of crime and violence. Poor urban planning creates an environment more susceptible to victimization of residents. Residential crowding, deterioration or lack of public recreational spaces, and insufficient basic public services, compounded with limited access to educational and job opportunities, are very well-known risk factors for violence and crime, including the involvement in illicit activities and association with criminal or delinquent groups, which also results in the victimization of residents in the region. Other factors associated with urban living also play into higher levels of violent crime, such as income inequality and the possibility to remain anonymous within denser and more highly populated places. For instance, UNODC's *Global Study on Homicide 2013* states that settlements with a population of over 50,000 register a disproportionate number of homicides in the Central American countries.

The causes of increased criminal violence and a larger perception of insecurity in Central America are many and multidimensional. Research has narrowed them down to three main drivers: (i) illicit drug trade, (ii) expansion of

Figure 1.13 Homicide Rates per 100,000 People in Central America, 2000–2012/13, by Country

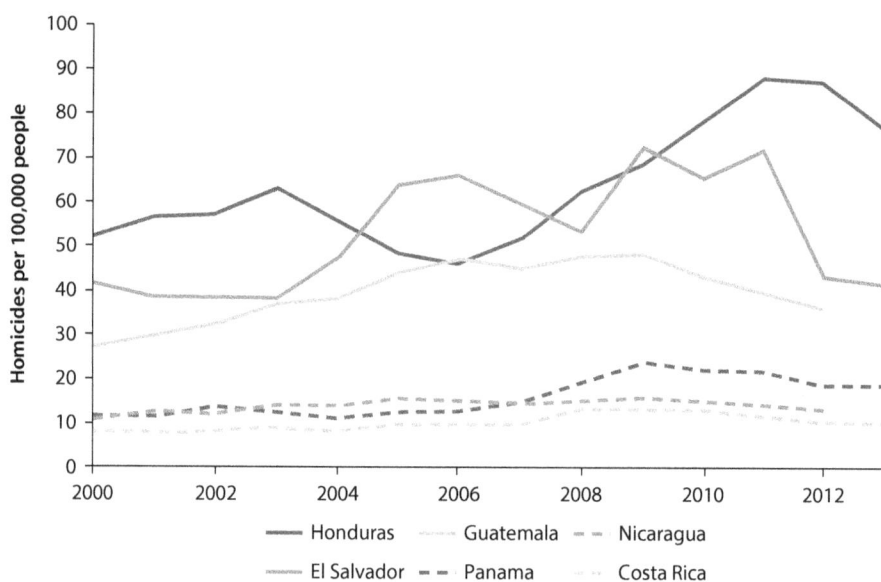

Sources: Berge and Carranza 2015; UNODC 2012, 2014; World Bank 2010, 2011.

local gangs, and (iii) wide availability of and easy access to firearms (World Bank 2011; Shifter 2012). Among the three, drug trafficking is the dominant factor explaining the hike and prevalence of violence in the region. At present, Central America is heavily affected not only for operating as a drug trade corridor between cocaine producers in South America and the consumer market in the United States and abroad, but also for recently evolving into a production center for other synthetic drugs. Homicide rates are 65 percent higher in areas with widespread drug trafficking activity than in other areas of a country (World Bank 2010).

The heavy presence of gangs or *maras* throughout the region—more than 900 currently operating in the region—can be explained in part by the limited education and employment opportunities available for the youth. In the case of Honduras, rising levels of urbanization and migration beginning in the 1980s made cities more susceptible to violent crime. Crime is geographically concentrated in the country, with 65 percent of homicides taking place in only 5 percent of urban municipalities in 2013. Urban areas have not been able to cope adequately with the incoming population, leading to insufficient infrastructure to accommodate all migrants and marked inequality in services provision. Additionally, competition over jobs and inequality may contribute to heightening the risk of violence. New incomers are also facing limited job opportunities as supply does not meet demand, causing high levels of unemployment, particularly among the youth (Berge and Carranza 2015).

Figure 1.14 Average Losses Due to Extreme Weather Events

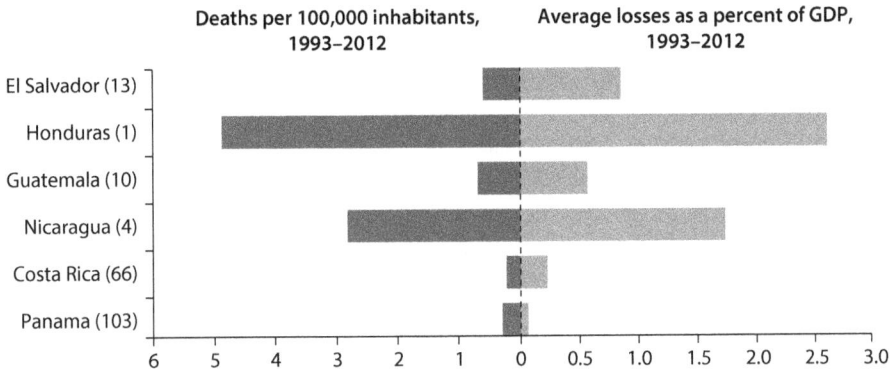

Deaths per 100,000 inhabitants,
1993–2012

Average losses as a percent of GDP,
1993–2012

El Salvador (13)

Honduras (1)

Guatemala (10)

Nicaragua (4)

Costa Rica (66)

Panama (103)

6 5 4 3 2 1 0 0.5 1.0 1.5 2.0 2.5 3.0

Source: Global Climate Risk Index 2014.
Note: Numbers in parentheses indicate worldwide ranking.

Resilient Cities Can Improve and Sustain Economic Growth

The increasing concentration of population and economic activity in high risk areas have resulted in rising vulnerability to natural catastrophic events. As shown in figure 1.14, in Central America, disasters generated from extreme weather events[14] have had devastating and disruptive effects on the foundations of a country's economy, reversing hard-won development gains. The increasing concentration of population and firms in urban areas has resulted in rising exposure and vulnerability to natural catastrophic events, with annual average losses accounting for between 0.7 percent and 2.6 percent of national GDP in El Salvador, Honduras, and Nicaragua. These factors, combined with global climate change and increased climatic variability, are likely to exacerbate Central America's exposure to hurricanes, floods, erosion, landslides, and droughts.

Building resilient cities can help countries withstand shocks and adapt to changing situations. In the context of the region's changing demographics, rapid urban growth, and certain unpredictable climatic trends, integrating disaster risk reduction policies and measures into local, national, and regional development practices is critical to build the future resilience of Central American cities. Increasing vulnerability to risks and high exposure in urban areas requires taking better informed financial decisions and policy priorities based on evidence-based research. Given the current regional institutional and regulatory context for risk management, improving the tools and policies for timely risk identification, as well as planning and financing instruments for better managing the impacts of disasters, will be needed.

Urban Pollution and Congestion Hinder Agglomeration Economies

In the absence of regulations, congestion and pollution costs can slow economic growth and reduce livability in cities. Unmanaged urban sprawl can lead to greater energy use for transport, lower labor productivity, and higher costs for energy and water supply. Other countries also experience the burden associated with the negative externalities of urbanization. Annual congestion costs in comparable cities in rapidly urbanizing Africa[15] are between US$255 million and US$400 million annually, including socioeconomic and environmental costs. Overall, minibus drivers lose around US$164.7 million in income and an estimated US$15.9 million in fuel costs yearly, while employers lose US$74.8 million in paid wages to workers who are not working because they are trapped in traffic jams (Kiunsi 2013; Ng'Hily 2013). Similarly, growing traffic congestion in urban areas carries significant environmental and health implications, which reduce the quality of life. A recent study by the Harvard Center for Risk Analysis (HCRA) estimated that emissions from traffic congestion in the 83 largest urban areas in the United States resulted in more than 2,200 premature deaths in 2010 with a value of US$18 billion in public health and social costs (Levy, Buonocore, and von Stackelberg 2010).

Traffic congestion in Central America has become an economic burden. In Central America, traffic congestion on main trading routes has been determined to increase road freight transport costs and prices, affecting trade and overall economic growth (Osborne, Pachón, and Araya 2014). Transportation costs are especially high in Costa Rica. A study analyzing the agglomeration economies and urban diseconomies in the greater metropolitan area (GMA) of San José identifies the city's transportation infrastructure and networks as an important urban diseconomy, with the potential of reversing the gains accrued from economies of scale (Pichardo-Muñiz and Chavarría 2012). Existing road conditions of the city's transport system are conducive to serious road congestion and have cost US$3.8 billion between 2005 and 2009, representing 2.8 percent of the country's annual GDP. Table 1.10 lists the monetary costs of the main transport system diseconomies in the GMA.

Table 1.10 Cost of Traffic Diseconomies in Greater Metropolitan Area of San José, 2005–09

US$, millions

Costs	2005	2006	2007	2008	2009	Total
Lost time due to traffic congestion	505	515	531	578	590	2,719
Additional fuel in traffic congestion	46	46	48	52	53	245
Traffic accidents	86	101	106	1,245	122	540
Air pollution due to motor vehicle emissions	54	59	59	634	656	301
Total	690	721	744	8,189	831	3,805
Percent with respect to GDP	2.64%	2.63%	2.66%	2.79%	2.84%	13.56%

Source: Pichardo-Muñiz and Chavarría 2012.

If Well Managed, Urbanization Can Improve Service Delivery and Boost Livability

High population density in cities brings cost savings in service provision. The proximity of physical structures and people brings efficiencies to the provision of network services such as drainage, sewerage, solid waste management, and transport connectivity. In Santiago de Chile, the cost of developing a new residential unit in the outskirts of the city is ten times higher than that in the city core, when accounting for the cost of water pipes, sewage, equipment, and other basic infrastructure. In the Latin America and Caribbean region, the average per capita cost for providing sewer connection ranges from US$120 to US$160 per household (UNEP 2010; WSP 2013). Yet in high-density areas such as cities, the household cost of both conventional and simplified sewerage drops up to population densities of around 80 people per hectare.

To improve the quality of life for residents, municipalities in the region are faced with a dual challenge of addressing a significant backlog of infrastructure needs and at the same time coping with rapid population growth. This puts growing stress on the administrations, particularly at the local level. In providing policy recommendations to tackle these challenges, chapter 2 presents the legal and institutional frameworks of city management in Central America in terms of division of functions between levels of government, municipal finance, and the provision of local goods and services. This chapter then addresses the needs for further vertical and horizontal coordination of government activities, that is, coordination between local and central governments, and the need for further coordination among the local governments in major agglomerations (metropolitan areas).

Failing to improve the living environment in cities could prevent the region from harnessing the economic benefits of an emerging demographic dividend. Along with rapid urbanization throughout the region, the proportion of children and seniors relative to the working-age population will soon reach a historical low. Thanks to its demographics, the region faces a unique development opportunity during the next 20 years (2015 to 2035, the period between the two vertical lines depicted in figure 1.15). As other regions have shown, low dependency ratios[16] create great economic opportunity (Bloom and Williamson 1998; Li, Zhang, and Zhang 2007). But to take advantage of this window, Central American cities must provide human capital and labor market opportunities to their growing population. Building livable cities is needed in order to attract and retain highly skilled workers in high-productivity sectors. But today the proportion of youth that neither works nor attends school in Central America is among the highest in Latin America. In El Salvador and Honduras, one of every four youth between the ages of 15 and 24 is out of school and not working, with the large majority, close to 75 percent, living in cities (Hoyos, Rogers, and Székely 2016).

Understanding the urban dynamics between the main metropolitan centers and those that take place outside the capital regions could present important opportunities for advancing toward a more sustainable urbanization model. Urbanization requires making large infrastructure investments that will lay the

Figure 1.15 Dependency Ratios Will Reach a Historic Low in the Next 20 Years

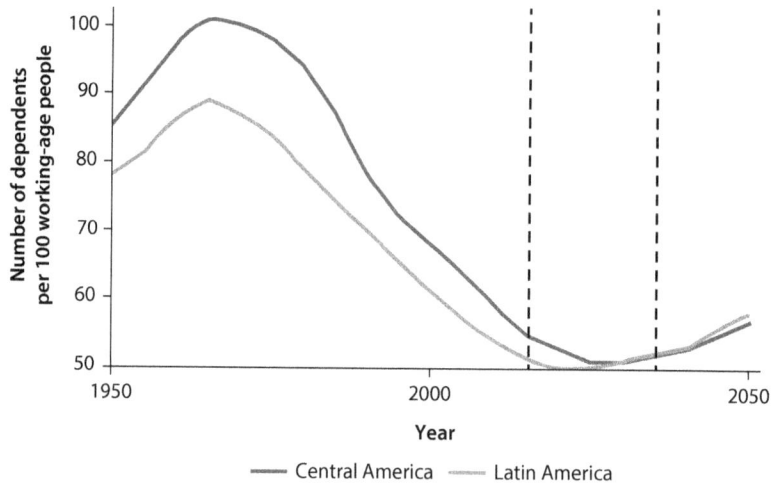

Source: Hoyos, Rogers, and Székely 2016.
Note: The dependency ratio is defined as the ratio of the population ages 0–14 and 65 or over to the population ages 15–64.

ground for a city's ability to transport goods and services more efficiently, facilitate the exchange of knowledge and ideas, and provide good quality of life for its residents. Larger cities need to prioritize investments in connecting infrastructure in order to maximize the economic and social returns of agglomeration. At the same time, smaller cities invest in basic infrastructure to ensure a sustainable growth pattern. Further, in order to maximize the social and economic returns of these investments, infrastructure provision must be tuned with the spatial layout of people and land. An accompanying piece to this report, *Morphology of Secondary Cities in Central America*, offers a comparative look at the evolution of the form and function of urban areas in the region, with a special focus on secondary or intermediate cities.

Notes

1. World Bank calculations and World Bank's Latin America and Caribbean Region Probabilistic Risk Assessment Program (CAPRA).

2. Central American countries arranged in order of most to least urbanized as of 2014 are as follows: Costa Rica (75.9 percent), Panama and El Salvador (tied at 66.3 percent), Nicaragua (58.5 percent), Honduras (54.1 percent) and Guatemala (51.1 percent) (WDI 2015).

3. It is important to note that, while the WDI figures are based on a population aggregation within certain administrative boundaries, the estimates showed in this report are derived from a definition based on built-up area and population. Because the model used in this work allocates a larger share of population to developed land and built areas, it is possible that these figures over estimate the share of urban population concentrated in urban areas, while the official figures may be under estimating population in cities.

4. Built-up area is defined as areas characterized by developed land due to human intervention such as buildings, concrete, asphalt, and suburban gardens (that is, any land or buildings and non-building structures which are present as part of a larger developed environment, such as an illuminated section of a road) (USGS 2012).

5. Urban land cover, or urban extent, is typically measured by the total built-up area (or impervious surface) of cities, sometimes including the open spaces captured by their built-up areas and the open spaces on the urban fringe affected by urban development (Angel et al. 2010).

6. World Bank calculations using GHSL 1975, 1990, 2000, 2014.

7. In situ urbanization is urbanization that is driven by natural population growth, by the reclassification of a settlement from rural to urban, or both. Such urbanization differs from that driven by net rural–urban migration.

8. A review of the World Bank's most recent SCDs for Costa Rica, El Salvador, Guatemala, Honduras, Nicaragua, and Panama was conducted for this report aiming to identify the most pressing development challenges and policy priorities in the region.

9. Per capita income figures were calculated by taking the GDP per capita average (at 2011 constant prices), weighted by the country's total population in each year.

10. One potential limitation of this approach is that it does not consider the regional variations in electrification rates within the region and countries. Therefore, it is difficult to disentangle the share of the variation in total brightness that is explained by differences in electrification rates from the one that can be attributed to increases in economic activity.

11. Underemployed workers include those that are highly skilled but working in low paying or low-skilled jobs, and part-time workers that would prefer to be full-time. Source: "U.S. Strategy For Engagement in Central America." Communication from the White House in support of The Alliance for Prosperity.

12. UN-Habitat, Urban Database.

13. Concejo Centroamericano de Vivienda y Asentamientos Humanos (CCVAH), "Estrategia Centroamericana de Vivienda y Asentamientos Humanos 2009."

14. *Weather events include*: meteorological events (tropical storms, winter storms, severe weather, hail, tornado, local storms); hydrological events (storm surges, river floods, flash floods, landslides); climatological events (freeze, wildland fires, droughts).

15. In Tanzania, congestion and lack of infrastructure investments threaten to erode the potential benefits associated with rapid urban growth in Dar es Salaam—the country's largest and most vibrant city with a population of over 4.3 million residents.

16. The dependency ratio is an age–population ratio that measures the rate of dependency between the population that is not in the labor force (the dependent) and those that are able to work. The ratios are calculated as the sum of population ages 0–14 and over 65 years old, divided by the population able to work (ages 15–65).

Bibliography

Angel, S., J. Parent, D. L. Civco, and A. M. Blei. 2010. *Atlas of Urban Expansion.* Cambridge, MA: Lincoln Institute of Land Policy.

Bashir, S., T. H. Gindling, and A. M. Oviedo. 2012. *Better Jobs in Central America: The Role of Human Capital.* Washington, DC: World Bank.

Berg, Louis Alexandre, and Marlon Carranza, 2015. *Crime, Violence, and Community-Based Prevention in Honduras: Research Report.* Justice, security, and development series. Washington, DC: World Bank Group.

Bloom, D. E., and J. G. Williamson. 1998. "Demographic Transitions and Economic Miracles in Emerging Asia." *The World Bank Economic Review* 12 (3): 419–55.

CCVAH (Consejo Centroamericano de Vivienda y Asentamientos Humanos). 2009. *Estrategia centroamericana de vivienda y asentamientos humanos 2009–2012.* Nicaragua.

GHSL (Global Human Settlement Layer). 2016. European Commission. Global Human Settlement. http://ghslsys.jrc.ec.europa.eu/index.php.

Hsu, F., K. Baugh, T. Gosh, M. Zhizhin, and D. Elvidge. 2015. DMSP-OLS Radiance Calibrated Nighttime Lights Time Series with Intercalibration." *Remote Sensing* 7 (2): 1855–76.

Henderson, J. V., A. Storeygard, and D. N. Weil. 2012. "Measuring Economic Growth from Outer Space." *American Economic Review* 102 (2): 994–1028.

Hoyos, R. D., H. Rogers, and M. Székely. 2016. *Out of School and Out of Work: Risk and Opportunities for Latin America's Ninis.* Washington, DC: World Bank.

Hsu, F., K, Baugh, T. Gosh, M. Zhizhin, and D. Elvidge. 2015. DMSP-OLS Radiance Calibrated Nighttime Lights Time Series. Remote Sensing Journal.

IMF (International Monetary Fund). 2015. *Regional Economic Outlook.* Western Hemisphere: Northern Springs Southern Chills. Washington, DC: IMF.

Inter-American Development Bank. 2012. *Room for Development: Housing Markets in Latin America and the Caribbean.* Washington, DC: Inter-American Development Bank.

Kessides, C. 2005. "The Urban Transition in Sub-Saharan Africa: Implications for Economic Growth and Poverty Reduction." Africa Region Working Paper Series. World Bank, Washington, DC.

Kiunsi, R. B. 2013. "A Review of Traffic Congestion in Dar es Salaam City from the Physical Planning Perspective." *Journal of Sustainable Development* 6 (2): 94–103.

Klaufus, C. 2010. "Watching the City Grow: Remittances and Sprawl in Intermediate Central American Cities." *Environment and Urbanization* 22 (1): 125–37.

Kreft, S., and D. Eckstein. 2014. "Global Climate Risk Index 2014. Who Suffers Most from Extreme Weather Events? Weather-Related Loss Events from 1993 to 2012." Germanwatch. Bonn, Germany.

Levy, J. I., J. J. Buonocore, and K. von Stackelberg. 2010. "Evaluation of the Public Health Impacts of Traffic Congestion: A Health Risk Assessment." *Environmental Health* 9 (65): 1–12.

Li, H., J. Zhang, and J. Zhang. 2007. "Effects of Longevity and Dependency Rates on Saving and Growth: Evidence from a Panel of Cross Countries." *Journal of Development Economics* 84 (1): 138–154.

Negroponte, Diana Villiers, Alma Caballero, and Consuelo Amat. 2012. *Conversations with Experts on the Future of Central America: Summary Report.* Washington, DC: Brookings Institution.

Ng'Hily, Dickson. 2013. "How Dar Traffic Jams Cost 411bn/-annually." IPP Media.

Osborne, T., M. C. Pachón, and G. E. Araya. 2014. "What Drives the High Price of Road Freight Transport in Central America?" Policy Research Working Paper 6844, World Bank, Washington, DC.

Pichardo-Muñiz, A., and M. O. Chavarría. 2012. *Agglomeration Economies versus Urban Diseconomies: The Case of the Greater Metropolitan Area (GMA) of Costa Rica*. INTECH Open Access Publisher.

Prensa Libre. 2015. "103 call centers operan en Centroamérica, 75 de estos en Guatemala" (accessed 19 May 2016), from http://www.prensalibre.com/economia/103-call-centers -operan-en-centroamerica-75-de-estos-en-guatemala.

Proceso Digital. 2016. "Solo en enero surgieron unos 30 mil nuevos pobres en Honduras, según el Fosdeh" (accessed 19 May 2016), from http://www.proceso.hn/nacionales /item/118705-solo-en-enero-surgieron-unos-30-mil-nuevos-pobres-en-honduras -segun-el-fosdeh.html.

Shifter, M. 2012. "The Shifting Landscape of Latin American Regionalism." *Current History* 111 (742): 56.

UNEP (United Nations Environment Programme). 2010. *The Central Role of Wastewater Management in Sustainable Development*. UNEP.

UN-Habitat Urban Data. 2016. (accessed 19 May 2016), from http://urbandata.unhabitat .org/.

UNODC (United Nations Office on Drugs and Crime). 2012. *Transnational Organized Crime in Central America and the Caribbean: A Threat Assessment*. UNODC.

———. 2014. *Global Study on Homicide 2013: Trends, Contexts, Data*. UNODC.

United Nations. 2014. *World Urbanization Prospects 2014*. United Nations Publications.

USGS (U.S. Geological Survey Land Cover Institute). 2012. Washington, DC. US Department of Interior. http://landcover.usgs.gov/urban/umap/htmls/defs.php.

WFP (United Nations World Food Programme) and IOM (the International Organization for Migration). 2015. *Hunger Without Borders: The Hidden Links Between Food Insecurity, Violence and Migration in the Northern Triangle of Central America*. WFP and IOM.

World Bank. 2009. *World Development Report 2009: Reshaping Economic Geography*. Washington, DC: World Bank.

———. 2010. *Crime and Violence in Central America*, Vol II. Washington, DC: World Bank.

———. 2011. *Crime and Violence in Central America: A Development Challenge*. Washington, DC: World Bank.

———. 2013. *Planning, Connecting, and Financing Cities—Now: Priorities for City Leaders*. Washington, DC: World Bank.

———. 2015a. *Competitive Cities for Jobs and Growth: What, Who, and How*. Washington, DC: World Bank.

———. 2015b. "Costa Rica: Systematic Country Diagnostic." World Bank, Washington, DC.

———. 2015c. "El Salvador—Building on Strengths for a New Generation: Systematic Country Diagnostic" World Bank, Washington, DC.

———. 2015d. "Honduras—Unlocking Economic Potential for Greater Opportunities: Systematic Country Diagnostic." World Bank, Washington, DC.

———. 2015e. "Panama—Locking in Success: Systematic Country Diagnostic." World Bank, Washington, DC.

———. 2016. "Building Bridges in Guatemala: Systematic Country Diagnostic." World Bank, Washington, DC.

———. 2016. World Development Indicators. Washington, D.C.: The World Bank (producer and distributor). http://data.worldbank.org/data-catalog/world-development-indicators.

World Bank LCR Probabilistic Risk Assessment Program—CAPRA. "Gross Domestic Product Disaggregation Methodology and applications in Disaster Risk Management." WB Working Paper in preparation by P. Blanchard, B. Blankespoor, J. Rivera-Fuentes, R. Gunasekera, O. Ishizawa and L. F. Jiménez-Salazar.

WSP (Water and Sanitation Program). 2013. Water and Sanitation Program Website. https://www.wsp.org/content/latin-america-and-caribbean. Washington, DC: The World Bank.

CHAPTER 2

Managing Cities and Agglomerations: Strengthening Institutions for Effective Planning and Service Delivery

Mats Andersson

Overview

Improving how cities are managed is essential to harnessing the benefits of urbanization and addressing its costs. Improved city management is critical to enhance the reach and quality of service delivery, finance the investments required to accommodate an increasing urban population, and coordinate infrastructure and service provision with territorial development plans. In Central America, central and municipal governments are the key institutions involved in managing cities. The ongoing decentralization process in Central America has extended the responsibilities of municipalities, but their ability to fulfill these increasing functions is constrained by their limited institutional and financial capacity. The central government has an important role in strengthening local institutions through capacity building and financial incentives to enhance their performance in managing the development of urban areas.

This chapter presents a diagnostic of the institutional and financial framework of municipalities and identifies policy options for Central American countries to improve how cities are managed. Section 2 presents an overview of the institutional framework for city management in the region. Section 3 discusses current efforts of intermunicipal coordination in the region. Section 4 presents an overview of the existing financial capacities of municipalities in the region. Last, section 5 identifies priorities for leveraging the potential of Central American cities through improved city management.

Key Messages

Central American countries can focus on the following key actions to improve city management and ensure better investments in urban areas.

- Empowering local governments, both institutionally and financially, is critical in order to enhance their performance in delivering key services and financing necessary investments for a growing urban population.
- Intermunicipal cooperation mechanisms can be strengthened to offer adequate service delivery and territorial planning within agglomerations covering various local government jurisdictions.
- Central and local governments can enhance coordination in areas where functional responsibilities intersect, particularly in spatial development and service delivery.

Improving City Management in an Increasingly Urban Central America

Improved management at the city level can help address some of Central America's most pressing challenges by making cities more prosperous and livable. While Central America has benefitted largely from urbanization, it has also been subject to numerous urban diseconomies, most visible in terms of congestion, poor services provision, and precarious housing. To tackle urbanization's negative impacts and reap its intended benefits (as those discussed in chapter 1), management at the city level is key. Effective city management is contingent upon strengthened municipalities and can go beyond the provision of basic services and infrastructure to also shape the efficiency, sustainability, and resilience of cities through territorial planning, capital investment, and articulation of public policies at the local level. Through these actions, municipalities are better positioned to make cities work in favor of existing residents or newly arriving urban residents.

There is an ongoing process of decentralization throughout the region, but it can be further strengthened. The level of decentralization differs across Central American countries, with Nicaragua and Panama being the most and least decentralized countries, respectively. New and recent laws have extended and better defined functions, responsibilities, and resources at the subnational level, but overall, their enactment has moved fairly slowly and has been confined mostly to basic services provision. Full implementation of the decentralization process has been hindered mostly by the relatively weak institutional and financial capacities of municipalities. Strengthening the decentralization process will allow municipal governments to have a more active role in city management by assuming greater responsibilities in spatial development, expanded service delivery, capital investments, and revenue mobilization. This calls for the active engagement of the central government, which will be key in supporting municipalities by facilitating the mechanisms to build their planning and management capacities to enhance performance.

In the Central American context, strengthening institutions for city management means strengthening municipal governments' capacities for territorial planning, financial management and investing, improving the coordination with the central government, and developing intermunicipal cooperation for efficient management of urban agglomerations. Municipalities are the focus of improved city management. Strengthening their planning, financial, and executing capacities will not only enhance their performance in their current role of basic services providers but will also prepare them to assume greater urban functions, which will be informed by, and benefit from, a local perspective. Municipal governments can coordinate with central government policies, initiatives, and operations to ensure coherent development of urban areas, and at par with other municipal governments for efficient service delivery and territorial planning.

The Central Role of Municipalities in City Management

All Central American countries are unitary states, and municipalities are the predominant form of subnational government. Power resides mainly in the central government, with only some powers devolved to politically autonomous local governments, namely municipalities. Other territorial subdivisions exist, such as provinces and departments, but these are not administered by autonomous governments, and act as deconcentrated extensions of the central government with no real executive powers. With the exception of specific autonomous regions in Nicaragua and Panama,[1] municipalities are the autonomous local administrations in the six Central American countries. The extent of devolution of powers to municipalities varies from country to country, and it is more or less reflective of when decentralization laws were adopted. Since the second half of the 1980s, Guatemala and Nicaragua, two of the most decentralized countries, passed legislation granting greater autonomy to subnational governments. In contrast, a decentralization law was recently approved in 2015 in Panama—the most centralized country in the region. Table 2.1 summarizes the territorial subdivisions in each of the countries and references the existing legal framework for decentralization.

Decentralization policies are underway in the Central American region, yet at varying rates. For a relatively homogenous group of countries in terms of size, population, and history, the region presents a variety of approaches to, and degrees of, decentralization and city management. Panama is by far the most centralized, and Nicaragua the most decentralized. Newer laws (for example, Panama) build on earlier examples and better define subnational functions, responsibilities, and resources. However, implementation of decentralization policies has been consistently slow in the region and it has been confined primarily to basic services provision.

Table 2.1 Territorial Subdivisions in Central American Countries and Underlying Framework

	Main territorial subdivisions	*Underlying legal framework*
Costa Rica	The national territory is divided into *Provinces, Cantons,* and *Districts* (Art. 168 CRCR)	Constitution of the Republic of Costa Rica (CRCR), Title XII—El Regimen Municipal
	7 Provinces, with no executive office	Municipal Code (Law 7794/1998)
	81 Cantons, with Municipal Governments	General Law on the Transfer of Powers from the Executive Government to the Municipalities (Law 8801/2010)
El Salvador	The Republic is divided into *Departments* (Art. 200 CRES), and these are further divided into *Municipalities* (Art. 202 CRES)	Constitution of the Republic of El Salvador (CRES), Title VI, Chapter VI—Gobierno Local
	Municipalities are autonomous economically, technically, and administratively (Art. 203 CRES)	Municipal Code (Decree 274/1986)
	14 Departments further divided into 39 Districts	Law of Development and Territorial Planning of the Metropolitan Area of San Salvador and Nearby Municipalities (Law 732-1993)
	262 Municipalities	The decentralization process follows the National Decentralization Policy of 2007
Guatemala	Municipalities act by delegation of the State (Art. 134 CRG).	Constitution of the Republic of Guatemala (CGR), Title V, Chapter VII - Regimen Municipal
	The territory is divided into *Departments*, and these into *Municipalities* (Art. 224 CRG)	Municipal Code (Law 12-2002)
	22 Departments	Preliminary Law of Regionalization (Law 70-1986)
	335 Municipalities	
Honduras	The national territory is divided into *Departments* and these into autonomous *Municipalities* administered by *Corporations* elected by the people (Art. 292 CRH)	Constitution of the Republic of Honduras (CRH), Title V, Chapter XI—Del Regimen Departmental y Municipal
	78 Municipalities	Law of Municipalities (Decree 134-1990)
Nicaragua	The national territory is divided into *Departments, Autonomous Regions of the Atlantic Coast,* and *Municipalities* (Art. 175 CRN)	Constitution of the Republic of Nicaragua (CRN), Title XI Political-Administrative Division
	The Municipality is the basic unit of the political-administrative division of the country (Art. 176 CRN)	Law of Municipalities (Law 40/1988)
	15 Departments + 2 Autonomous Regions (No executive government)	
	153 Municipalities	
Panama	*Municipalities* are defined as "the fundamental entity of the political-administrative division of the State, with a self-government that is democratic and autonomous." (Art. 233 CRP)	Constitution of the Republic of Panama (CRP), Title VIII—Regimenes Municipales y Provinciales
	Provinces are essentially extensions of the Central Government	Law 106/1973 on the Municipal Regime
	The provinces are divided into *Districts (Municipalities)*, and these are further divided into *Corregimientos.*	Law 2/1985 on the functions of provincial governors
	10 Provinces + 3 Indigenous *Comarcas* at the level of provinces	Congress approved a new Decentralization Law in 2009, but the president did not sign it (Law 37/2009)
	2 other smaller Indigenous *Comarcas* at the level of *Corregimiento*	A Decentralization Law was approved in 2015 (amended Law 37/2009)
	77 Municipalities	

Legal decentralization frameworks assign roles and responsibilities to municipalities, but these are only partially implemented. All countries guarantee subnational policy making in their constitutions, but the level of detail of these guarantees differs throughout the region. Specific laws, commonly Municipal Codes, specify subnational responsibilities and designate municipalities as the subnational institutions empowered to solve local problems. However, significant heterogeneity exists throughout the region in terms of actual municipal competence. In practice, the role of municipalities is limited, and central governments across the region are still responsible for some local service provision. Table 2.2 below summarizes the roles and responsibilities for provision of municipal services in the metropolitan areas of capital cities in Central America. As illustrated, municipal governments in Nicaragua and Guatemala have the broadest scope of responsibilities, while in Panama and Costa Rica, the central government is in charge of most local service provision. The situation in El Salvador and Honduras falls somewhere in between. Aside from San Salvador, no metropolitan entity is currently responsible for coordination of service provision at the metropolitan level.

Table 2.2 Service Provision in the Metropolitan Area of Capital Cities in Central America

Level	Costa Rica	El Salvador	Guatemala	Honduras	Nicaragua	Panama
Central government	• Cadaster • Building Permits • Water Supply • Sanitation • Local Roads • Drainage • Transport • Public Safety[b]	• Cadaster • Water Supply • Sanitation • Local Roads • Drainage • Transport (regulation) • Public Safety	• Cadaster • Public Safety[b]	• Cadaster • Transport (regulation) • Public Safety[b]	• Water Supply • Sanitation • Public Safety	• Cadaster • Water Supply • Sanitation • SWM • Local Roads • Drainage • Transport • Public Safety[b]
Metropolitan entity	–	• Building Permits • Solid Waste Management (disposal)	–	–	–	–
Local government	• SWM • Local Roads[a] • Drainage[a] • Public Safety[b]	• SWM (collection) • Local Roads[a] • Drainage[a] • Transport	• Building Permits • Water Supply • Sanitation • SWM • Local Roads • Drainage • Transport • Public Safety[b]	• Building Permits • Water Supply • SWM • Local Roads • Drainage • Transport • Public Safety[b]	• Cadaster • Building Permits • Solid Waste Management • Local Roads • Drainage • Transport	• Building Permits • Public Safety[b]

a. Secondary function.
b. Shared public safety responsibility.

Roles and responsibilities for municipal service provision vary substantially across countries and sectors. Some examples to highlight include:

Water and sanitation—This sector shows the largest inconsistency between what is stated in the respective laws and what occurs in practice. Although all countries in the region—with the exception of El Salvador—legally assign water and sanitation provision to municipalities; only Guatemala City provides this service, through its company EMPAGUA.[2] Despite the legal provisions in place, national agencies are the actual providers of water and sanitation services.[3]

Solid waste management—In most countries, municipalities provide solid waste management services, either directly, or through private concessions. The exception is Panama, where the service is centralized, and currently provided by the Authority of Urban and Household Sanitation (AAUD). In the case of San Salvador, solid waste management services are provided through a mechanism of metropolitan coordination. Through a public-private partnership, the Council of Mayors of the Metropolitan Area of San Salvador (*Consejo de Alcaldes del Área Metropolitana de San Salvador*, COAMSS) and private sector investors created the company MIDES (*Manejo Integral de Desechos Sólidos*) to offer integrated solid waste management services to a total of 87 municipalities.

Roads—Responsibility for the construction and maintenance of roads varies considerably across the region. For instance, municipalities in Guatemala, Honduras, and Nicaragua are in charge of this service, while national-level agencies oversee interurban connectivity networks. On the other hand, in Costa Rica and El Salvador it is a shared responsibility between the central and local governments. Similar to many other local services in Panama, the central government is also responsible for the management of urban roads.

Public safety—National police forces are the main providers of public safety in all Central American countries. However, Costa Rica, Guatemala, Honduras, and Panama are complementing national forces with police departments managed at the municipal level. In these cases, a clear division of responsibilities and adequate coordination among both levels of police are mostly lacking.

Municipal governments have a central role to play in territorial planning in Central America. Although many municipalities do not have the technical capacity to prepare territorial development plans, they play a key role in their implementation as the responsibility of issuing building permits lies with them (except in Costa Rica). Territorial planning is an area where coordination between central and local governments is critical for sustainable urbanization to take place in Central America. Given the limited capacity at the local level, territorial development plans are often developed by central agencies, which results in limited appropriation of these instruments at the local level. This diminishes the potential impact of these plans, not only through partial implementation of the territorial control provision they contain, but also through a lack of coordination between spatial development and capital investment planning. Central America offers examples of intermunicipal cooperation mechanisms which can contribute to solving this challenge by providing the adequate geographical scale to build local capacity for territorial planning. The following section discusses the current situation and opportunities for such arrangements.

Managing Agglomerations through Intermunicipal Coordinating Mechanisms

Local governments need to seize opportunities for coordinated planning and service delivery across agglomerations. Chapter 1 showed how the growth of capital and secondary cities is increasingly extending over formally defined municipal boundaries. As a result, cities are becoming more economically interdependent with other surrounding urban and rural areas, constituting agglomerations or metropolitan areas. While these areas can benefit from economies of scale in service provision, they are also more vulnerable to negative spillovers. For example, clogged storm drains in one area can cause flooding in another, or water pollution in an area can bring health risks in another. This pattern of growth and greater interconnectedness among cities calls for development at the metropolitan scale, which can be achieved by establishing stronger intermunicipal coordination and cooperation arrangements.

As economically dynamic regions outgrow their local political boundaries, each municipality usually continues delivering services within its own jurisdictions only, even though most urban services spill over the municipal boundaries. Intermunicipal coordination is critical for adequate service delivery, managing growth, and ensuring environmental sustainability across municipal boundaries. Moreover, the governance structure of agglomerations that include multiple municipalities is known to have a direct impact on overall productivity. Work by the Organisation for Economic Co-operation and Development (OECD) shows, for instance, that a metropolitan area of any given size with twice the number of municipalities is associated with around 6 percent lower productivity rates, but the existence of an effective governance mechanism at the metropolitan level can cut this effect by almost half (OECD 2015). In Central America, where agglomerations span multiple municipal administrative boundaries, several scales of metropolitan regions are formed.

However, Central American agglomerations have few supramunicipal coordinating institutions. There are only a few instances, where service provision has been decentralized, that formal coordinating mechanisms have been established between neighboring local governments. In general, metropolitan-level dialogue and collaborative efforts among municipalities are limited in most of the capital regions. One exception, and the strongest example of metropolitan coordination in the region, is COAMSS, a formal coordination mechanism entrusted with urban planning responsibilities (described in detail in box 2.1). Tegucigalpa is a unique case, given that the metropolitan area (made up of two cities) coincides with the area of the Central District Municipality, facilitating metropolitan-wide

Box 2.1 COAMSS in El Salvador

The Council of Mayors of the Metropolitan Area of San Salvador (*Consejo de Alcaldes del Área Metropolitana de San Salvador,* COAMSS) is an autonomous institution established in July 1987. Its objective is to fuel and facilitate inclusive social, economic, and territorial development of the Metropolitan Area of San Salvador to improve the quality of life of its inhabitants. The size of the area is composed of 14 municipalities with a population in 2012 of 2.2 million, 36 percent of the population in El Salvador at the time. The size of the area is 610 km² (about 3 percent of the national territory); the urban (built-up) area is about 175 km² (29 percent). Although a large part of the metropolitan area is rural land, 97 percent of the population is considered urban. The gross domestic product (GDP) of the area is about a third of the national GDP.

This institutional arrangement was born out of the earthquake of 1986, and from the real-ization that the area had become a metropolis whose problems could not be tackled by the various local governments independently, hence the need for a coordinated and united reconstruction approach for the area.

The mission of COAMSS is "To be a collegial body that formulates, regulates, coordinates and leads the policies and programs that allow for the integral development of the territory and the inhabitants of the metropolitan area of San Salvador."

The initial solution was for COAMSS to create in 1988 the Planning Office of the Metropolitan Area of San Salvador (*Oficina de Planificación del Área Metropolitana de San Salvador,* OPAMSS), a technical advisory entity charged with investigating, analyzing, and proposing solutions to the area's urban development. OPAMSS also functions as an executive secretariat of the Council. In 1994, COAMSS reformed the statutes of OPAMSS making it a separate legal entity, an administra-tively and financially autonomous municipal institution. COAMSS appoints the Executive Director of OPAMSS, and its administration is overseen by the General Coordinator and Executive Committee of COAMSS. OPAMSS is funded by municipal contributions, user charges for services it provides in the metro area, and by project implementation resources from national and inter-national cooperation agencies.

With the approval of Law 732/1993[a] OPAMSS was also charged with regulating urban land use and approving building permits in the area. In time, COAMSS has also served as the responsible coordination mechanism for various projects in the area, most notably on public safety, and solid waste management. In 2015 a Council for Metropolitan Development (*Consejo de Desarrollo Metropolitano,* CODEMET) was established within the COAMSS frame-work to propose public investment projects for metropolitan development, and be the entity focused on collaboration with the central government.

Source: www.opamss.org.sv.
a. La Ley de Desarrollo y Ordenamiento Territorial del Área Metropolitana de San Salvador y de los Municipios Aledaños, with related regulations issued in 1995.

coordination. Table 2.3 briefly describes the metropolitan arrangements of capital regions and the extent to which metropolitan coordination exists, particularly in the form of territorial plans. Although certain territorial plans were conceived by some metropolitan areas, the lack of strategic coordination between investment and territorial planning in key sectors has prevented their successful execution.

Table 2.3 Metropolitan Arrangements and Coordination in Territorial Planning

Capital city	Metropolitan arrangement	Examples of territorial plans
Guatemala City	The Metropolitan Area of Guatemala (AMG) comprises 3 large municipalities, each with more than one million people, and 14 other small municipalities. Despite being an area with intensive daily commuting to, and from, Guatemala City, there is very limited coordination among the 17 municipalities. The exception is the *Mancomunidad del Sur Villanueva* formed by six municipalities in the metro area. Further metropolitan-level dialogue might be triggered in the future around (i) heavy transit going through the core city; (ii) pollution of the river; and (iii) the potential extension of an existing Bus Rapid Transit system beyond Guatemala City.	In 2009, the Municipality of Guatemala City launched a Land Management Plan (*Plan de Ordenamiento Territorial*, or "POT"), but this had a limited metropolitan perspective.
Managua	Metropolitan areas are defined at two scales: (i) The *Zona Metropolitana de Managua* (ZMM) composed of 7 municipalities, including Managua, Ciudad Sandino, Tipitapa and Mateare[a]; and (ii) the *Región Metropolitana de Managua* (RMM), covering 30 local authorities in the departments of Managua, Granada, Masaya, and Carazo (an area accounting for about 40 percent of Nicaragua's population). Intermunicipal dialogue is mainly in conjunction with a weekly meeting in Managua with all the mayors in the country.	Although municipalities in Managua's Metro Region have achieved some progress in territorial development, there are no strategic guidelines and concrete land management instruments to carry out projects at a supra-municipal level (IDB 2014). Currently, there is no articulation between existing territorial development plans such as the Municipal Plan for Territorial Development and Managua's Master Plan (*Plan Regulador*).
Panama City	The Panama City Metropolitan Area (*Area Metropolitana del Pacífico*) contains four municipalities (Panama City, San Miguelito, Arraigan, and La Chorrera), which represent close to 40 percent of the population in the country.	A territorial Metropolitan Plan was developed in 2012 by the Ministry of Housing and Territorial Planning (MIVIOT), but has had very limited developmental impact to date.[b]
San José	Three scales of metropolitan areas exist: (i) *four main municipalities* considered local metropolitan areas (San José, Alajuela, Heredia, and Cartago); (ii) the *Area Metropolitana de San José* (14 municipalities); and (iii) the *Gran Area Metropolitans* (GAM), or Valle Central (31 municipalities).	A "Territorial Plan GAM 2013-2030" was prepared in 2013 but was not formally approved by the Institute of Housing and Urbanism (INVU).
San Salvador	Fourteen municipalities make up the Metropolitan Area of San Salvador. They are organized through an autonomous coordinating entity, COAMSS (explained in detail in box 2.1).	The "Municipal Plan for Territorial Planning of the City of San Salvador" was recently approved in 2015.

table continues next page

Table 2.3 **Metropolitan Arrangements and Coordination in Territorial Planning** *(continued)*

Capital city	Metropolitan arrangement	Examples of territorial plans
Tegucigalpa	The Central District of Tegucigalpa, containing Tegucigalpa and its neighboring city Comayaguela, represents the metro area of the capital city. It is by far the largest among the municipalities in Honduras, at almost eight times the size of the average municipality in the country. The metro area is confined to the Central District administration (with two cities), thereby reducing the problem of coordination compared to metro areas with many municipalities.	The Central District elaborated a Municipal Development and Territorial Plan (*Plan de Desarrollo Municipal y Ordenamiento Territorial*, PDMOT), approved in 2014. The plan was developed in consultation with public, private, and civil society stakeholders. However, no mechanisms have been put in place to ensure the plan's implementation nor to guide the metro area's urban development (IDB 2016).

a. A *Plan de Desarrollo Urbano de la Capital*, covering parts of the ZMM, is under development with support of the Emerging and Sustainable Cities Initiative of the Inter-American Development Bank (IDB).
b. Territorial scenarios were recently developed for Panama City and its neighboring areas with support of the Emerging and Sustainable Cities Initiative of the Inter-American Development Bank (IDB).

Municipalities in Central America are increasingly organizing, and establishing mechanisms for intermunicipal coordination. The most notable forms of coordination and cooperation among municipalities are *mancomunidades* (legal entities formed by member local governments) and associations of mayors or local governments (for example, based on legal agreements known as *convenios*). These mechanisms are being established in all the countries to various extent, including in some cross-border settings. They are a reflection of current municipal efforts to strengthen decentralization as municipalities lack sufficient capacities to assume some responsibilities alone. The use of such voluntary arrangements in the respective country is summarized in table 2.4. See box 2.2 to learn about Colombia's efforts in interjurisdictional coordination within agglomerations.

These intermunicipal coordinating structures are a good starting point, but they can be strengthened and applied more broadly in the Central American countries. A municipality's association to a *mancomunidad*, or *convenio*, alone is not sufficient. It needs to actively use the structure to foster effective coordination among the member municipalities on critical subjects. Stronger institutional platforms (for example, the staffing of a secretariat or administrative unit) and financial resources are needed in most cases for these coordinating entities to reach their maximum potential (see box 2.1 on San Salvador as a good example). In some cases, and for specific sectors, a separate metropolitan authority may be considered a stronger arrangement. Taking full advantage of coordination and cooperation efforts among local governments will help municipalities achieve four important objectives: (i) seize economies of scale, (ii) address negative spillovers, (iii) address equity concerns, and (iv) become stronger by acting jointly. Below is a brief explanation of these objectives, and a few examples of existing *mancomunidades* and existing supramunicipal institutions working toward their achievement.

Table 2.4 Intermunicipal Coordination Mechanisms in Central American Countries

Country	Description
Costa Rica	*Mancomunidades*, as separate intermunicipal legal entities, have not been set up in Costa Rica to date. Instead, *Convenios* are sometimes established for the purpose of metropolitan-level coordination.
El Salvador	For over twenty years, the country has worked in forging intermunicipal arrangements, referred to as microregions, *mancomunidades,* or associations of municipalities. About 90 percent of the country's municipalities are members of one or more association. Currently, about 50 such entities exist, with memberships ranging from 2 to 25 municipalities for each.
Guatemala	Approximately 25 *Mancomunidades de Municipios* and local associations of municipalities exist in Guatemala.[a] Some of them focus on one specific function such as solid waste management or joint training programs, while others have prepared strategic plans supported by the EU. Others function as political alliances for joint proposals to the central government. About 40 percent of the municipalities in the country are members of one or more such arrangement.
Honduras	The national government as well as the National Association of Municipalities (AMHON) in Honduras have for many years promoted the formation and strengthening of Mancomunidades (or micro-regions) as a means of increasing the administrative capacity of the smaller municipalities in the country. As per the Municipal Law, by municipal council vote of two thirds, the municipalities can form associations for territorial or sectoral reasons, or for the purpose of rendering services.
Nicaragua	Intermunicipal dialogue in Nicaragua is mainly in conjunction with a weekly meeting in Managua attended by all the mayors in the country. These meetings are chaired by the president of the Nicaraguan Institute for Municipal Development (*Instituto Nicaragüense de Fomento Municipal*, INIFOM). Within departments, intermunicipal interaction tends to be mainly along party lines. However, a few subject-specific coordination initiatives exist.
Panama	Only a few small *mancomunidades* exist at present, mainly for coordination of solid waste disposal. More intermunicipal cooperative initiatives may emerge in coming years since the municipalities will be able to implement more investments based on significant property tax funds being distributed to the municipalities by the central government as of 2016.

a. Both forms are legal entities as stipulated in the Código Municipal. In addition, a couple of cases exist of "empresa municipal de tipo asociativa". For example, EMAPET a water and wastewater company serving the two municipalities Flores and San Benito in northern Guatemala since 1997.

Box 2.2 Interjurisdictional Coordination in Colombia: Law of Territorial Planning

International experience indicates that national governments are able to reduce coordination costs by offering municipalities incentives for interjurisdictional coordination in metropolitan areas. Colombia is one example of a country that introduced instruments for coordination within a context of decentralization. Similarly to the majority of Central American countries, decentralization in Colombia was consolidated under the national constitution, but the process was lacking a framework for interjurisdictional coordination—a tool to strengthen municipal capacity and to drive projects that cross boundaries.

After more than 20 years of debate to create integrated approaches to land use management and provision of infrastructure for cities that extended beyond their municipal borders, Colombia enacted the Law 1454 of 2011 (*Ley Orgánica de Ordenamiento Territorial*, LOOT for its acronym in Spanish). The law provides the legal, administrative, and financial framework for coordinating spatial units across the country. In a country as decentralized as Colombia—with more than 1,000 municipal governments having identical responsibilities—appropriate incentives for intermunicipal coordination become essential to avoid forgoing the benefits from economies of scale and minimize costs from urbanization.

box continues next page

Box 2.2 Interjurisdictional Coordination in Colombia: Law of Territorial Planning *(continued)*

The new law reinforces municipal authority over local projects and creates commissions to collaborate on territorial planning issues. It creates various schemes for voluntary territorial association (*esquemas asociativos territoriales*) for metropolitan areas, allowing municipalities to work together in joint projects and to create spaces for voluntary, collaborative interjurisdictional arrangements.

Source: Samad, Lozano-Gracia, and Panman 2012.

1. Seizing opportunities for *economies of scale*, to save on costs. Examples include solid waste disposal to one (or a few) sites in the area and integrated water and sanitation networks (provided the various urban areas are close enough). The Metropolitan Federation of Municipalities (*Federación Metropolitana de Municipalidades*, FEMETROM) in Costa Rica, formed in 2004 by 12 municipalities in the Metropolitan Area of San José, addresses their solid waste management jointly. The *Región Metropolitana de Managua* (RMM), an informal association of fourteen municipalities, has also come together to jointly address their solid waste management. A third regional example of cooperation among local governments is the *Mancomunidad del Sur Villanueva*, formed in 2013 by six suburban municipalities south of Guatemala City. This *mancomunidad* conducts joint initiatives and addresses a variety of subjects through studies and other preparatory work, including a potential joint landfill, water resource management, transport studies, and providing land for a local university, among others.

2. Addressing *spillovers* (externalities). Such a case occurs when activities in one local jurisdiction have negative or positive impacts in neighboring local jurisdictions, and raises a question of "fairness." For instance, air and water pollution and flooding tend to disregard jurisdictional boundaries. Similarly, tourism attractions may exist in one jurisdiction while accommodations are mainly located in another. The *Asociación de Municipios de la Subcuenca del Lago de Managua* (AMUSCLAM), an alliance of the municipalities of Managua (three districts), Crucero, Concepción, Tecuantepec, and Nindiri are focused on water and other environmental issues south of Lake Managua.

3. Addressing *equity concerns*. Large differences may exist in the tax base among the local jurisdictions, creating significant differences in the service provision. People may live (and pay local taxes) in one city, but work and spend most of their time in another, using services they do not pay for. Such situations may raise questions of "compensation."

4. Becoming *stronger by acting jointly*. This may include pooling of funds for a facility or equipment for shared use, jointly attracting investments or major events to the area (rather than locally competing for them among each other), and carrying out joint procurement to achieve better price and lower transaction costs.

Municipal Finances in Central America

The financing of municipalities in Central America reflects the overall decentralization scenario in the respective countries. Figure 2.1 presents local governments' and central government revenues[4] as a percentage of gross domestic product (GDP) in the six countries. The weight of local government revenues, both in terms of percent of GDP and as percent of total government revenues, varies significantly between the countries, with Panama and Costa Rica being the most centralized countries, and Guatemala and Nicaragua the most decentralized. In 2012, revenues of municipalities in Panama represented the smallest percentage, both in terms of a percentage of GDP (0.5 percent), and in comparison to the central government revenues (municipal revenues represented around 2 percent of total government revenues). Nicaragua is the country in which municipal revenues are the most significant, representing around 4 percent of GDP.

Although the financial weight of municipalities is significant, their resources remain limited in absolute terms. The wide range that can be observed in the region, in terms of the share of total government revenues assigned to the municipalities, mirrors the diversity both within Latin America and across the world. However, all countries in Central America have relatively low levels of public spending, with Guatemala being the country with the lowest percentage of public expenditure as a percentage of GDP. As a result, in spite of receiving a significant share of public revenues in some of the countries, the revenues per capita of Central American municipalities are uniformly low. Figure 2.2 presents total revenues per capita by level of government. In 2012, average local government revenues per capita ranged from US$90 in Panama to US$185 in Guatemala.

Figure 2.1 Total Revenue by Level of Government in Central America as a Percentage of GDP, 2012

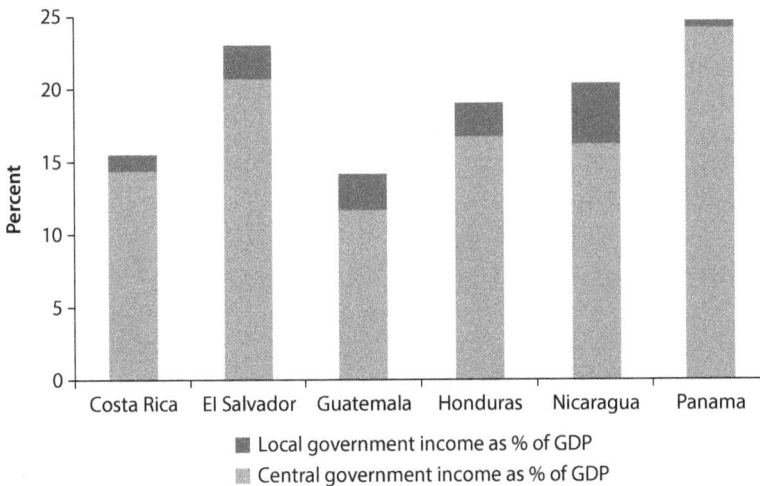

Local government income as % of GDP
Central government income as % of GDP

Source: Based on data from the countries' central banks and ministries of finance.

Figure 2.2 Total Revenue per Capita by Level of Government in US$ PPP, 2012

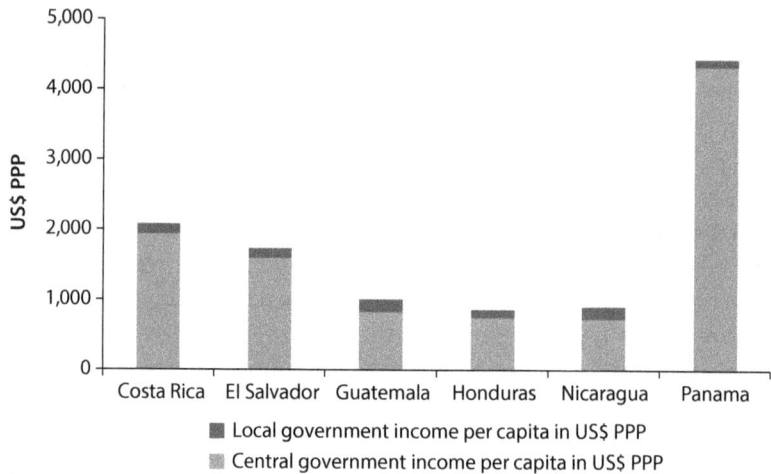

■ Local government income per capita in US$ PPP
▨ Central government income per capita in US$ PPP

Source: Based on data from countries' Central Banks and Ministries of Finance, and the World Bank.
Note: PPP = purchasing power parity.

The allocation of tax revenues between central governments and municipalities varies significantly within the countries. Municipalities with the most limited revenues are in countries where the central government collects and keeps the property tax, as in the cases of Costa Rica and Panama. However, the situation in Panama is changing following the enactment of the 2015 decentralization law which provides for the creation of a decentralization fund, financed by the revenues from the property tax, and directed to the financing of municipal investments. Table 2.5 summarizes the taxes allocated to municipalities in the six countries.

Most Central American countries have been using formula-based transfers as the main source of financing for their municipalities. The most common design of transfer is one where municipalities receive a percentage of the central government budget. As presented in table 2.6., in El Salvador and Guatemala, the transfer is based on the total current income, while in Honduras and Nicaragua it is based on the tax income only. For many of these recurrent transfers, minimum requirements exist for their use on capital (not current) expenditures. These capital expenditure requirements can be up to 90 percent. No central approvals are required for the projects for which the transfers are used. A second transfer design is based on agreements between the central government and municipalities. This is mainly the case in Costa Rica, although other countries also have such transfer mechanisms to complement the main recurrent transfers. Finally, a third design is recurrent capital transfers. The best example is Panama, where a set amount is transferred based on approved projects. This is also the case in Costa Rica with a complementary transfer for roads based on fuel taxes.

The largest source of financing for capital cities[5] is their own-source income, consisting mostly of local taxes and fees. This is true both for municipalities that are relatively strong and relatively weak financially speaking (see figure 2.3). The relative weight of taxes and fees in local income varies significantly between

Table 2.5 Local Taxes of Municipalities in Central America

	Main locally collected taxes and fees	Centrally collected taxes
Costa Rica	Business patents (Art. 79 Municipal Law 7.794/1998). For the Municipality of San José the National Tax Directorate (DGT) has transferred the collection of the property tax. Municipalities can collect fees for public lighting, solid waste management, park maintenance, police services, and other services it deems necessary (Art. 74 Municipal Law 7.794/1998).	Property tax is collected by the central government DGT (Law 7.509/1995).
El Salvador	Municipalities can collect taxes on local businesses and property (Art. 125 Law 86/1991) Municipalities can collect fees on public services such as public lighting, solid waste management, park maintenance, paving of public roads, and markets, among others (Art. 130 Law 86/1991).	
Guatemala	Municipalities collect an annual tax from citizens based on their income for maintenance of local infrastructure (*Boleto de Ornato*, Law 121/1996), as well as taxes on economic activities (Municipality-specific regulation).	The central government collects the property tax (IUSI) through the Tax Administration Superintendence (SAT), but directly transfers most of the collection to municipal governments (Law 15/1998).
Honduras	Taxes are: property tax, personal income tax, tax on economic activities, tax on extraction or exploitation of mineral resources, and tax on cattle (Art. 75 Law 134/1990). Fees on municipal services; use of public property and administration fees (Art. 84 Law 134/1990).	
Nicaragua	Property tax (Decree 3/1995). In Managua there is a tax on economic activities and a patent register tax (Decree 10/1991). There are fees and rights for municipal services (including electricity, telephone, solid waste. management), cattle, markets and use of municipal property (Decree 10/1991).	
Panama	Taxes on economic activities, the sale of alcoholic beverages, and butchering. Fees and rights on the use of municipal goods and services; and rights on public spectacles and extraction of sands, other non-metallic mining, wood, and exploitation of forests (Law 106/1973).	Property tax is collected by the central government through the National Authority for Public Income (ANIP).

Table 2.6 Transfers to Municipalities in Central America

	Current/mixed transfers	Conditional capital transfers
Costa Rica	The law contemplates transfers to municipalities based on agreements with the central government on transferred competencies (Law 8.801/2010). There are no unconditional transfers to municipalities.	7.5 percent of the Tax on Fuels is transferred to municipalities for building and maintenance of local roads (Law 8.114/2001).
El Salvador	The central government transfers 8 percent of its current net income to the Municipal Economic and Social Development Fund (FODES) (Art. 1 Law 74/1988). FODES is managed by the Salvadorian Institute for Municipal Development (ISDEM). The FODES in turn transfers funds to municipalities; 80 percent of funds must finance infrastructure, and 20 percent for current expenditures.	

table continues next page

Table 2.6 Transfers to Municipalities in Central America *(continued)*

	Current/mixed transfers	*Conditional capital transfers*
Guatemala	The central government must transfer 10 percent of its operating budget to municipalities. At least 90 percent of the transfer must be invested on programs in education, preventive health, infrastructure, and public services; the remaining up to 10 percent can finance functioning expenditures (Art. 257 CRG). 1.5 percent of value added tax collection must be transferred to municipalities. Up to 25 percent can finance functioning expenditures, with the remaining 75 percent for investment (Law 27/1992). Various other laws include current transfers to municipalities including on gasoline, agricultural products, and liquor (see Law 6/1991).	The central government collects a tax on vehicles, and transfers a share to municipalities. This transfer must be spent on road maintenance and construction (Law 70/94).
Honduras	The central government must transfer 5 percent of total tax income to Municipalities. Of this, up to 15 percent can be spent on current expenditures, while 85 percent or more should be spent on investment (Art. 91 Law 134/90).	
Nicaragua	The central government must transfer a percentage of tax income to Municipalities, starting with 4 percent in 2004 and increasing 0.5 percentage points a year up to 10 percent in 2010 (Art. 5 Law 466/2003). Municipalities must spend most transfers on investment, with the required percentage changing according to a government classification of municipalities by total income. For the top category of municipalities (of four) it is 90 percent, and for the bottom category 60 percent (Art. 12 Law 466/2003).	
Panama		The National Program for Local Development (PRONADEL) makes yearly fixed-amount capital transfers to municipalities and communal juntas based on specific preapproved projects (Law 84/2012)

Figure 2.3 Total Income of Capital City Municipalities in Central America by Source, 2013

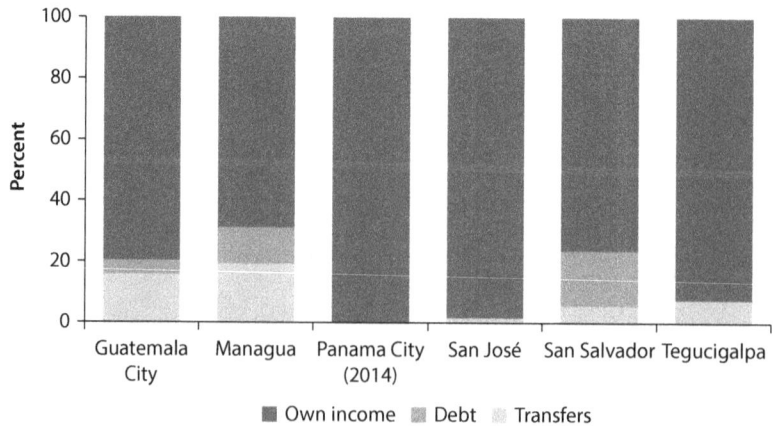

Source: Based on budgets of capital city municipalities.

Figure 2.4 Own Income by Source of Capital City Municipalities in Central America, 2013

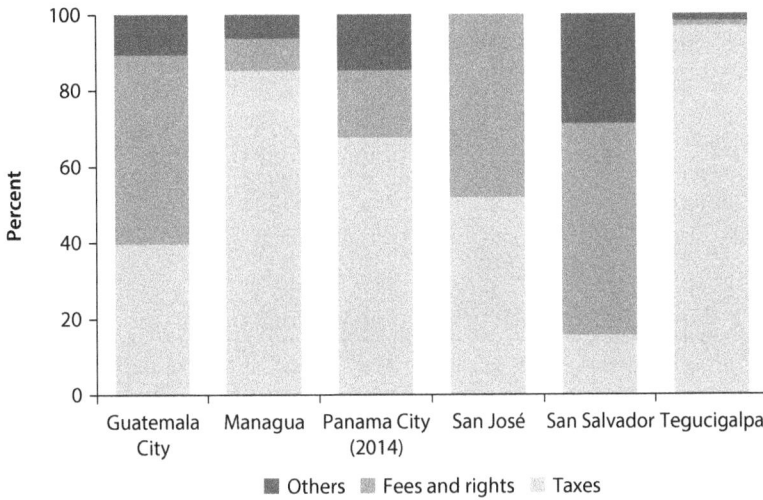

Source: Based on budgets of capital city municipalities.

capital cities. Taxes–mainly property taxes—are the predominant source of own income in San José, Tegucigalpa, Managua, and Panama City, while local service fees generate most income in San Salvador and Guatemala City (see figure 2.4). However, in Costa Rica tax revenues are kept by the central government. This was also the case in Panama until 2016 when property tax revenues are scheduled to be transferred to the municipalities (to be used for capital investments only). Other common taxes collected at the municipal level in all Central American countries include business taxes, patents, and a percentage of sales (turnover tax). Transfers represent more than 10 percent of total income only in Managua and Guatemala City, while debt is a notable source in San Salvador and Managua.

Basic local government functioning is the largest expenditure item in Central American capital cities. This is common across Latin America. Resources allocated to government day-to-day operations are particularly large in San José and Guatemala City, and notably low in Managua, leaving significant space for other types of expenditures. Figure 2.5 shows the breakdown of expenditures in the capital cities for the year 2013 (2014 for Panama City). The second-largest item is capital expenditures, which is a notably large part of the budgets in Managua and Panama City, while essentially nonexistent in San José. San Salvador spends the most on debt service and transfers. San José is the only capital city that had no debt service expenditures in its budget in 2013 (see figure 2.5).

Municipalities can contract debt but usually only after approval or rating by a central entity. All capital cities have contracted short-term debt in recent years to various degree (see figure 2.3).[6] Except in Costa Rica, municipal debt needs to be approved or rated by a central government–controlled mechanism. This gives the central government some fiscal and political control over the public indebtedness of local governments. In most countries there are also restrictions on how much

Figure 2.5 Total Expenditures of Capital City Municipalities in Central America by Type, 2013

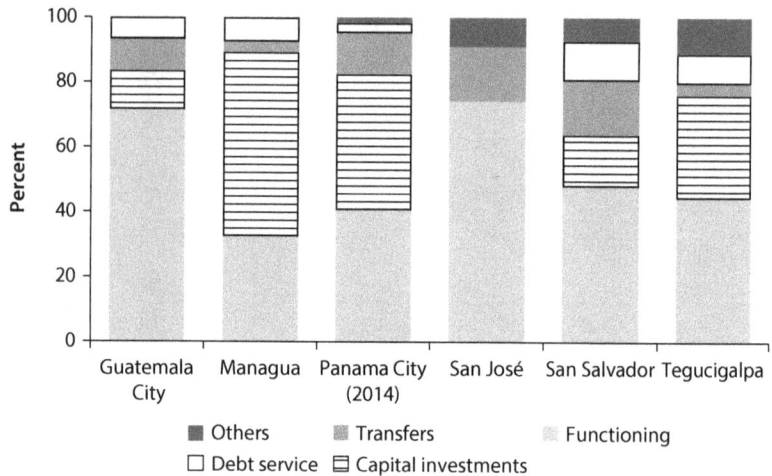

Source: Based on budgets of capital city municipalities.

a municipality can borrow. Limits are set in terms of: (i) length (loan maturity); usually the term in office of local officials; or (ii) amount; by capacity to pay, as a ratio of the municipal income. The more restrictive designs limit the total amount of debt by operating income, or short-term necessities, while the less restrictive ones limit the amount of budgeted income that can be used for debt service payments. In Costa Rica and Panama there are no formal specific limits.

Priorities for Leveraging the Potential of Central American Cities: Strengthening Municipalities for Efficient City Management

Strengthening Municipalities Institutionally and Financially

The central government has an important role to play in enhancing local capacity. Capacity building at the local level is a mutual responsibility between the central and local governments (particularly in unitary states). As mentioned above, ongoing urbanization puts additional stress on local capacity, and further decentralization is often constrained by the capacity of local governments to assume new responsibilities. It is frequently most cost-effective to arrange capacity-building programs on a national basis, rather than in a piecemeal fashion by each municipality. However, it is not only the number and skills of local staff (as important as these may be) that determine the institutional strengths or weaknesses of a local government, but its performance is also a function of the policies applied, the manual and automated processes and workflows used, and related financial allocations. In conjunction with capacity-building initiatives, it is often opportune to also revisit policies and procedures, introduce reasonable standards for service performance, and, to the extent possible, create concrete incentives for good performance.

The Central American countries need to strengthen their local capacity building by enhancing their technological, human, and financial capabilities. All Central

American countries have central agencies and/or local government associations providing technical assistance and capacity-building services to the municipalities in the respective country. This is a critical role during and following any governance change such as implementation of decentralization reform. Therefore, it is recommended that central authorities pay further attention to strengthening and supporting these entities and ensure that they can effectively execute their important functions. At the municipal level, it is essential that adequate capacity—both in terms of human resources and financial capacity—exists to assume new responsibilities. This remains a prerequisite to make the devolution work without detriments (at least early on) for residents and other beneficiaries.[7] This may involve realignment of the number of staff and their skill sets, introduction of new procedures and computer applications, and related training. All Central American countries have central agencies and local government associations providing assistance and training to municipalities, functions which will be critical to ensure effective continued decentralization in light of the challenges that municipalities already face. Continuous improvement programs at the municipal level are also needed, for example as applied for some time in the municipality of Cartago in Costa Rica, in COAMSS (San Salvador), and lately by Panama City in its attempt to become ISO certified.

Central American municipalities need to be financially strengthened to play a more active role in urban development. Municipal finance largely affects the ability of local governments to fulfill their obligations. The financial autonomy of municipalities in Central America has decreased, while the dependence on transfers from national governments has increased. While the scope of the functions performed by municipalities has grown over time, the devolution of spending responsibilities has not been matched by increased revenues. In the absence of adequate sources of revenues, the increase in responsibilities has given rise to unfunded mandates. Municipal expenditure has not been increasing in parallel with own-source revenues, leading to a deepening of the vertical imbalance. Decentralization of functions in the region can be accompanied by a larger budgetary role in order for municipalities to build on urban investments.

Central American countries can build on existing transfer mechanisms to increase the municipalities' capacity to finance required investments while strengthening administrative and technical capacity as well as accountability. As mentioned in the previous section, most Central American countries are using formula-based transfers as the main source of financial support for their municipalities. This type of transparent and predictable intergovernmental fiscal transfer mechanism is an important component of a sound municipal finance framework. International experience offers examples of how national governments can build on these foundations to develop programs that integrate financial support to municipal investment, capacity building, and incentives for improved institutional performance at the municipal level. An approach increasingly adopted by other countries to raise municipal resources is through performance-based programs, a mechanism through which national governments allocate investment grants to municipalities for local capital expenditures (see box 2.3 for an overview of the international experience). A key element of these programs is the performance framework used to monitor the municipalities' performance annually and determine the transfers of performance-based capital grants. Examples of such performance framework already exist in Central America (see box 2.4 for a description of the municipal performance ranking in Guatemala). These programs provide incentives to improve institutional performance as resource transfers are conditional on a city's performance on an array of areas, including service delivery, accountability, participation, budgeting, and planning. Comprehensive capacity-building support is also provided to municipalities and closely articulated to the municipal performance framework. The introduction of transparent, equitable, and predictable sources of finance for municipal investment allows municipalities to shift from a piecemeal project-by-project approach, to a more programmatic approach to municipal investment planning.

Big cities should generally have more fiscal autonomy, and finance should follow function.[8] Certain characteristics of large cities and agglomerations have

---

Box 2.3 Performance-Based Programs: International Experiences

Over the last two decades, various countries across different regions have developed programs to strengthen the institutional performance of municipal governments through performance-based grants. One of the earliest examples of such programs can be found in Indonesia. Since 2001 Indonesia has gone from being one of the most centralized countries in the world in administrative, fiscal, and political terms to one of the most decentralized, with local governments now carrying out more than half of all public investment. Performance-based grants have also been introduced in Ethiopia, India, Tanzania, Tunisia, Uganda, and Vietnam.

These programs share the following characteristics:

- Support to municipal investment is channeled through capital investment grants using transparent, equitable, and predictable allocation mechanisms.
- The use of grant funds is decided by the municipalities following a pluriannual and/or annual participatory planning process aligned with the municipalities' budgeting cycle.
- Eligible investments are defined through a menu of investments corresponding to the municipalities' core functions.
- Municipalities' access to the grants is conditioned on a set of minimum conditions that ensure the required level of fiduciary accountability from municipalities on the use of funds.
- Municipalities' institutional performance in key areas is defined under a municipal performance framework, and participating municipalities are evaluated through an Annual Performance Assessment.
- Institutional performance improvements are incentivized through performance-based grants.
- Comprehensive capacity-building support is provided to municipalities and closely articulated to the municipal performance framework.

box continues next page

Box 2.3 Performance-Based Programs: International Experiences *(continued)*

Figure B2.3.1 shows a typical structure of a performance-based program.

Figure B2.3.1 Performance-Based Program Overall Scheme

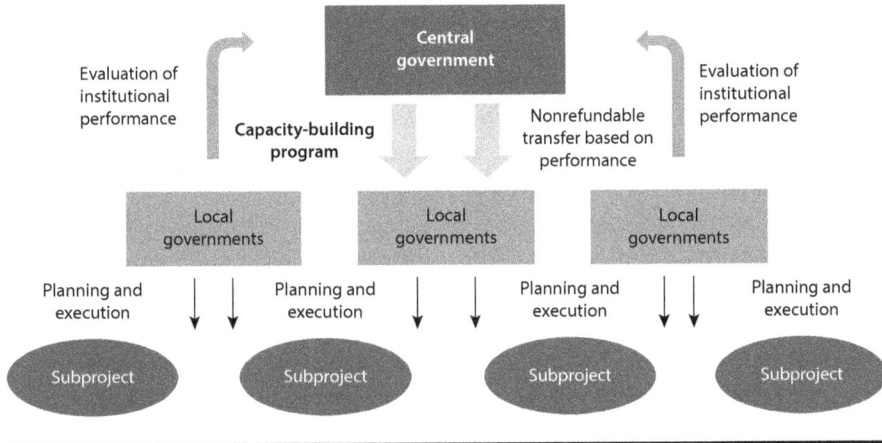

Box 2.4 Municipal Performance Ranking in Guatemala

Since 2008, the government of Guatemala has worked on developing tools for measuring municipal performance, with the objective to strengthen and advance the concept of governance. In 2012, the Planning and Programming Secretariat of the Office of the President of Guatemala (*Segeplán*, for its acronym in Spanish) proposed to institutionalize the National System of Planning (an articulation between the central and municipal governments' planning and territorial development processes) by promoting a policy to strengthen municipalities. This paved the way for the institutionalization and launching of the 2012 Municipal Management Ranking.

Segeplán convened a working group composed of 21 public institutions to formulate the Municipal Strengthening Policy (*Política de fortalecimiento de las municipalidades*). The group agreed on the Municipal Management Ranking as one of the policy's main instruments. The ranking of municipalities makes it possible to have updated information on the performance of municipalities in an array of different subjects, and helps determine the progress and limitations of local governments in areas considered to be conducive to "good governance."

The 2013 Ranking collected information through 277 variables that were organized around six thematic indicators: (i) administrative management; (ii) financial management; (iii) basic municipal services; (iv) strategic management; (v) citizen participation; and (vi) disclosure of information to the public. Municipalities received a score based on their performance in each of these themes. The information that is gathered informs the Municipal Strengthening Policy, and is used to define or redirect the national government's capacity building and technical assistance to local governments.

Source: Ranking de la gestión municipal 2013. (2015). Subsecretaría de Planificación y Ordenamiento Territorial de Segeplán, Secretaría de Planificación y Programación de la Presidencia.

implications for metropolitan public finance. For example, high population density could in some cases reduce the per capita cost of service provision due to economies of scale, but large cities also concentrate a larger number of problems (for example, congestion and pollution) and expenditure needs (for example, public transport and sanitation). Accordingly, large cities and metropolitan areas generally have higher expenditures per capita than smaller municipalities. Local governments usually also have stronger human resource capacity, and greater ability to raise revenues (through taxes and fees). Therefore, they should generally have more fiscal autonomy than other areas, such as in the application of user charges, property taxes, local income and/or business taxes, and fuel taxes, among others. Such policies would be applicable to the capital municipalities of all the Central American countries, in particular when new responsibilities are assigned to them.

Developing Intermunicipal Cooperation

Cities in Central America are becoming more interdependent with their surrounding areas, calling for improved intermunicipal coordination and cooperation. As cities continue to expand beyond their jurisdictional boundaries, the need for metropolitan-level management increases. Local governments must work collaboratively to ensure effective planning and equity in service delivery. Provision of some public services, such as drainage, waste disposal, and sewage collection, are often fragmented, resulting in higher costs and financing challenges for local governments in the region. A lack of any formal or informal metropolitan arrangement tends to reflect missed opportunities in cost savings, which can be achieved through a fair monetary contribution from all municipal governments sharing common issues. The essence of a metropolitan approach is for local governments to cooperate on certain, not all, initiatives or services. As a minimum, a forum for periodic intermunicipal dialogue among local government executives is needed. See box 2.5 for a variety of arrangements for metropolitan governance applied by cities around the world.

Municipalities can benefit from greater coordination among them on a number of different subjects, including:

- Area-wide strategic planning and/or integrated territorial (land use) planning
- Coordinated area-wide economic development
- Joint arrangement for the delivery of one or more services (to gain efficiencies) or to address a specific sector or subject matter jointly (for example, public transport system, flood protection, tourism promotion, disaster risk management, emergency service, and so on)
- Harmonization of local taxes or fees, or arrangement of area-based revenue-sharing (beyond what is being addressed through the intergovernmental fiscal transfer system) to address inequality in service provision among the local jurisdictions
- Ad hoc coordination related to a particular event, incidence or matter concerning the metropolitan area as a whole

Box 2.5 Metropolitan Governance Arrangements from around the World

A variety of arrangements for metropolitan governance are applied by cities around the world, albeit mostly in OECD countries. A classification of these institutional arrangements is presented below.

A. Intermunicipal coordination—horizontal cooperation among local governments

- Ad hoc cooperation/case-by-case joint initiatives/contracting among local governments
- Committee, association, partner agreement, consortium agreement (for example, in Brazil), and so on
- *Mancomunidad* (legal entity)
- Metropolitan council, or "council of governments" (common in the United States)

B. Metropolitan authority—sometimes called "special purpose district"

- Metropolitan authority, for a single or multiple sectors, such as a metropolitan planning authority, a service delivery authority, or a planning & service delivery authority (for example, Buenos Aires Metropolitan Transport Agency)

C. Second-level metropolitan local government

- Second-level metropolitan local government for certain functions (for example, Metropolitan District of Quito)

D. Consolidated local government

- Through territorial annexation or amalgamation of local governments (that is, one local government covering all—or most of—its metropolitan area)

E. Regional/provincial government

- Some metropolitan coordination needs being addressed by a regional/provincial government (for example, by state governments in Mexico and the Intendant of the Santiago Metropolitan Region).

Ensuring a basic legal framework and clarity on roles and responsibilities are key steps in establishing a well-functioning metropolitan arrangement. "Metropolitan area," as conceptually defined in a country's constitution or other legislation, gives credence to the concept, and forms a base for forming institutional arrangements (depending on the actual legislative provisions). In most countries, as in all the Central American countries, basic legal provisions do exist for local governments to form intermunicipal cooperation arrangements to address their needs in the most efficient way. In any metropolitan governance arrangement, there needs to be clarity about functions and responsibilities among the involved parties, particularly if any new authority is introduced. This includes both what the expenditure responsibilities are and what revenue sources a new entity would have. It needs to be effectively communicated to the constituency in the area, for them to know who to hold accountable for what. If a metropolitan agency is not given *any* independent authority (that is, having an advisory function only), a risk of limited effectiveness tends to exist.

Enhancing Coordination between the Central and Local Governments

Enhanced coordination between the central and local governments is critical, but the scope and emphasis depend on the local context. Municipalities and central government agencies work together on a multitude of subjects, ranging from spatial planning and municipal finance to shared local service provision and emergency response. In some sectors, municipalities may have an executing function within a national regulatory framework, with oversight by a central agency (for example, education and health sectors). As shown in table 2.2, the scope of functional responsibilities devolved from the central government to the local governments varies quite significantly among the countries in Central America. Therefore, the need for and approaches to coordination between the two levels of government may differ by country. In Costa Rica and Panama, where the central government is carrying out most local public services, coordinated spatial (land use) planning is critical, particularly related to transport and housing development. In Guatemala and Nicaragua, where the municipalities already carry out most local services, emphasis need to be on finance in the vertical relationship (that is, effective tax regimes, and intergovernmental fiscal transfer system, ideally with built-in incentives for good local governance revenue collection and expenditure management).

Municipalities and central government agencies need to coordinate their operational activities on a multitude of functions. For example, major works on a street or local road need to get synchronized with entities responsible for such services as public transit, power, water, and telecom. Depending on the sector and country, the context is usually one of the following (in some sectors, more than one of the situations may exist):

- *Service provision at the local level is shared between the local and central governments.* Examples are functions such as policing, social protection, and cultural facilities. This requires ongoing coordination in addition to clarity on policies, responsibilities, and rules.
- *Central government agencies are carrying out their responsibilities within municipal jurisdictions.* This may apply to implementation of capital investments and maintenance as well as ongoing service provision. An example is water supply in the capital cities in all the Central American countries except Guatemala (and since 2015 in Honduras). These activities need to be done in coordination with any function the local government is performing in the area to prevent potential complications and inefficiencies.
- *The municipalities have an executing function within a national regulatory framework*, with oversight provided by a central agency (for example in the education and public health sectors). Coordination in these cases tends to include dialogue on policy development and compliance.

The Central American countries need permanent forums and processes for coordinating land use planning with economic development and investment plans. Since planning processes in the region are often spearheaded by a central or a local government body,[9] coordination between the two levels of governments is essential. Each country needs a predefined, permanent forum and process for periodic coordination particularly of land use plans. A similar approach needs to be ensured for economic development plans, capital investment programming, and by sector for transport and other infrastructure subjects where both the central and local governments are involved. Existing vehicles, such as the weekly meeting between the central government and all mayors in Nicaragua and the K'atun process in Guatemala, can possibly be built upon to this effect.[10]

Notes

1. The North Caribbean Coast Autonomous Region (RACCN) and the South Caribbean Coast Autonomous Region (RACCS) are the two autonomous regions in Nicaragua. Panama has five semiautonomous administrative units, organized as indigenous *comarcas* (or territories), which include Emberá-Wounaan, Kuna Yala, Ngöbe-Buglé, Kuna de Madugandí, and Kuna de Wargandí.

2. EMPAGUA was created in 1972 tasked with the provision of water; in 1984 sanitation and drainage were added to its mandate. It is owned by the Municipality of Guatemala. EMPAGUA also serves other municipalities in the metropolitan area.

3. The service provision was passed to municipalities in Honduras in 2015.

4. Local government revenues presented here include both own-source revenues and transfers.

5. The rest of the discussion on financing is done only for the capital cities because of data availability.

6. However, in 2013 San José did not reflect any debt service expenditures in its financial statement. Panama City has only limited long-term debt.

7. However, it is important not to make this an "excuse" for delaying decentralization indefinitely. Rather, concrete actions—with support of the central government—should be taken to increase the local capacity and enable the local authorities to retain trained staff, maintain new processes, and apply capacity development continuously.

8. Reference for this section: Bahl, Roy W., Johannes F. Linn., and Deborah L. Wetzel, eds. 2013. "Financing Metropolitan Governments in Developing Countries," Lincoln Institute of Land Policy, Cambridge, MA.

9. In some metropolitan areas, significant planning functions are carried out by a nongovernmental organization, for example, in the New York Metropolitan Area by the Regional Plan Association (RPA), and in the past in the Greater ABC Region in Sao Paulo.

10. The K'atun 2032 process in Guatemala is a multilevel planning framework including prioritized investment projects, applying a bottom-up approach, with financing being provided "top down" through regional governors.

Bibliography

Andersson, M. 2014. *Metropolitan Governance and Finance. Municipal Finances–A Handbook for Local Governments.* Washington, DC: World Bank.

Bahl, R. W., J. F. Linn, and D. L. Wetzel, eds. 2013. *Financing Metropolitan Governments in Developing Countries.* Cambridge, MA: Lincoln Institute of Land Policy.

IDB (Inter-American Development Bank). 2014. "Plan de Acción: Managua Sostenible." IDB.

———. 2016. "Tegucigalpa and Comayagüela: Capital Sostenible, Segura y Abierta al Público." IDB.

ICMA (Asociación Internacional de Administración de Ciudades y Condados). 2004. "Situacion y Analisis de la Cooperacion Intermunicipal en El Salvador." Document prepared for the U.S. Agency for International Development.

INVU (Instituto Nacional de Vivienda y Urbanismo). 2010. "Plan de Ordenamiento Territorial de la Gran Área Metropolitana. National Institute forHousing and Urbanism, Costa Rica." INVU.

OECD (Organisation for Economic Co-operation and Development). 2015. *The Metropolitan Century, Understanding Urbanization and Its Consequences.* Paris: OECD Publishing.

Samad, T., N. Lozano-Gracia, and A. Panman, eds. 2012. *Colombia Urbanization Review: Amplifying the Gains from the Urban Transition.* Washington, DC: World Bank.

Subsecretaria de Planificacion y Ordenamiento Territorial de Segeplan, Secretatia de Planificacio y Programacion de la Presidencia. 2015. "Ranking de la Gestión Municipal 2013." Guatemala.

UNFPA (United Nations Population Fund). 2009. "Escenarios para la Región Metropolitana de Managua al Año 2020." United Nations Population Fund, Nicaragua.

CHAPTER 3

Making Cities Inclusive by Improving Access to Adequate and Well-Located Housing

Jonas Ingemann Parby and David Ryan Mason

Overview

The availability of adequate and well-located housing is a key challenge for the region and directly impacts economic competiveness, quality of life, human development, and urban resilience. Today, more than a quarter of Central American residents live in slum conditions and a significant share of housing stock is situated in hazardous areas and subject to conditions of overcrowding. The proliferation of informal settlements with the low-density urban expansion contributes to the reduction in access to health and education services, aggravates congestion, and tempers the economic benefits of agglomeration. Adequate and well-located housing provides long-term social and economic benefits to cities through enabling social inclusion, attracting investment, and supporting green growth.

This chapter focuses on the components necessary to produce and finance housing, drawing attention to key constraints in the sector that policy makers can address to propel a more efficient, inclusive, and sustainable model for provision of housing, integrated with urban development. Section 1 portrays the role of housing in Central America's future. Section 2 presents an overall diagnostic of the situation of housing in the region. Section 3 offers a comprehensive value chain approach to tackle the housing challenges. Section 4 delves into government involvement in the housing sector. Last, section 5 identifies priorities at national and city levels to leverage housing as a catalyst for urban prosperity.

Key Messages
- Housing policies need to strengthen the overall system of housing delivery to improve housing quality and affordability for all, across income groups.
- Housing policies need to be better aligned and coordinated with national and local development planning, spatial planning, and management in order to promote sustainable and inclusive cities.

The Role of Housing for Central America's Urban Future

Ensuring the availability of quality housing will help Central America maximize the gains of urbanization. Where people live in a city is directly linked to the availability and access they have to jobs, schools, health care facilities, and other public services that cities provide. Cities in the region have been expanding to accommodate migration and population growth, but the quality of the housing stock, particularly in terms of infrastructure access, has not kept pace with the need. These conditions, along with the incidence of overcrowding and the siting of new settlements in hazardous locations, indicate that quality housing is limited and inaccessible to the urban poor. The current trend of urban expansion in Central America detailed in chapter 1 has placed new housing further from employment centers and has raised the cost to the government of providing infrastructure connections to these developments. Without improvements to housing quality and affordability, residents will miss out on the economic and human development and social benefits that cities can provide.

Housing investment also plays a substantial role in promoting sustained and inclusive economic growth. Across Latin America, housing investment comprised an average of 8.8 percent of gross domestic product (GDP) from 2001 to 2011. Where data are available in Central America, housing supply averaged 4.6 percent of GDP in Honduras and 15.5 percent of GDP in Panama during this period. Globally, housing investment increases alongside GDP, with the highest rates of investment occurring between per capita income levels of US$3,000 and US$36,000 in urbanizing countries (Dasgupta, Lall, and Lozano-Gracia 2014).[1] Per capita gross domestic income (GDI) levels in most of Central America presently fall within this range, suggesting that housing investment and consumption is an important component of economic growth, and, as incomes rise, households tend to spend more on housing.

The housing sector also has important positive spillover effects into other parts of the economy. Housing investment increases the demand for construction materials production, development services, and construction labor in addition to banking and other financial services, which stimulates employment. In El Salvador, the construction sector has contributed to 46 percent of investment and 6.7 percent of employment generated over the past decade (UN-Habitat 2014). In Costa Rica, the construction industry grew nearly twice as fast (6.4 percent) as the overall economy (3.5 percent) in 2013 (MINVAH 2014). In Panama, the construction sector generated either directly or indirectly 232,159 jobs, or about 18 percent of total employment (CAPAC 2014).

While cities are engines of growth, urbanization can contribute to the concentration of poverty in slums and informal settlements. Urban land is expensive due to proximity to infrastructure and employment opportunities, which in turn raises the cost of housing. These factors, along with low and irregular incomes, limit the resources households have to afford housing. As a consequence, informal settlements emerge in response to a lack of affordable housing options, and are characterized by deficiencies including nondurable structure, lack of tenure, overcrowding, and the lack of access to water and sanitation. Across Latin America, the share of people living in slums has declined from 35 percent in 1990 to 23 percent (UN 2014). However, in Central America, the available data suggest that about 29 percent of urban residents live in slums, which is close to the global average of 32 percent and higher than other regions including East Asia and the Middle East. Figure 3.1 below compares the proportion of urban residents living in slums to GNI per capita and suggests a negative relationship between urban slum incidence and incomes.

Cities have a critical role to play in ensuring access to quality affordable housing. While housing policies are articulated at the national level, cities are key partners to help ensure the achievement of policy goals. For example, cities can support housing markets by encouraging density and diversity of land uses and the proximity of housing to transportation facilities and infrastructure connections. These will not only improve the housing options available to residents but will also make the city attractive to new investment (as detailed further in chapter 5). Cities can help assemble underutilized land for housing investment and use value capture instruments to sustainably finance basic infrastructure and social services to new developments (as discussed in chapter 2). Standards and permitting functions can be improved to reduce costs and uncertainty for housing developers and self-builders. Improved planning can enable future growth to occur in areas with lower exposure to disaster risks such as earthquakes and flooding (as presented in chapter 4).

However, there are several constraints to housing delivery across the region. The most prevalent challenge is the lack of adequate infrastructure, especially in informal urban settlements, resulting in relative deprivation in access to services.

Figure 3.1 Share of Urban Dwellers in Slums, 2005–09, and GNI per Capita, 2014

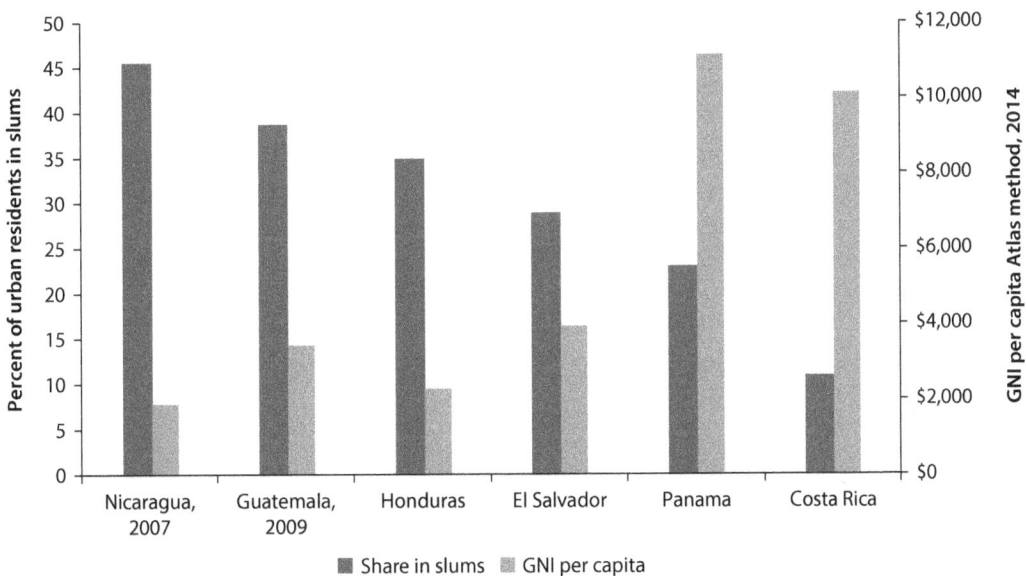

Source: Calculations from UN-Habitat 2014; World Bank 2015.

This qualitative deficiency is a result of (i) the underprovision of trunk infrastructure, particularly sewer systems, to new settlements, and (ii) the inability of low-income groups to afford new formal housing. Second, housing subsidies do not reach the poorest groups and may also be further encouraging urban expansion because they do not align with local-level planning functions.

- The lack of planning and enforcement at the municipal level has enabled low-density expansion to areas where land costs are lower, including land at risk from flooding, landslide, or earthquake damage. This trend also occurs through the formal sector through mortgage subsidy interventions that lower the effective price of housing, but that encourage developers to build in peripheral areas in order to lower unit prices.
- Mortgage subsidies have been largely directed to middle- and upper-income groups, while the urban poor are often not eligible for these subsidies because of limited formal savings with banks and irregular or informal incomes.
- There is a need to improve public sector coordination for strategic investments to support housing delivery. Quality housing delivery requires coordination between local- and national-level policy makers as well as across sectors and line ministries involved in infrastructure, finance, housing subsidies, and market regulation.

The qualitative housing deficit is a key challenge across the region. Informal housing covers a range of both physical and structural conditions and degrees of legal and regulatory compliance. Slums represent an extreme deprivation of infrastructure, land tenure, and shelter quality. Nicaragua has the region's highest share of qualitative housing deprivation, particularly in terms of improved water and sanitation access, and more than one-third of Guatemalan households live in overcrowded conditions or in homes that are located in hazard areas. Targeted infrastructure provision can improve housing quality and support the formalization of low-income settlements. For quantitative deficiencies, the supply of quality housing options need to be expanded to relieve overcrowding and settlements in hazardous or precarious areas may need to be assessed for resettlement options.

Policies also tend to focus on supporting homeownership while overlooking alternative solutions that could address the broader segment of the market. Homeownership is supported through mortgage subsidies for the purchase of a new, complete house. While the subsidies have expanded homeownership, they benefit mostly middle-class households that have formal employment rather than low-income, informal sector workers. Other forms of expanding access to affordable housing include neighborhood upgrading and rental programs.

- Housing quality, in the form of infrastructure deficits, can be addressed through upgrading programs. National governments have recognized the importance of upgrading and improvement of informal settlements, but the need remains far greater than what has been delivered. Community organizations and non-profits in partnership with local governments have also piloted examples of neighborhood upgrading, but these projects have not achieved the scale necessary without sustained involvement from key ministries.

- Renters constitute a significant proportion of urban residents, though housing policies do not support improvements to the quality and availability of formal rental housing supply as well as improving the regulatory framework for rental housing. Rental housing is a desirable option for new migrants who cannot afford to purchase a home or need flexibility to follow new employment opportunities. Informal rental arrangements provide flexibility for tenants and landlords but preclude enforcement of standards for housing or fair rental agreements for either party.

Taking Stock: The Delivery of Formal and Informal Housing

In coming years the need for urban housing in the region will grow. A quantitative deficit is the total amount of housing units required to meet the need for housing based on urban migration and household formation rates, but which has not been addressed with the current supply of housing. Estimates from United Nations (UN) data on projected urban migration and urban household formation suggest the need for housing will be greater within the next 15 years, leveling off by 2030. Precise long-term estimates of quantitative deficits are difficult to make because of changes in household formation rates which are influenced by a number of different socioeconomic factors. Currently, formal housing production is limited in countries where need will be highest; in Guatemala, the region's most populous country, annual production is between 20,000 and 30,000 units, similar to that of Costa Rica. In Honduras, production averaged about 32,000 units per year in the period 2000–2008, which only accommodated new demand, rather than expanding future supply.

About 10 to 20 percent of the current housing stock in the region is in high-risk areas or is overcrowded. Table 3.1 below shows the most recent estimates of absolute need based on housing that is located in a risk zone or that is overcrowded, which represents the share of housing units that need to be replaced and built to meet existing need. It shows that lower-income countries, in particular

Table 3.1 Housing Stock Needed to Reduce Current Overcrowding or Resettlement

Country	Year	Share of dwelling in risk zones (%)	Households in overcrowded conditions (%)	Combined (%)
Costa Rica	2013	0.16	0.25	0.41
El Salvador	2013	4.20	12.50	16.70
Guatemala	2011	10.80	26.50	37.30
Honduras	2013	3.30	4.90	8.20
Nicaragua	2009	3.40	24.50	27.90
Regional Average		**4.3**	**13.7**	**18.1**

Source: SEDLAC 2015.
Note: Overcrowding defined as 3 or more persons per room.

Guatemala and Nicaragua, have the highest share of absolute housing need. Costa Rica has the lowest incidence—less than 1 percent—of overcrowding or inappropriately located housing.

Homeownership is the most common housing tenure form. The majority of households report owning their home or the plot on which their house is built (see table 3.2). While renting is less common overall, tenants do so for a variety of reasons, such as better access to job locations, students needing temporary accommodations for university, or the high cost of mortgages. Indeed, global experience suggests a wide variation in homeownership rates; homeownership in Latin America is around 64 percent, which is actually lower than other regions such as Asia and Eastern Europe.[2] Apart from Panama, most who rent are in the lowest income quintile, and the majority of renters are in cities rather than rural areas because of housing cost differentials (IDB 2012b). However, in a review of rental across the Latin America and Caribbean (LAC) region, a recent study finds that the incidence of renting does not necessarily decline as incomes rise, suggesting that there may be demand for rental housing across income groups (IDB 2014).

More attention to current housing stock conditions and qualitative gaps is needed. Precise estimates of future quantitative housing deficits are difficult to make due to data constraints and varying assumptions about household formation, crowding, and housing quality (Monkonnen 2013; Rojas and Medellín 2011).[3] First, quantitative deficits assume a lack of housing units of a certain standard that is often poorly defined or that may differ across countries. Second, household formation rates are likely to decrease as incomes rise, urbanization continues, and populations age, which also vary across countries and over time (Bonvalet and Lelievre 1997).[4] Finally, quantitative deficits should be addressed not only through the addition of new formal units; alternative considerations, such as improving existing stock or providing options for other tenure arrangements such as renting, are also critical. Furthermore, qualitative housing deficiencies, including built structure, infrastructure connections, and overcrowding can be addressed through targeted interventions, including access to land, planning and regulatory standards, construction materials, and utility provision. These span both ownership and rental tenures and also permit different housing producers (self-builders, private developers) to accommodate different needs, and allow governments to better target subsidies to low-income groups.

Table 3.2 Housing Tenure by Country, 2009–13
Percent

Country	Owner occupied	Rental/rent free	Year
Costa Rica	71.9	28.1	2013
El Salvador	70.1	29.9	2013
Guatemala	78.7	21.3	2013
Honduras	80.1	19.9	2013
Nicaragua	83.3	16.7	2009
Panama	82.6	17.4	2013

Source: SEDLAC 2015.

Housing policies in the region are generally progressive, but interventions do not reach the lowest income groups. Most government approaches to housing subsidies focus on homeownership, mirroring the ABC (*ahorro*/savings, *bono*/subsidy, *crédito*/credit) approach pioneered in Chile during the 1980s. Under an ABC scheme, housing subsidies are allocated up-front and linked to a mortgage, typically from a commercial bank, provided that beneficiaries meet certain savings or eligibility criteria, usually a minimum down payment. While these types of mixed-finance programs could also be used for financing home improvement and expansion, they are most often used for new home purchases. The subsidy increases affordability for consumers and reduces risk for lenders, which creates incentives for the construction sector to increase the supply of new units (Bredenoord, Van Lindert, and Smets 2014).

Urban planning and land administration are key challenges for governments in the regions. Local governments have been afforded greater powers as part of a series of decentralization reforms that occurred during past decades, but they tend to lack technical and fiscal capacity to produce and implement planning and investment activities in support of new growth, as described in chapter 2. Indeed, from the period 2002–05, local governments in Costa Rica, El Salvador, Honduras, Nicaragua, and Panama averaged total expenditures less than 10 percent of all government spending; compared to Brazil (16.6), and Colombia (17.0). At the regional level, only San Salvador and San José have a coordinating body charged with planning and land use decisions at the metropolitan level. Local governments have an important role in identifying and implementing appropriate land use plans, revenue-capture tools, and infrastructure access to ensure inclusive urban growth.

In Central America, a large segment of housing is produced and consumed informally. Informal housing refers to units that do not meet legal and regulatory standards that govern the formal access and use of land and buildings (UN-Habitat 2003). It also constitutes a wide range of housing conditions which can include, but are not necessarily the same, as slums (see figure 3.2 below). It includes land tenure that is either perceived, contested, or not held (squatting)

Figure 3.2 A Continuum of Informality in Housing

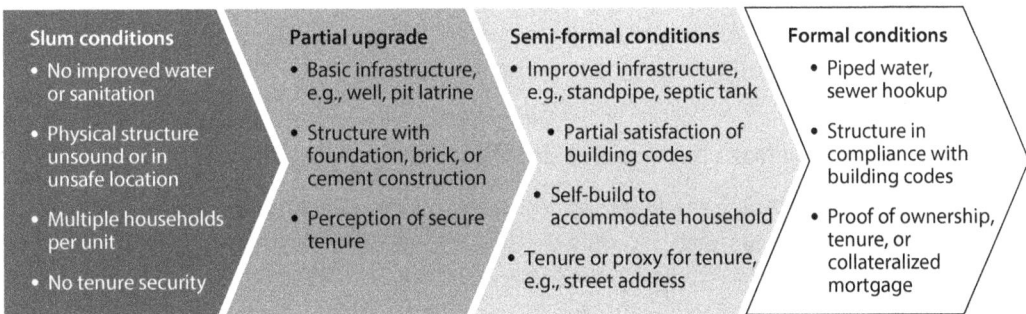

Slum conditions	Partial upgrade	Semi-formal conditions	Formal conditions
• No improved water or sanitation	• Basic infrastructure, e.g., well, pit latrine	• Improved infrastructure, e.g., standpipe, septic tank	• Piped water, sewer hookup
• Physical structure unsound or in unsafe location	• Structure with foundation, brick, or cement construction	• Partial satisfaction of building codes	• Structure in compliance with building codes
• Multiple households per unit	• Perception of secure tenure	• Self-build to accommodate household	• Proof of ownership, tenure, or collateralized mortgage
• No tenure security		• Tenure or proxy for tenure, e.g., street address	

Source: World Bank.

as well as housing units that are built without formal finance and that do not meet applicable standards. By contrast, formal housing meets standards, is consumed through mortgage lending or rental contracts, and is built and maintained by a specialized construction sector. Informal housing covers a range of physical and regulatory conditions, and international experience has shown that the quality and security of informal dwellings can be improved over time through both private investment, infrastructure upgrading, tenure regularization, and flexible building and planning standards (Bredenoord, Van Lindert, and Smets 2014; Fergusson and Smets 2010).

Informal housing is especially prominent in urbanizing areas of lower-income countries. In nearly all countries, one-third or more of urban households do not have access to improved toilet or sanitation facilities. In El Salvador, 64 percent of homes were built progressively and 34 percent of poor households report incremental investment in home improvement (UN-Habitat 2014). Approximately 80 percent of housing units in Nicaragua are in some degree of informality. In Guatemala, 39 percent of housing is without permits, three-quarters of which are built and occupied by those without tenure or who are squatters on public lands or who live in hazardous locations, such as canyon slopes or areas prone to flooding. A recent estimate in Panama identifies a total of 450 informal settlements housing approximately 185,000 people, nearly two-thirds of whom live in Panama City, the rest in other medium sized cities (IDB 2008). Similarly, in Costa Rica the majority of informal settlements are located on public land possessed by city governments in and around the San José metropolitan area.

The lack of adequate housing is a combination of low incomes and weaknesses in the housing delivery systems. Housing informality covers a wide range of shelter conditions and is a product of the systems through which housing inputs (land, materials, labor, and finance) function. Land is an important component of housing (around 20 percent or more of total costs) and the function of land markets, along with the regulations and rights afforded to landholders are critical for investment decisions. The cost of materials and the quality of the construction sector also influence the price and quality of housing. The availability of improved infrastructure (water and sanitation) along with schools and health facilities also influence housing prices and convey key long-term benefits to household welfare. Finally, the options for housing finance on both the developer and consumer side also influence the price, location, and quality of housing that can be built by developers or owner-occupiers.

Building from the Ground Up: Housing Value Chains

A value chain framework can identify key constraints to the provision of quality affordable housing. Housing is the product of a complex set of supply and demand value chains which directly influence the quality and availability. Whether it is produced through formal or informal channels, housing requires the same inputs (land, construction, materials, infrastructure, and finance).

In Central America, housing costs and quality vary widely. A value chain approach allows for policy makers and stakeholders in each to better understand particular links in the chain and their influence on housing delivery across country contexts. This will improve and coordinate policy reforms aimed at improving access to quality housing, particularly for the urban poor, who face the greatest challenges in finding adequate housing options.

The value chain approach highlights how housing is delivered (from both the supply and demand sides) and identifies key areas of policy attention for improvement by highlighting the linkages between supply and demand inputs. The supply value chain consists of key inputs such as land, infrastructure, and construction. The demand side consists of the finance options available to both developers and to housing consumers. A formal housing delivery system is complex and requires an integrated sequence of inputs (for example, land, materials, and infrastructure) along with regulatory, institutional, and financial capacities to support them. Figure 3.3 summarizes the conceptual relationships for the

Figure 3.3 Supply and Demand Value Chains for Formal Housing Delivery

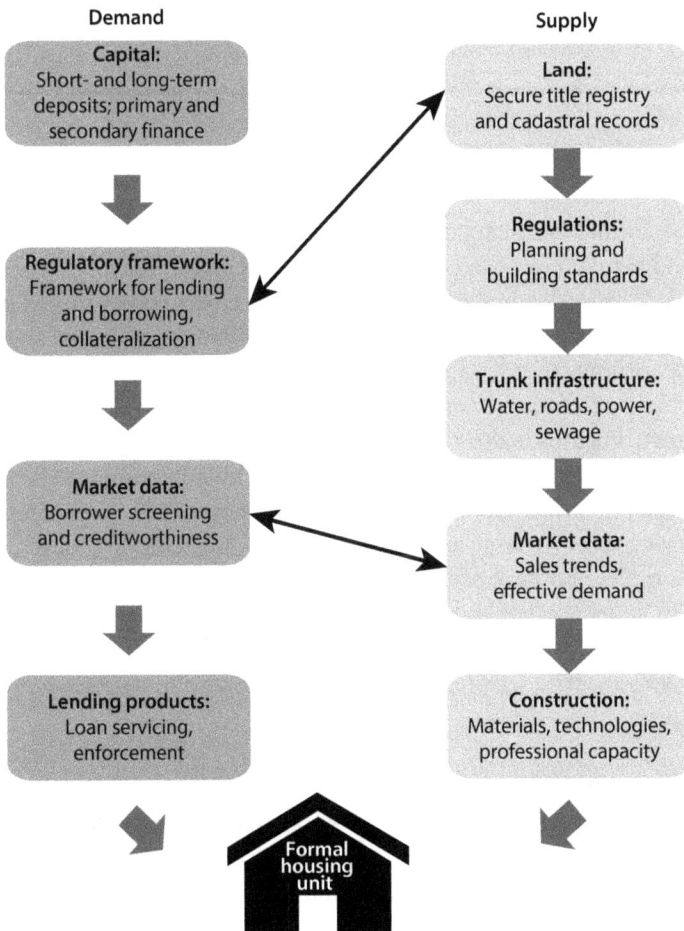

Box 3.1 Methodology and Data Sources

The chapter draws from a desk review of existing research, recent national-level household survey data from the Socio-Economic Data Base for Latin America and the Caribbean (SEDLAC), and two in-depth case studies. Unfortunately, housing data from this set do not fully cover Panama, which is not included in parts of the analysis, though current descriptive data is supplied where available. It also develops two country case studies (Costa Rica and Nicaragua) based on interview data with government, private sector, nonprofit, and civil society groups involved in the housing sector. The cases were selected to examine differences in housing policy and needs between two countries with very different poverty levels and per capita GDI figures, but with a common border.[a]

Across Central America, however, available data do not capture the full scope and scale of the housing sector, making it difficult to compare trends and needs across the region. Data on housing market activity, particularly new housing starts, prices, sales volumes, and numbers of rental, ownership, or other tenure arrangements are limited. In poorer areas, housing is largely consumed informally, making analysis and stocktaking more difficult.

a. For Nicaragua, per capita GNI is US$1,850 (2014), with 42.5 percent of the population living below the national poverty line (2009). Costa Rica's per capita GNI is US$10,124 (2014) with a national poverty rate of 22.4 percent (2014). In 2009 the most recent year where comparable data are available, 10.8 percent of the population of Nicaragua was below the international poverty line of US$1.90 and in Costa Rica 3.3 percent was below this line.

---

delivery of formal housing, including links between the two chains where demand and supply links can be mutually reinforcing.

Inputs such as land, infrastructure, design, and construction proceed in parallel with a corresponding set of demand side inputs related to housing finance. The supply side assumes that land and property markets are active and widespread, that legal claims to property are clear and enforceable and price information is widely known. Further, it also requires that a reasonable set of construction, planning, and infrastructure standards are supported by governments and to which private development activity conforms. On the demand side, construction firms must also have access to large amounts of capital from banks in order to assemble land and complete housing projects and to sell them to consumers via mortgage products. In order for banks to create mortgages, they have to have access to sources of long-term capital and must be supported by an appropriate financial regulatory system. Box 3.1 presents the methodology and data sources followed in the chapter.

Land, Property, and Planning Standards

Land administration responsibilities are fragmented across levels of government and different ministries.[5] Land administration policies establish the rights and protections afforded to the circulation and development of property and have direct consequences on investment levels and housing affordability.

Investment in housing, whether from formal developers or self-builders will be less likely where property rights are constrained, contested, or unclear (Payne 2005). Diminished investment can reduce the quantity and quality of the housing stock. Furthermore, land governance systems including maps and registry databases tend to be incomplete (El Salvador) and not easily available to the public (Guatemala, Honduras) (World Bank 2014c, 2015). This reduces incentives for investment because information about property availability is difficult to obtain and verify, and there is less clarity on property claims, which discourages collateralization of property for mortgages or development finance.

At the sub-national level, property registration practices tend to be consistent in terms of time, procedures, and costs. This is to be expected given land administration policies, such as property registration, are dictated at the national level. Ease of property registration influences the cost and interest in property investment. Registration procedures that are reliable and efficient can encourage investment or collateralization of property for housing or other type of private development. Table 3.3 summarizes subnational rankings in the region related to property registration.[6] It shows that city-level registration procedures mirror country-level patterns to a large degree. However, there can be a large variation in time required; registration in Choluteca takes three times as along as in other Honduran cities. Furthermore,

Table 3.3 Procedures, Time, and Costs to Register Property, Subnational Level, 2015

City (Country)	Rank	Procedures (number)	Time (days)	Cost (% of property value)
San José (Costa Rica)	1	5	19	3.4
San Salvador (El Salvador)	2	5	31	3.8
Panama City (Panama)	3	7	22.5	2.4
Quetzaltenango (Guatemala)	4	6	25	3.6
Escuintla (Guatemala)	5	6	24	3.8
Guatemala City (Guatemala)	5	6	24	3.8
Cobán (Guatemala)	7	6	25	3.8
San Miguel (El Salvador)	8	6	21	4.1
Santa Ana (El Salvador)	9	6	23	4.1
Soyapango (El Salvador)	10	6	30	4.2
Puerto Cortés (Honduras)	11	6	25	4.7
San Pedro Sula (Honduras)	12	6	27	4.7
Tegucigalpa (Honduras)	13	6	22	5.7
Choluteca (Honduras)	17	6	66	4.7
Estelí (Nicaragua)	18	8	54	3.9
Managua (Nicaragua)	20	9	58	5
Juigalpa (Nicaragua)	21	9	73	4.2
León (Nicaragua)	22	10	62	4.4

Source: Doing Business 2015.

apart from Tegucigalpa and Managua, capital cities tend to rank highest, with fewer procedures (five to six) and time required for obtaining registration (about a week).

The lack of a strategic urban planning framework encourages low-density expansion. Low-cost land on urban fringes drives both formal and informal housing development. However, this type of growth places additional burdens on transportation networks as commute times to the central business district increase. It also increases the marginal cost for governments to provide networked infrastructure to these areas. In San José, a study found that population density in the built-up area of the metropolitan region from 1997 to 2010 increased from 71.4 to 75.3 persons per hectare. However, in comparative terms it is still more dispersed than most major cities in Latin America due in part to a consolidation of formerly disparate settlements (Pujol-Mesalles and Pérez Molina 2013). Between 1990 and 2000, population densities (in terms of persons per hectare) in the built-up areas of both Guatemala City and San Salvador have declined 7 percent and 2 percent respectively, which, while modest compared to most major cities in developing countries, still suggests a trend toward population dispersion (Angel et al. 2010).

Urban planning and land use regulations are applied unevenly. Planning regulations can increase the cost of formal housing. Regulations of building material types, construction permits, minimum lot sizes, and density requirements can unnecessarily add to the cost of construction by imposing additional costs to developers for compliance. A recent study found that, among households that cannot afford housing in San Salvador, 20 percent identify the minimum lot size requirement ($60m^2$) as the main impediment (IDB 2012b). In Nicaragua, for example, planning and construction regulations are often ignored by informal builders, and smaller towns lack the technical capacity to review projects for compliance. They may also be incompatible with efficient land use principles; central city areas of Managua and San José for example, tend to have large, wide lots, buildings with two stories or less, and a lack of street hierarchies, which worsens circulation and increases housing costs.

Without enforcement of existing plans or coordination with utility and service providers, local governments have few tools to direct urban growth, capture revenue from land, or encourage infill development in areas that can be connected to infrastructure. Rather, the lack of available urban land along with rising congestion costs (in terms of commute times, environmental degradation, and so forth) encourages new development in fringe areas due to the low cost of land. Infrastructure and transportation connections are then expected to follow these investments though resources for the public investments required may be absent for years. Apart from Costa Rica, local-level planning in the region is often disconnected from regional- or national-level plans, or lacks medium- or long-term strategic goals. For example, urban land development issues in Guatemala are addressed from several agencies, including the Planning and Programing Secretariat of the Office of the President (*Segeplán*), the Municipal Development Institute (INFOM), and the Ministry of Communications, which can have overlapping or competing goals and priorities (World Bank 2015). Box 3.2 reviews Colombia's experience with a legal framework that provides municipalities with mechanisms to harness urban growth to finance public infrastructure while cities grow. This allows local governments, service providers, and developers to coordinate investment priorities.

The steps required for obtaining building permits can add substantially to costs and time required for completing new construction. This can deter investment and discourage full compliance with standards. However, there is substantial variation in the time and costs for these regulatory activities within countries. Table 3.4 details subnational indicators for ease of obtaining construction permits for a warehouse facility. This can be used to assess permitting and regulatory capacity,[7] which are also land and infrastructure intensive.

The results suggest a large variability in the standards and review procedures employed at the local level. For example, while León (Nicaragua) ranks the lowest in property registration, it issues construction permits three times faster than Managua and for about one-quarter the cost of Juigalpa. Guatemalan cities rank at or near the bottom of the region with approval times of more than 130 days and costs of up to 14 percent of the project value. In Costa Rica, for example,

---

Box 3.2 Colombia: Tools for Linking Planning with Infrastructure Finance

Colombia's Territorial Development Law 388 (passed in 1997) provides a strong foundation for improving planning in infrastructure investment across the country. The law provides a framework for the development of coordinated spatial and sector plans for municipalities and also permits these entities to plan at the neighborhood level through overlay zones with an emphasis on urban design and land use. To date, more than 90 percent of cities have completed local plans. The law also provides that public actions that improve urban land (for example, zoning changes and increasing density) also allow local governments to capture a share (30–50 percent) of the resulting increase in market land values (*plusvalías*). These gains can be used to offset infrastructure costs for servicing newly designated areas for development. The law also provides other tools for land value capture, such as the auctioning of underutilized public lands and land readjustment.

Medellín in particular has experimented with land pooling/readjustment approaches to improve density, redevelop vacant or abandoned space, and provide quality housing (Smolka 2013). Land pooling/readjustment is also an option for Colombian cities providing infrastructure to informal settlements while minimizing resident displacement and necessary government expenditures. Under a land readjustment approach, residents allow for the redistribution of their parcels, provided that a portion of each parcel is pooled together for infrastructure corridors and community facilities. Governments pay the up-front costs for infrastructure, but can recover costs through sale of excess land. While residents receive a smaller plot, its value is increased because of the infrastructure improvements.

Table 3.4 Obtaining Construction Permits, Select Cities, 2015

City (Country)	Rank	Procedures (number)	Time (days)	Cost (% of value)
León (Nicaragua)	1	11	62	2
San Pedro Sula (Honduras)	2	9	68	4.8
Puerto Cortés (Honduras)	3	14	32	3.2
Estelí (Nicaragua)	4	16	41	2
San José (Costa Rica)	5	13	113	1.7
Panama City (Panama)	6	15	101	2.1
Santa Ana (El Salvador)	8	15	132	3.1
Juigalpa (Nicaragua)	9	14	70	7.6
Tegucigalpa (Honduras)	12	15	82	7.2
Guatemala City (Guatemala)	13	11	158	7.9
San Miguel (El Salvador)	14	18	144	3.7
Managua (Nicaragua)	15	16	207	2.7
Soyapango (El Salvador)	16	17	163	5.6
Quetzaltenango (Guatemala)	17	15	210	5.2
San Salvador (El Salvador)	19	25	115	4.6
Choluteca (Honduras)	20	13	100	17.6
Cobán (Guatemala)	21	22	133	9.5
Escuintla (Guatemala)	22	18	196	14.1

Source: World Bank 2014a.

new housing developments can take between three and four years for final completion, with permit reviews representing 7.4 to 13.9 percent of the project cost. In El Salvador, new housing developments can take up to 850 days (and up to 3.5 percent of the total project value) for completion, varying on the size of the project and the institutions involved (UN-Habitat 2014).

Connecting Housing to Infrastructure

Infrastructure is an important determinant of housing quality, though access is limited especially to the urban poor. Infrastructure, both in terms of trunk utility connections and basic services including health, education, and public safety are important determinants of housing value and quality of life. For example, targeted investment in water and sanitation has demonstrable effects in improving literacy and incomes while reducing household health care expenditures (Barnejee and Duflo 2012). However, infrastructure investments are large and capital intensive, especially when they are provided after housing settlement has occurred. A study of slum upgrading in Brazil found that basic infrastructure upgrading is 2.5 times the cost of providing these investments prior to development (Abiko et al. 2007). This underlines the need for coordination of planning and infrastructure investments before supporting new housing development.

Access to improved sanitation is the most critical infrastructure deprivation for poor urban households in the region. Across the region, electricity access is nearly universal and for most countries approaches or matches averages across Latin America. Potable water access, especially in urban areas, also approaches regional averages. However, improved sanitation systems, especially sewers, are absent from a substantial share of urban dwellings, even in wealthier countries such as Costa Rica. Table 3.5 shows the percentage of households with infrastructure coverage for both urban and rural areas. Figure 3.4 below summarizes infrastructure coverage for the poorest 40 percent of urban residents. It shows that, while a majority have access to clean water at levels that approach urban averages, most poor households do not have improved restrooms and sewer connections. In Nicaragua, the urban poor have about half the level of coverage; in Guatemala and El Salvador it is 20 percent less than the average for all urban households. Improved sanitation systems, particularly contained sewage networks, reduce the incidence of contamination and exposure to communicable diseases. Unprotected and untreated sewage may otherwise seep into groundwater, rivers, or storm runoff.

The lack of trunk infrastructure connections is reflective of weaknesses in planning and coordination. This impacts both new formal developments as well as incremental, self-built housing. Housing development should proceed in line with infrastructure planning and provision, but in the case of informal settlements, infrastructure comes last. However, infrastructure access remains a barrier even for formal developers. In Nicaragua, for example, private developers cite the lack of finance and technical capacity by state-run utility providers as a major impediment to infrastructure provision in new developments, along with the limited revenue capture capacity afforded to local governments in order to extend municipal services to newly built developments (*urbanizaciones*).

Infrastructure investment also has significant impacts on urban land markets. Commitments to extend infrastructure or publication of development plans can spur speculative development that will capture the enhanced market value that these services will provide. In select cities across Latin America, serviced urban land is worth five times more than unserviced

Table 3.5 Percentage of Households with Infrastructure Coverage, 2013

Geography	Water		Hygienic restrooms			Sewerage		Electricity	
	Urban	Rural	Urban	Toilet in dwelling	Rural	Urban	Rural	Urban	Rural
Costa Rica	99.9	97.9	99.5	99.3	94.4	34.0	8.2	100.0	99.1
El Salvador	85.0	56.7	71.2	72.2	15.3	57.6	0.8	97.9	90.6
Guatemala	90.0	57.3	74.8	77.1	15.3	69.5	7.7	95.0	71.6
Honduras	96.6	77.2	73.5	73.5	23.3	60.9	4.5	99.0	74.9
Nicaragua	89.8	25.3	46.1	47.8	2.6	35.3	0.3	98.0	45.0
LAC Region	94.4	68.9	84.8	–	45.2	62.1	8.1	99.1	85.5

Source: Calculations from SEDLAC 2015.
Note: Data for Panama are not available. LAC = Latin America and the Caribbean.

Figure 3.4 Coverage of Urban Infrastructure for Bottom Income Quintiles, 2009–13

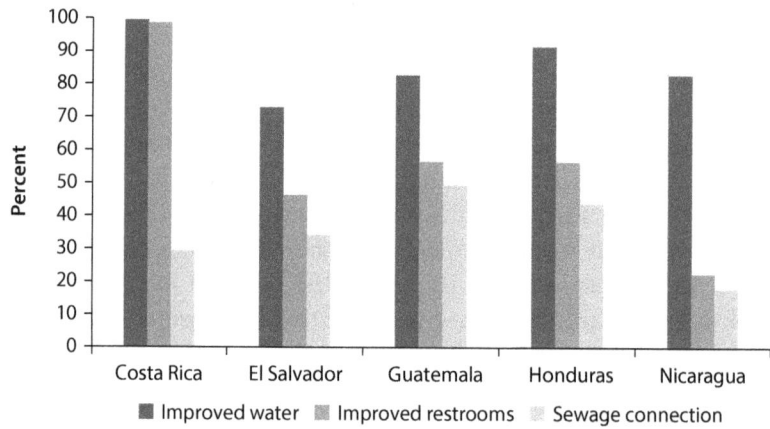

Source: Calculations from SEDLAC 2015.
Note: Data for Nicaragua are from 2009, all others from 2013.

urban land (in San Salvador, the value is 2.6 times higher) (IDB 2011, 148). This cost is reflected in the market value of housing units, which reduces affordability for lower-income groups. The retroactive extension of network infrastructure connections to these areas can be both disruptive to residents and even more expensive for governments due to additional construction and possible resettlement costs. The declining access to services speaks to the importance of establishing proper rights of way and prioritizing infrastructure expansion during the urban growth that Central America is experiencing. It also underscores the important link between reliable tenure security and infrastructure, since most basic services are unlikely to expand into areas where people may not have secure tenure or the capacity to pay for these services. The extension of these services can be seen as a signal of de facto formalization and can in turn drive land speculation and displacement.

Parts and Labor

The construction sector is a major economic driver across the region. In most countries, the construction industry has grown consistently, likely due in part to housing policies that encourage new housing construction through mortgage subsidies (or in the case of Panama provide tax holidays), along with growth in the higher end residential markets and the influx of remittances for consumption.[8] In El Salvador since 2004, about 6 percent of the labor force is engaged in construction work, but of these 84 percent are in the informal sector (UN-Habitat 2014). Formal and informal construction sectors also draw from the same labor pool, and in lower-income countries such as Nicaragua, construction laborers, engineers, and architects tend to pursue higher-paying work either domestically in resort or luxury projects or abroad (such as Panama or Costa Rica) where wages for the same work are higher.

New formal housing units are targeted toward middle- and lower-middle-income groups with access to finance. The lowest-cost formal house provided by developers in the region ranges from between US$12,000 and US$ 25,000.[9] Outside of Managua for example, new fringe subdivision developments offer housing units starting at US$18,000 (for 38m²) ranging to more than US$60,000 for larger units. In El Salvador, such starter units would start at US$28,500 (UN Habitat 2014).[10] While these units allow expansion, the structures do not support an additional story. By contrast, used houses in Managua usually cost at least US$50,000 because of the location premium they afford. This reduces the tendency for older homes to filter to lower-income groups over time and effectively prices lower-income groups out of the market. Furthermore, consumer mortgage subsidy programs create incentives for developers to supply new houses and to reduce prices in order to fit into eligibility criteria, often by purchasing and subdividing low-cost peripheral land.

Nonprofit and community groups have partnered with governments for housing purchase and upgrading programs. Nonprofit providers supporting self-built housing can assist with housing quality improvements for less than the cost of new housing. El Salvador's Foundation for Development and Low-Cost Housing (FUNDASAL) pioneered an approach later adopted by governments and nongovernmental organizations (NGOs) in neighboring countries (see box 3.3 below). Through donor assistance beginning in the 1980s, Costa Rica, El Salvador, Guatemala, Honduras, and Nicaragua each established housing development organizations that provide technical assistance and act as second-tier finance organizations for banks, microfinance institutions (MFIs), and cooperatives (Stein and Vance 2008). Habitat for Humanity, a nonprofit developer, provides self-help 40m² housing units for families in smaller towns and the urban periphery of Managua for a cost of about US$175–200/m²

Box 3.3 Slum Upgrading: The Case of FUNDASAL in El Salvador

The Foundation for Development and Low-Cost Housing (*Fundación Salvadorena de Desarrollo y Vivienda Mínima*, FUNDASAL) is an NGO that was created in 1968 to address housing need following urban flooding damage in San Salvador. The organization experimented with pilot projects in financing and upgrading low low-income neighborhoods through organizing residents and providing access to serviced land to allow incremental self-built home improvements. In 1974 it obtained a World Bank loan to take the program to a national scale, benefitting 12,000 households over nine years. Since its inception and with the support of the World Bank and European donor agencies, the organization has financed the construction and improvement of 44,868 houses, benefitting 267,650 people.

box continues next page

Box 3.3 Slum Upgrading: The Case of FUNDASAL in El Salvador (*continued*)

More recently, FUNDASAL has developed a microfinance arm (*Credihábitat*) for housing improvements targeted to low-income and informal sector workers with home-based enterprises. Loans are used for home purchase, incremental construction, and land purchase or regularization. FUNDASAL provides technical assistance including site planning and design and sells construction materials for use at a discount. The case demonstrates both the complementary role that civil society actors can have in sustainable low-income housing provision and also the existing technical capacity and institutional experience in large-scale upgrading schemes including lot purchase and legalization, basic service provision, and progressive housing improvements.

(excluding land cost and infrastructure connections).[11] These are based on prefabricated designs utilizing a concrete floor, brick walls, and corrugated zinc roof panels.

Most basic building materials are sourced locally and are not a major impediment to affordability. Cement bricks are the most common building material and are made locally or distributed through large suppliers such as Cemex and Holcim.[12] Imported materials include steel, ceramics, and furnishings. Quarried stone (*piedra cantera*) and adobe are also used by lower-income groups as a less costly alternative, especially in rural areas, though the quality and strength of these blocks is not inspected. Newer building technologies for houses, such as cold form steel frame construction, are new and comparatively more expensive, but reduce construction times and offer strength and durability especially to weather or seismic hazards that occur in the region. Most informal builders do not obtain permits or inspections for construction, especially in smaller towns where technical capacity is low.

Buying a Home

Apart from Costa Rica, access to formal finance in the region is low. Figure 3.5 below shows housing-related indicators of finance penetration. It shows that Costa Rica, Panama, and Guatemala have the highest levels of formal finance participation. However, across the region, the proportion of the population (older than 15) with a savings account is at or below 20 percent. Among the poorest 40 percent, it is even lower: just 4.1 percent in El Salvador and 2.9 percent in Nicaragua. Mortgage penetration is also low, averaging 9.7 percent across the region or about one-third the rate of Organisation for Economic Co-operation and Development (OECD) countries. This is also shown in figure 3.6 where national-level mortgage-to-GDP levels are slightly higher than the regional average and comparable to that of Georgia, a country of similar per capita GDP, but far below that of Spain. In El Salvador, Guatemala, and Honduras, mortgage debt among the wealthiest 60 percent is nearly twice as common as among lower-income groups. The difference is smaller in Costa

Figure 3.5 Selected Access to Finance Indicators, 2014

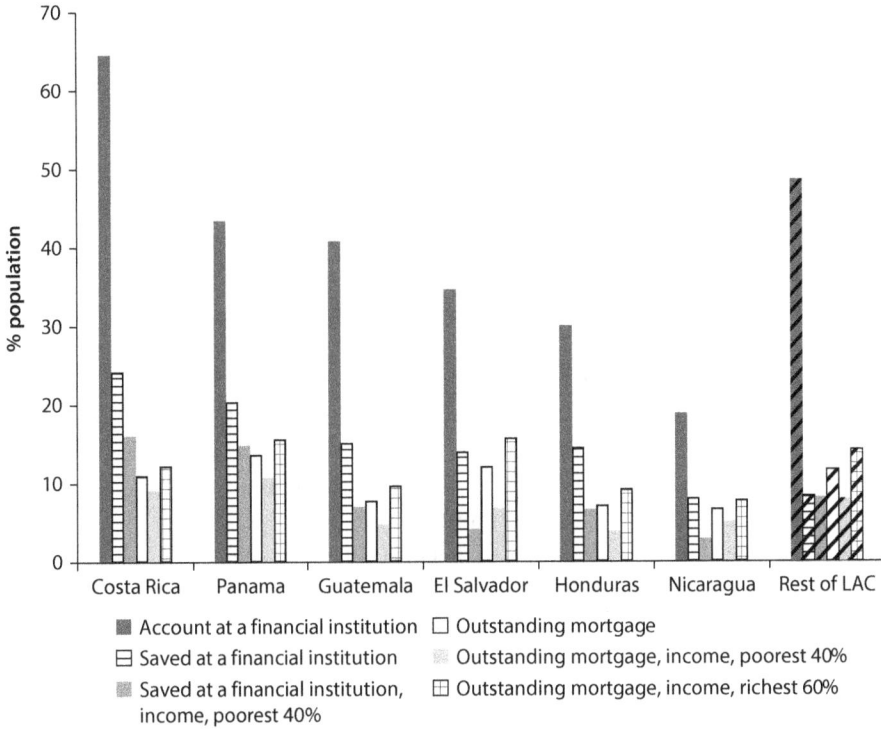

■ Account at a financial institution ☐ Outstanding mortgage
⊟ Saved at a financial institution ▨ Outstanding mortgage, income, poorest 40%
▨ Saved at a financial institution, ⊞ Outstanding mortgage, income, richest 60%
  income, poorest 40%

Source: Global Findex.
Note: LAC = Latin America and the Caribbean.

Figure 3.6 Total Outstanding Mortgages as a Percentage of GDP

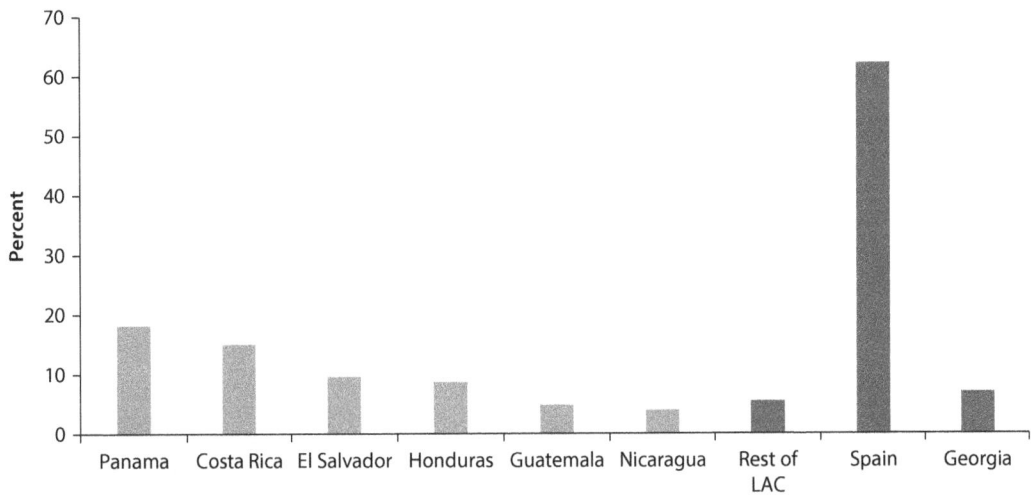

Source: Hofinet.
Note: Data are current values and are from most recent year (Costa Rica: 2009; Panama 2012: other Central American countries 2013; Spain: 2012; and Georgia: 2013). LAC = Latin America and the Caribbean.

Rica, Nicaragua, and Panama, which have introduced mortgage subsidy programs to make these loans more affordable.

Formal mortgages are not within reach of the informal sector and low-income groups. Mortgage terms range between 15 and 25 years, require down payments of between 5 and 20 percent, and feature interest rates of between 8 and 15 percent. These terms are favorable for middle- and upper-income consumers given typical housing costs, but they would represent significant burdens to poor households.[13] Commercial mortgages in Costa Rica, El Salvador, Guatemala, Nicaragua, and Panama can be—and sometimes are only—issued in dollars. Lower-income groups, especially those in the informal sector, are not paid in dollars; and should they have the option to obtain a mortgage in local currency, as in Costa Rica, the interest rate can be twice as high as the dollar-backed alternative (IDB 2012a).

Lower-income groups also tend to work in the informal sector and lack proof of or regularity of income. Figure 3.7 below shows the estimated urban population that would not be able afford a sample house with a mortgage because of income and access-to-finance constraints,[14] and the extent to which mortgage finance is unavailable to households because of either low or undocumented incomes, compared with other major cities in Latin America, showing that in most cases these factors are significant barriers for would-be home owners. Proof of property ownership is required for mortgage lending, which is often difficult to

Figure 3.7 Estimated Housing Affordability Gap for Mortgage Finance Based on Low or Undocumented Income, Select Cities, 2011

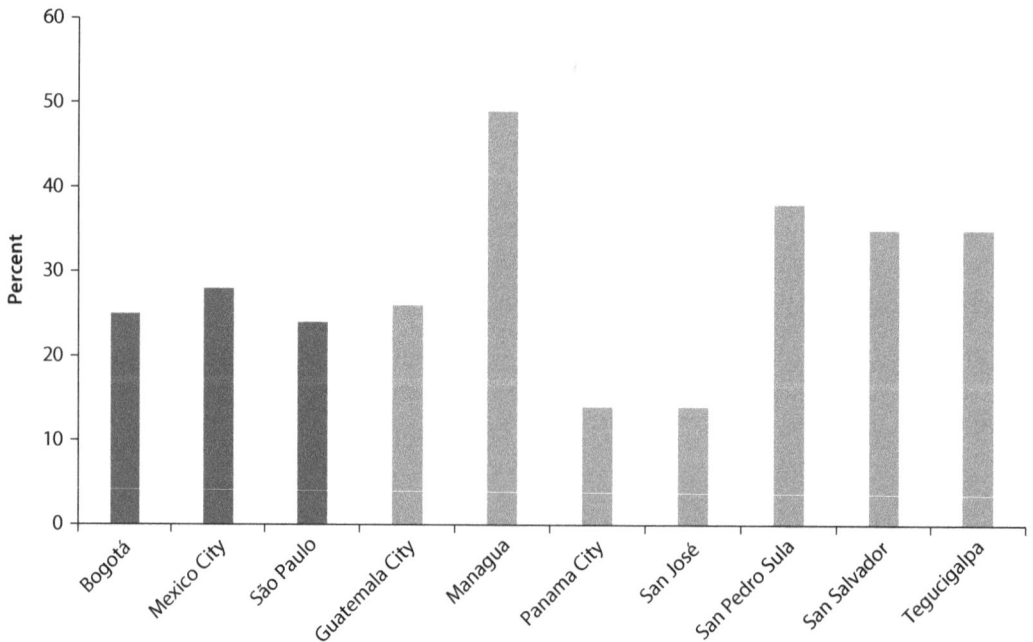

Source: IDB 2011.

Box 3.4 Extending Housing Finance to the Urban Poor

Nicaragua: RAFCASA

RAFCASA began in 2007 with the goal of introducing informal sector workers (particularly those earning four minimum salaries or less) to financial access. The company provides a platform for demonstrating household savings capacity with the purpose of developing credit history for mortgage loans. It requires steady savings for a period of 24 months for an amount of approximately US$1,500, with interest accrued to the participant. The organization works with a large commercial bank (Banco de Finanzas, BDF), which provides mortgages to program participants who complete the program without missing a savings installment, of which 98 percent of participants pay fully and on time. The bank has also partnered with five private housing developers to link beneficiaries with new units for purchase. Participants may also be eligible for mortgage subsidies, including the down payment subsidy and mortgage interest subsidy, provided the value of the house meets eligibility requirements.

Colombia: *Credifamilia*

Credifamilia began in 2011 with a focus on extending housing finance to low-income groups that have traditionally been unable to access commercial mortgages through strategic partnerships with developers and microfinance lenders. They have developed innovative tools such as assistance to clients in estimating household earning and savings patterns, requiring small savings contributions for loan eligibility and using an innovative credit scoring system that includes records of payments for utilities and other services as a proxy for payment reliability. Participants are also able to apply for government subsidies applied to their down payment, which further reduces the cost of home purchase. *Credifamilia* also offers a range of products from small loans of US$3,000 over 5 years for home improvement to larger loans of around US$30,000 (15 years) for home purchase or construction. After three years of operation, the company disburses between 3 and 4 million per month in mortgages, 80 percent of which are directed to the poor (IDB 2014).

---

obtain in informally or illegally settled areas or where and registries are incomplete. For example, in El Salvador, 16.6 percent of informal households own their unit but not the land it is on (UN-Habitat 2014). In Guatemala, some 39 percent of homeowners do not have title (IDB 2011), while in Nicaragua 80 percent of owners have at least partial claim to their land but lack title registration (Stein and Vance 2008).

Low-income groups rely on savings, informal borrowing, or microcredit for home improvement and expansion. While mortgage finance is concentrated among higher-income groups, foreigners, and expatriates, most lower-income groups access finance for housing through personal savings, remittances, credit cooperatives, and microfinance sources (box 3.4 provides examples of microfinance initiatives for low-income housing). As table 3.6 below demonstrates, microfinance is popular in Guatemala, Honduras, and Nicaragua, where there are many providers and loans tend to be small. Higher-income countries such as Costa Rica and Panama have fewer providers, but loans tend to be larger. Remittances

Table 3.6 Select Indicators of the Microfinance Sector, 2013

Country	Number of MFIs	Active borrowers	Gross loan portfolio (US$)	Outstanding portfolio per capita (US$)
Costa Rica	14	25,032	74,184,950	2,964
El Salvador	11	139,787	368,458,455	2,636
Guatemala	15	356,825	189,154,072	530
Honduras	23	181,109	387,892,273	2,142
Nicaragua	22	316,024	313,034,496	991
Panama	6	43,473	178,961,839	4,117

Source: MixMarket.
Note: MFI = microfinance institution.

are also an important source of household consumption generally and for housing in particular. Nicaraguans received US$1.07 billion in remittances in 2015 (BCN 2015). UN-Habitat (2014, xviii) estimates that US$390 million in remittances are used for housing investment in El Salvador each year.

Housing microfinance products have gained traction as an option for home improvement and expansion. In Nicaragua, several MFIs offer housing microfinance bundled with technical assistance provided by NGOs such as Habitat for Humanity and PRODEL. These loans are typically around US$1,000 with an interest rate of 30 percent and a term of 18 months to two years. The target market are households with incomes at around US$300 per month, or around 3–4 minimum salaries. The high interest rate is a reflection of the risk undertaken by the MFI for these loans as they do not require collateral or a guarantor but rather a credit assessment based on borrowing history with the institution. Furthermore, MFIs undertake additional costs in borrowing from secondary capital markets to package these longer-term loans, which lenders cited as a major impediment to reducing the cost and availability of the products, which constitute only about US$20 million of the country's microfinance portfolio.

Enabling Ownership: Government Involvement in Housing

All countries have a housing policy that aims to provide housing to low-income groups by placing the government as a housing sector facilitator. All countries have constitutional provisions for a national housing policy with emphasis on providing housing for low-income and vulnerable options (Cuenin et al. 2012).[15] The key difference between policies is the depth of the role of government in housing provision; Costa Rica, El Salvador, and Panama have tended to support the private provision of housing foundational support for housing markets including securing property rights for land, improving the flexibility of regulatory standards, and developing a supportive legal framework for housing finance. Guatemala, Honduras, and Nicaragua have also experimented with these interventions, though at a policy level adequate housing is viewed more explicitly as a *right* for all citizens worthy of more direct intervention.

In the past, this included government-built social housing, though this is no longer widespread in the region. These policies are broadly consistent with an "enabling approach" toward housing that provides government a role in overseeing housing markets and correcting their failures (Buckley and Kalarickal 2006; World Bank 1993).[16]

Intergovernmental coordination and continuity is a key challenge for housing policy implementation. National-level housing agencies also tend to be primarily involved in implementing subsidy programs and typically operate independently of the needs or demands of municipal governments. There is little incentive to coordinate subsidy disbursements with, for example, parallel investment in infrastructure or transportation, or in areas identified in local long-term planning documents. For example, while Costa Rica's housing policy calls for the participation of municipal governments alongside the Ministry of Housing and Human Settlements, there is little incentive for them to do so in practice (see box 3.5). While Guatemala has recently updated its housing policy, the lack of coordinating authority has slowed implementation. Nicaragua has also faced a discontinuity and a short-term horizon in housing policy priorities, which is further limited by a lack of legal clarity, limited budget resources, and a shifting set of public sector actors charged with implementing housing policies since the 1990s.

Box 3.5 Access to Housing through Subsidies

Costa Rica is the only country in the region that has been able to consistently meet or exceed quantitative formal housing deficits, largely through its direct demand subsidy program (Held 2000). The subsidy program is the product of a longer-term commitment to improving social welfare outcomes, including housing since the 1950s (Gutierrez et al. 1993). The centerpiece of Costa Rica's approach to housing is a one-time subsidy to qualifying households (*bono familiar de vivienda*), introduced in 1986 during a period of economic instability and political pressure for more affordable housing (Jenkins and Smith 2001).

Under this system, the Ministry of Housing and Human Settlements oversees two state-owned financial institutions, the National Housing Finance System (SFNV), which channels subsidies in partnerships 23 banks, credit cooperatives, and other lending organizations, and the Housing Mortgage Bank (BANHVI), a second-tier lender capitalized by international donors and a 3 percent budget set aside that provides financing for the mortgage subsidies

Developers propose housing projects to the SNFV for subsidy eligibility based on the unit cost, receiving short-term development finance to complete construction. Low-income families are eligible for a one-time subsidy in the amount of US$12,000 to cover the purchase of a completed house, a plot, or self-construction, with any remaining portion requiring a commercial loan (the subsidy amount depends on the household income, though those making more than US$2,820 are not eligible). In cases of extreme poverty or emergency, households can receive a subsidy of up to US$50,000. A savings contribution of 15 percent of the housing

box continues next page

Box 3.5 Access to Housing through Subsidies *(continued)*

cost is also required. Since the beginning of SNFV, more than 260,000 subsidies have been disbursed. Subsidies for developers support the delivery of around 10,000 units annually.

While the subsidies are well targeted to low-income groups, there remain several challenges to the long-term sustainability of the SNFV. First, there is no coordination between housing project location and subsidy criteria. Developers indicated that the high cost of urban land must be integrated into the unit cost, which raises prices and makes the units less affordable to low-income groups (even with the subsidy). Indeed, the cost of housing encourages many families to use the *bono* to acquire a plot rather than a completed unit; since 2001, 52 percent of subsidies have gone for plot purchase and housing and 63 percent have been used in rural areas (IDB 2011). Second, the subsidy relies in part on a budget commitment that has steadily declined in recent years as the government has sought to reallocate funds or has simply been slow to disburse them (IDB 2011). Finally, there is a risk that subsidized mortgages could crowd out competition; currently subsidized mortgages represent about 53 percent of formal housing and nearly all mortgages are between 15 and 20 years. A guarantee mechanism could support greater competition among commercial banks to offer longer-term loans at lower interest rates.

Table 3.7 below summarizes major housing programs from the region. It shows that subsidies for mortgages, both on the consumer side (through down payment assistance) and on the lender side (interest rate subsidies and mortgage guarantees), are common. Settlement upgrading programs are also typical (though they are relatively small in scale and as a share of government investment in housing) as are support for plot acquisition and home improvement, though these also tend to be more modest in scale and public investment compared to mortgage subsidies. Apart from Panama, supply-side interventions such as the direct provision of housing are rare. The majority of workers do not have access to formal banking and are unlikely to meet the qualifications for commercial mortgages to access subsidies.

Despite the need for settlement upgrading, efforts to date do not meet current and future need. In El Salvador, government-led neighborhood upgrading programs have benefitted just 8,626 families from 2004 to 2010 (UN-Habitat 2014). Similarly, Honduras' Housing Solidarity Program (*Programa de Vivienda Soldaria*) started in 2006, has only improved 3,500 units for low-income families. Guatemala's national subsidy program, which includes several subsidy-based schemes for housing purchase, and reduced financing options for home improvement and land acquisition, disbursed for only 13,466 units in 2014. Nicaragua's Neighborhood Improvement Program (*Programa de Mejoramiento de Barrios*) has upgraded neighborhoods in 14 cities since 2012, with contributions from the government, municipalities, and each household (US$2,600 per lot) to provide street lighting, drainage, power, sanitation, and water treatment for 3,902 households. In each case subsidies are targeted to low-income communities and assist with improving housing quality, but at a scale too small for significant improvement of the housing stock.

Table 3.7 Housing Policies in Central America

Summary of housing programs	Government-as-housing-supplier			→	Government-as-market-enabler		
	Financing for a unit with a price ceiling	Settlement upgrading and infrastructure	Finance for home improvement	Consumer mortgage subsidy (cash)	Financing for incremental improvement	Support for subdivision of land	Subsidies for lenders (interest rates, guarantees)
Costa Rica		✓	✓	✓			✓
El Salvador		✓		✓		✓	✓
Guatemala			✓	✓	✓		✓
Honduras		✓	✓	✓			✓
Nicaragua		✓	✓	✓	✓		✓
Panama	✓	✓	✓	✓	✓		✓

Source: IDB 2012b, with updates.

Mortgage subsidies reduce the cost of housing, but units remain unafford-able to the urban poor. Housing affordability is assessed in terms of household income dedicated for housing costs such as rent or mortgage service. International experience suggests that housing is unaffordable when it consumes more than 30 percent of expenditures. In Nicaragua, 47 percent of households earn less than US$350 per month (Hábitat para la Humanidad 2008). Assuming receipt of the US$1,500 down payment assistance and a 3 percent interest rate subsidy for the first 10 years, the initial monthly payments of US$132 would exceed the afford-ability levels for most households in this group.[17] In El Salvador, only the top two quintiles could afford subsidized monthly mortgage payments of US$118 required for a qualifying house (UN-Habitat 2014).[18] This may account for the slow take-up of mortgage subsidies for low-income groups: only 63,039 have been disbursed since 1992, a total expenditure of US$115 million (UN-Habitat 2014). The IDB (2012a) estimates that 90 percent of demand for improved housing is in El Salvador and Costa Rica among households earning four mini-mum wages (about US$800 and US$900, respectively) or less. In Panama half of housing need is for households making less than US$250 per month.

National-level housing policies and programs need to be coupled with improvements in local urban planning and management to avoid distorting land markets and urban development patterns. As discussed in chapter 2, improving the coordination and planning capacities among local governments and national-level agencies could improve the efficiency of housing subsidies and reduce urban service investment costs. Nicaragua's mortgage subsidy is tied to housing value, which encourages developers to reduce sale prices in order to allow con-sumers to qualify. However, where materials, labor, and permitting costs tend to be fixed, developers have focused on the urban fringe where land is cheap. In two new periurban developments near Managua, the highest demand is for units that are eligible for the mortgage interest rate subsidy (up to 70 percent or more of all units are financed with the subsidy, which is linked to unit price, not consumer income).[19] The developments also lack proximity to commercial and service uses, have limited public transportation services and require commutes of up to an hour each way. Mexico provides a case of how subsidies can be directed to encourage densification and infill development rather than continued low-density urban expansion (box 3.6). The United States provides a case on interinstitutional coordination in the provision of affordable housing (box 3.7).

Box 3.6 Linking Housing Subsidies with Urban Growth

Since 2000 both the types and overall volume of government subsidies in the Mexican housing sector have grown markedly. For example, in 2000, a total of 400,000 mortgages were originated; and by 2008 there were 1.4 million, with more than 60 percent coming from housing finance subsidy programs aimed at reducing the cost of mortgages for consumers and providing subsidies and guarantees for lenders.

Between 1980 and 2010, the urban population of Mexico doubled, but the urban footprint expanded seven times (SEDESOL 2011). This low-density growth not only exacerbated deficiencies in infrastructure coverage as piecemeal or leapfrogging development but also distorted land markets by increasing speculation and reducing available green space and agricultural land.

In 2013, the government reconsidered the subsidy allocations by including spatial criteria which increase the size of subsidies based on housing development in areas that are within or proximate to urban zones. The purpose of this adjustment was to control urban expansion, reduce housing deficits, and promote urban mobility and connectivity.

The criteria include:

1. Location (within one of three designated "zones" contornos)
2. Density (based on proposed density or Floor Area Ratio of the project)
3. Services (the presence of services and infrastructure connections)
4. Competitiveness (proposals that provided sustainable financial models)

In exchange for satisfying these criteria, a developer can receive technical assistance for environmental review and permitting, infrastructure financing guarantees, housing subsidies, and preferential support from land banks.

Despite the changes, developers have been slow to produce housing in urban contornos and that which has been built is not affordable for the lowest income quintile. There are two main reasons for this. First, serviced land, even in vacant or underutilized urban spaces, is expensive to assemble and develop, which reduces the incentive for developers to utilize the subsidy programs because it will not cover development costs. Second, the subsidy program originates at the federal level and local governments have had little involvement or incentive. Improving the coordination of local government involvement with land use regulations, land assembly and development controls, or incentives could lower the cost and risk for developers in providing housing in areas with existing proximity to infrastructure and jobs.

Box 3.7 United States: Improving Coordination for Affordable Housing Provision

The HOME Investment Partnerships Program (HOME) is an affordable housing program supported through the U.S. Department of Housing and Urban Development. The program was launched in 1990 and provides federal support to various affordable housing options for low-income populations through a system of block grants to state and municipal governments. The annual budget for the program is about US$1 billion, 40 percent of which is shared among 50 state governments and the rest allocated to local governments. Governments access the money by forming a "participating jurisdiction" (of which there are 643), which may include multiple governments across administrative boundaries, and by partnering with an experienced nonprofit group to implement the proposed housing project.

The HOME program focuses on improving the quality and availability of housing for low-income groups by providing funding for local governments to implement projects that would otherwise be too costly to complete. State governments develop their own housing needs assessments and plans based on local market and demographic needs for low-income groups. These criteria include the incidence of poverty, housing affordability gaps, and the overall quality of housing stock (age, overcrowding, infrastructure connection). Grants vary in size and are awarded for proposals based on how well they meet these plans and require a commitment to match 25 percent of the requested amount with other funding sources, which can include donations of money, property or labor.

Eligible activities include:

• Support for financing assistance for home purchase for low-income households
• Support for developers to build or renovate housing to accommodate low-income renters or buyers, including the offset of land assembly, demolition, or relocation expenses necessary to complete the project. A certain portion of the developments must be set aside for low-income households.
• Rental vouchers for eligible low-income tenants

The block grant approach provides support and flexibility to local governments in determining how best to address the scarcity of quality affordable housing. It relies on local governments to identify particular needs and work in partnership with civil society groups and the private sector to determine the location, scale, and type of housing solution given local demands and market conditions. Since 1992 the program has provided support to 274,944 renters and has produced over 1.1 million physical units, 42 percent of which are occupied by households with incomes less than 30 percent of the Area Median Income (AMI), the target beneficiary group.

Source: Gramlich 2014.

A Way Forward: Housing as a Catalyst for Urban Prosperity

The recommendations are linked to bridge the gap between the informal and formal housing delivery. There are three overlapping areas of policy intervention at the national level that provide an entry point to housing sector reform. These areas (detailed in figure 3.8 below) aim to strengthen the overall housing

Figure 3.8 Improving Housing Delivery across Income Groups

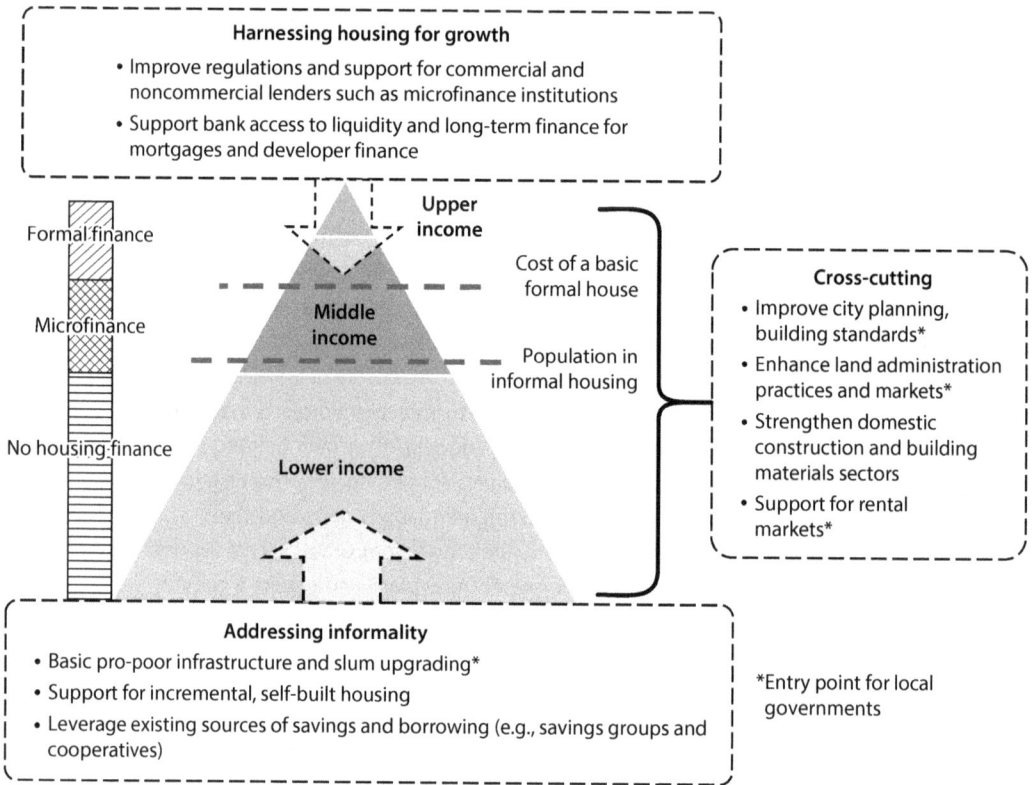

sector for all markets and housing types, reduce the cost of purchasing or financing formal housing, and improve the quality of informal housing for the poor.

Priorities at a National Level

Cross-cutting interventions can improve the overall function of the housing sector. This includes improvement in land administration and property registration systems used by municipal governments as well as introducing flexible or graduated standards to support incremental housing improvements and encourage density and infill development. Setting up national-level housing observatories can be instrumental in tracking land and property markets, particularly with data on prices, volumes, and sales trends. These data can assist both banks and private developers and can be useful for developing and targeting subsidies to low-income populations. Additionally, housing policy support for formalized rental housing provides an additional option and greater locational flexibility for residents.

Reform to the banking sector to reduce the cost and risk for formal housing finance is an important component for both housing production and consumption.

Governments can introduce reforms to encourage competition in mortgage lending and identify screening, and alternative qualification criteria for low-income borrowers. Support for development finance for rental housing or linking mortgage subsidies to housing location can better align housing supply with needs. Reforms can support smaller lenders such as MFIs and credit cooperatives to scale up lending for housing consumption for middle- and lower-income groups.

Targeted infrastructure upgrades can improve housing quality for low-income groups. Mapping and assessment of conditions in informal settlements can direct investment in basic services to those who need them the most. A national-level initiative for informal settlement mapping and pro-poor targeting of investments can assist municipal governments in identifying and addressing service gaps. Housing policy support for self-building, such as targeted subsidies for small loans and in-kind construction materials, or serviced "core" or "starter" units that can be incrementally expanded by owner-builders or local contractors, will also improve access to quality housing for the poor.

Housing policies need to incorporate and strengthen links between national-level programs and subsidies and the tools and capacities of local governments. They must also provide a framework for coordination between sub-national governments and relevant ministries including housing, transportation, finance, and infrastructure with the purpose of improving low-income neighborhoods. This will both reduce overlapping or redundant public investments and direct housing subsidies to urban areas that will be more environmentally and economically sustainable. Partnerships and alliances between local governments (*mancomunidades*) discussed previously would provide an important convening role for these dialogues. Similarly, housing policies should also support a plurality of housing and tenure options (apart from privileging single-family detached houses) in line with local and regional needs. Local governments should also obtain the tools and capacities to develop plans that would better allow them to coordinate long-term investment and housing needs planning with neighboring jurisdictions.

Housing interventions should be linked with land use planning in order to promote density. As discussed previously, primary cities in the region have been growing through low-density urban expansion, which reduces the economic advantages offered by urban agglomerations. Planning and land value capture tools can play a major role in improving the quality and stock of housing in large cities. This can be enhanced further when national-level housing programs or subsidy schemes include links to local land use and capital investment plans. In this way, local governments can direct subsidized housing investment to dense, serviced, and built-up areas of the city, rather than the urban periphery that lacks infrastructure. However, there is currently little if any legal or institutional support at the national level for developing these approaches for municipal governments.

Improving the quality of informal housing can encourage inclusive urbanization. Most countries have also provided subsidies for home improvement and expansions, and given the predominance of this approach in informal settlements, these efforts are worth bringing to scale through linking with technical assistance and community-upgrading programs. A stocktaking of the location and housing conditions within informal settlements could be used to guide priorities and targeting criteria for upgrading. More policy support at the national level should be given to nonbank financial institutions such as MFIs and savings groups as well as the role of housing cooperatives as an option for financing and developing low-income units. For most of the urban poor, these organizations represent the only option for developing savings or credit histories and would be well placed to leverage the extensive remittances received by households with migrant laborers. These institutions would benefit from a legal and regulatory framework that would allow for leveraging these sources of income and savings and would enable alternative creditworthiness assessments for the informally employed, such as the case of RAFCASA.

Priorities at a City Level

Cities can have a key place in developing an inclusive housing system. The differing sizes and forms of primary and secondary cities in the region should inform the policy options for supporting housing delivery in each. For primary and capital cities, a diversity of housing types in proximity to existing job centers and services is needed. Growing secondary cities will need to improve planning and coordination to ensure that new urban growth provides residents access to services and reduces the incidence of new informal settlements. The recommendations in the next section provide a general overview of solutions. More detailed, country-specific diagnostics of the housing sector would be needed to provide more specific recommendations and action plans for each country.

With proper support, municipal governments can assemble public land for private housing development. For example, vacant parcels can be taxed at higher rates in order to encourage development, as has been done in Mexico. Request for proposal (RFP) mechanisms can encourage competitive bids to build low-cost housing on underutilized local government land. Other tools such as Tax Increment Financing can encourage infill development by allowing cities to pay for infrastructure improvements through borrowing against future tax revenues. Informal settlements can be improved through the use of land readjustment, where residents release a portion of their plot to allow for infrastructure provision and receive a slightly smaller, but serviced (and higher-value) plot at the same location.

Cities also need to explore options for promoting or formalizing low-cost rentals. Large cities also tend to be the most supportive of rental markets, which can be an affordable alternative to home purchase. Legal protections and obligations for tenants and landlords can be further developed, along with subsidies or tax exemptions for petty landlords to let out spare rooms or units. Rental voucher programs can be included in housing policies and would allow lower-income renters additional mobility and choice.

Secondary cities will need prospective planning to accommodate new population growth. As urbanization trends continue, these local governments will play an important role in providing quality housing. Local governments will need technical support and capacity building to coordinate land use planning and housing by identifying areas for infrastructure provision and rights of way, a process called guided land development (Angel 2012). This will signal to housing developers where future public investments, such as sites and services, will be directed. At the same time, municipalities must also explore ways to use urban land to sustainably finance infrastructure and urban service investments to new areas. Such tools could include impact fees and special assessment districts where private developers share the cost of infrastructure provision. Local governments can also create and enforce plans to identify hazardous areas prone to natural disasters in order to discourage housing development in these places.

Cross-cutting interventions can support the function of the housing sector across income groups. Governments, especially at the local level, have an important role in developing the framework through which housing markets can function more equitably and efficiently. Strengthening land administration systems including land registries and cadasters that local governments use can reduce the time and costs for getting necessary approvals required for transferring or collateralizing property. For low-income groups, municipal governments can adopt a regulatory framework that allows for graduated standards or alternative materials and construction types to encourage the formalization of self-built units without unnecessarily high costs.

Notes

1. Above or below this interval, other consumption needs (food or durable goods) reduce the share of housing expenses.
2. In Europe, renting constitutes 30 percent of tenure, with Germany and Switzerland having rental rates of over 40 percent. In Latin America, Bolivia and Colombia have comparable rental rates (IDB 2014).
3. For example, INVUR, the Nicaraguan housing ministry, estimated a housing deficit of 400,000 units in 2005. By contrast, the Central American Housing Association places the deficit at 745,000 units when distinguishing between qualitative and quantitative deficits (Bredenoord and van der Meulen 2014).
4. There is evidence that high urban housing costs can discourage new household formation among young adults (Ermish and Jenkins 1999; Haurin, Hendershott, and Kim 1993). This can in turn actually increase the number of people per household in urban areas compared to rural areas (Stinner 1977), which requires that estimates of household formation and, by extension, future housing be well-calibrated.
5. Land administration refers to the legal/regulatory framework that applies to rights afforded to public and private lands. This includes cadaster records, property registries, public land management, and land use and zoning standards applied to land.
6. The rankings exclude four cities from the Dominican Republic that are included in the sample. For this reason, positions 14, 15, 16, and 19 are omitted.

7. Construction permits for the Doing Business indicators examine warehouse development. Residential developments, however, are similarly land and infrastructure intensive. This comparison is used as a general proxy for planning and permitting capacity.

8. Honduras is an exception, because political instability and a macroeconomic downturn have steadily contracted the level of formal construction activity since 2009.

9. These figures come from interviews with commercial developers and a review of available figures in secondary sources.

10. Data on comparative costs of housing inputs are scarce, though across the region costs for the same inputs may vary considerably; in San Salvador, infrastructure and administrative costs on new units are 40 percent of the total unit cost, but in Buenos Aires these inputs are only 20 percent. By contrast materials and labor are half the total unit cost in San Salvador while they are three-quarters of the cost in Buenos Aires (IDB 2012b).

11. Habitat has also piloted the introduction of mini-septic systems to replace unimproved latrines. These units cost US$600 and can be built and maintained by beneficiary households.

12. In El Salvador, for example, only 10 percent of concrete is imported (UN-Habitat 2014).

13. For example, the lowest-cost formal housing units in San José, Tegucigalpa, and Guatemala are equivalent to about one year's average household income in those cities respectively; ranging from between US$12,000 and US$18,000 (IDB 2011). Given standard mortgage finance assumptions at these income levels, the houses would likely not present an affordability challenge.

14. The table shows the estimated percentage of urban households that would be able to purchase a formal house. The estimates are based on data compiled from city-level household surveys measuring expenditures compared to a hypothetical formal housing unit price. The unit price is a composite estimate based on housing prices compiled from formal housing costs drawn from cities across the region; construction costs are assumed to be US$11,000 after US$4,000 for land acquisition, giving a final price of US$15,000. Finance terms are 10 percent down payment, with a 6 percent interest rate over 20 years. Housing affordability is calculated as a maximum of 30 percent of household income for housing/mortgage expenditure (IDB 2011, 61).

15. El Salvador has had a consistent policy of ensuring housing provision for all residents (UN-Habitat 2014). Similarly, Panama's Constitution (Article 117) allows for government involvement in housing. Guatemala's 2004 National Housing Policy provided citizens the right to decent housing and obligated the government in its provision.

16. This contrasts with an interventionist approach where the government provides housing directly at below-market prices and provides large or hidden subsidies through poorly designed interest rate subsidies, the application of price or rent ceilings, or other market distortionary measures (Chiquier and Lea 2009).

17. Assumptions include US$18,000 unit cost, 10 percent down payment, US$1,500 subsidy, mortgage interest subsidy of 3 percent for first 10 years of 20 year mortgage, and commercial lending rate of 12 percent interest for the final 10 years.

18. Assumptions include 25 percent affordability threshold, housing price of US$14,868, 5 percent down payment, and 25 year mortgage term at 9 percent interest.

19. The subsidy is targeted to loans of US$32,000 or less, with deductions from the market interest rate ranging from 3.5 to 2.5 percent depending on the value of the loan for 10 years. The larger the loan, the lower the interest rate subsidy awarded.

Linking the subsidy to housing value makes it difficult to estimate how many more low-income households are able to purchase a unit that otherwise could not afford it. It is possible that the subsidy is providing access to formal housing to those who could otherwise afford a market-rate mortgage.

Bibliography

Abiko, A., R. Azevedo, R. Rinalddelli, and C. Riogi. 2007. "Basic Costs of Slum Upgrading in Brazil." *Global Urban Development Magazine* 3 (1).

Angel, S. 2012. *Planet of Cities*. Cambridge, MA: Lincoln Institute of Land Policy.

Angel, S., J. Parent, D. L. Civco, and A. M. Blei. 2010. "The Persistent Decline in Urban Densities: Global and Historical Evidence of Sprawl." Lincoln Institute of Land Policy Working Paper.

Banco Central de Nicaragua. 2015. Cuentas Nacionales.

Barnerjee, A., and E. Duflo. 2012. *Poor Economics: A Radical Rethinking of the Way We Fight Global Poverty*. New York: Public Affairs.

Bonvalet, C., and E. Lelièvre. 1997a. "The Transformation of Housing and Household Structures in France and Great Britain." *International Journal of Population Geography* 3 (3): 183–201.

Bredenoord, J., and B. van der Meulen. 2014. Self-Help Housing and Upcoming Policies for Affordable Housing in Nicaragua. *Affordable Housing in the Urban Global South: Seeking Sustainable Solutions*, 300.

Bredenoord, J., P. Van Lindert, and P. Smets. 2014. *Affordable Housing in the Urban Global South: Seeking Sustainable Solutions*. Earthscan from Routledge.

Buckley, R. M., and J. Kalarickal. 2006. *Thirty Years of World Bank Shelter Lending: What Have We Learned?* Washington, DC: World Bank.

CAPAC (Camera Panamena de la Construccion). 2014. "Estadisticas de Empleo" http://www.capac.org/index.php/2015-03-17-15-34-21/estadi-sticas-de-empleo-agosto-2014.

Chiquier, L., and M. Lea. 2009. *Housing Finance Policy in Emerging Markets*. Washington, DC: World Bank.

Cuenin, F., C. Piedrafita, E. Rojas, and Nadin Medellin. 2012. "Hammering Out a Housing Policy that Works." In *Room for Development: Housing Markets in Latin America and the Caribbean*, edited by Bouillon, C. Washington, DC: Inter-American Development Bank, 239–280.

Dasgupta, Basab; Lall, Somik V.; Lozano-Gracia, Nancy. 2014. "Urbanization and Housing Investment." Policy Research Working Paper 7110, World Bank, Washington, DC.

Ermisch, J. F., and S. P. Jenkins. 1999. *Retirement and Housing Adjustment in Later Life: Evidence from the British Household Panel Survey*. Labour Economics. Vol 6. Institute for Social and Economic Research, University of Essex, Colchester CO4 3SQ, UK.

Fergusson, B., and P. Smets. 2010. "Finance for Incremental Housing: Current Status and Prospects for Housing in Latin America." *Review of Urban and Regional Development Studies*.

Gramlich, E. 2014. *HOME Investment Partnerships Program*. National Low Income Housing Coalition.

Gutierrez, J., W. Van Vliet, E. Arias, and R. Pujol. 1993. "In Defence of Housing: Housing Policies and Practices in Costa Rica." *Habitat International* 17 (2): 63–72.

Hábitat para la Humanidad. 2008. "Información clave sobre La Situación Actual de la Vivienda Social en Nicaragua". Retrieved January 28, 2016http://www.habitat.org/lc/lac/pdf/situacion_vivienda_nicaragua.pdf.

Haurin, D., P. Hendershott, and D. Kim 1993. "The Impact of Real Rents and Wages on Household Formation." *The Review of Economics and Statistics* 75 (2): 284–93.

Held, G. 2000. "Políticas de vivienda de interés social orientadas al mercado: Experiencias recientes con subsidios a la demanda en Chile, Costa Rica y Colombia." Proyecto Interdivisional CEPAL "Instituciones y Mercados" Santiago de Chile.

Hofinet (Housing Finance Information Network). Hofinet note. http://www.hofinet.org/index.aspx.

IDB. 2008. Programa de Mejoramiento de las Condiciones Habitacionales. Proyecto PN-L1002.

———. 2011. "The Missing Foundations of Housing Finance: Incomplete Markets, Fragmented Policies and Emerging Solutions in Guatemala." Technical Notes, No. IDB-TN-286. Inter-American Development Bank, Washington, DC.

———. 2012a. "Housing Finance in Central America: What is Holding it Back." Technical Notes, No. IDB-TN-285. Inter-American Development Bank, Washington, DC.

———. 2012b. *Room for Development: Housing Markets in Latin America and the Caribbean.* Washington, DC: Inter-American Development Bank.

———. 2014. *Se busca vivienda en Alquiler: Opciones de política en América Latina y el Caribe.* Washington, DC: Inter-American Development Bank.

Jenkins, P., and H. Smith. 2001. "An Institutional Approach to Analysis of State Capacity in Housing Systems in the Developing World: Case Studies in South Africa and Costa Rica." *Housing Studies* 16 (4): 485–507.

MINVAH (Ministerio de Vivienda y Asentamientos Humanos). 2014. Compendio Estadistico de Vivienda 2014. http://www.mivah.go.cr/Biblioteca_Estadisticas.shtml.

Monkonnen, Paavo. 2013. "Housing Deficits as a Frame for Housing Policy: Demographic Change, Economic Crisis and Household Formation in Indonesia." *International Journal of Housing Policy* 13 (3): 247–67.

Nickson, A. 2011. "Where is Local Government in Latin America? A Comparative Perspective." Working Paper No. 6, Swedish International Center for Local Democracy.

Payne, G. 2005. "Getting Ahead of the Game: A Twin-Track Approach to Improving Existing Slums and Reducing the Need for Future Slums." *Environment and Urbanization.*

Pujol-Mesalles, R., and E. Pérez Molina. 2013. "Urban Growth in the Metropolitan Region of San José, Costa Rica: A Spatial and Temporal Exploration of the Determinates of Land Use Change, 1986–2010."

Rojas, E., and N. Medellin. 2011. "Housing Policy Matters for the Poor."

SEDESOL. 2011. *La expansión de las ciudades 1980–2010.* SEDESOL, Mexico City.

SEDLAC (Socio-Economic Database for Latin America and the Caribbean. 2015. Center for Distributive, Labor and Social Studies (CEDLAS)/World Bank.

Smolka, M. 2013. *Implementing Valie Capture in Latin America: Policies and Tools for Urban Development.* Cambridge, MA: Lincoln Institute of Land Policy.

Stein, A., and I. Vance. 2008. "The Role of Housing Finance in Addressing the Needs of the Urban Poor: Lessons from Central America." *Environment and Urbanization* 20: 13–30.

Stinner, W. F. 1977. "Urbanization and Household Structure in the Philippines." *The Journal of Marriage and the Family.*

UN (United Nations). 2014. *World Urbanization Prospects 2014 Revisions*. United Nations.

UN-Habitat. 2003. *Global Report on Human Settlements 2003: The Challenge of Slums*. London: Earthscan.

———. 2014. *Perfil del Sector de Vivienda de El Salvador*. Nairobi: UN-Habitat.

United Cities and Local Governments (UCLG). 2008. *Decentralization and Local Democracy in the World: First Global Report by United Cities and Local Governments*. UCLG, Barcelona.

World Bank. 1993. "Housing: Enabling Markets to Work." Housing Policy Paper, World Bank, Washington, DC.

———. 2014a. *Doing Business 2015: Going Beyond Efficiency*. Washington, DC: World Bank.

———. 2014b. "Global Findex Database." http://datatopics.worldbank.org/financialinc.

———. 2014c. *Mejora de la Gobernanza de la Tierra en Honduras: Implementación del Marco de Evaluación de Gobernanza de la Tierra*. Washington, DC: World Bank.

———. 2015. *Mejora de la gobernanza de la tierra en Guatemala: Implementación del Marco de Evaluación de la Gobernanza de la Tierra – LGAF*. Washington, DC: World Bank.

CHAPTER 4

Making Cities Resilient to Reduce Central America's Vulnerability to Natural Disasters

Haris Sanahuja and Oscar A. Ishizawa

Overview

Making Central American cities more resilient is critical to reduce the long-term impact of natural disasters on the population and economies. Natural disasters not only have a significant negative impact on the lives of the urban residents in the region—especially the poor—but they hinder the national growth trajectory. Cities already represent 70 to 80 percent of the assets at risk in the different countries, and this concentration will further increase in the future along with increasing urbanization, rising population, and economic growth. Poorly managed urbanization leads to increased vulnerability to natural disasters: (i) precarious settlements usually develop in risk prone areas; (ii) inadequate building standards increase vulnerability to earthquakes; and (iii) sprawling urban areas with inadequate infrastructure increase flood risks.

This chapter focuses on characterizing the risks and exposure to risk in the region, especially in the urban areas. Disaster Risk in Central America presents an overall diagnostic on how vulnerable to disasters the countries in the region are, and what type of assets are at risk in urban areas. Enabling Factors for DRM and Urban Resilience discusses how countries have the opportunity to strengthen disaster risk management (DRM) and increase urban resilience by promoting actions to better *understand* urban patterns and disaster risk, *avoid* the generation of future risk, *reduce* existing risk, and develop instruments to *finance* inevitable risk. Finally, Moving Forward in Building Resilient Cities proposes a series of recommendations moving forward in building more resilient cities in Central America.

Key Messages

There are clear opportunities to promote policies that can avoid the generation of future risk, as well as reduce and manage the existing risk.

- To prevent future risk, municipalities need to be provided with adequate information capacity and incentives, to play the role in incorporating DRM criteria into local territorial development plans, investments plans, and building regulations.
- Reducing existing risk will require investments that will need the financial support of the central governments. However, cities will need to lead the prioritization of investments in new risk mitigation infrastructure, and retrofitting of existing critical infrastructure and buildings.
- To enhance the understanding of disaster risk, national governments need to improve the knowledge base of vulnerability exposure and hazard profiles at the city level and its availability to local actors.

Disaster Risk in Central America

Central America's geographic location makes it remarkably prone to disasters from adverse natural events, including hurricanes, droughts, floods, El Niño-Southern Oscillation (ENSO), and earthquakes. In the past 50 years, based on data from the International Disasters Database (EM-DAT),[1] the number of recorded natural events has increased (see figure 4.1) in the region, affecting almost all

Figure 4.1 Number of Events per Hazard in Central America

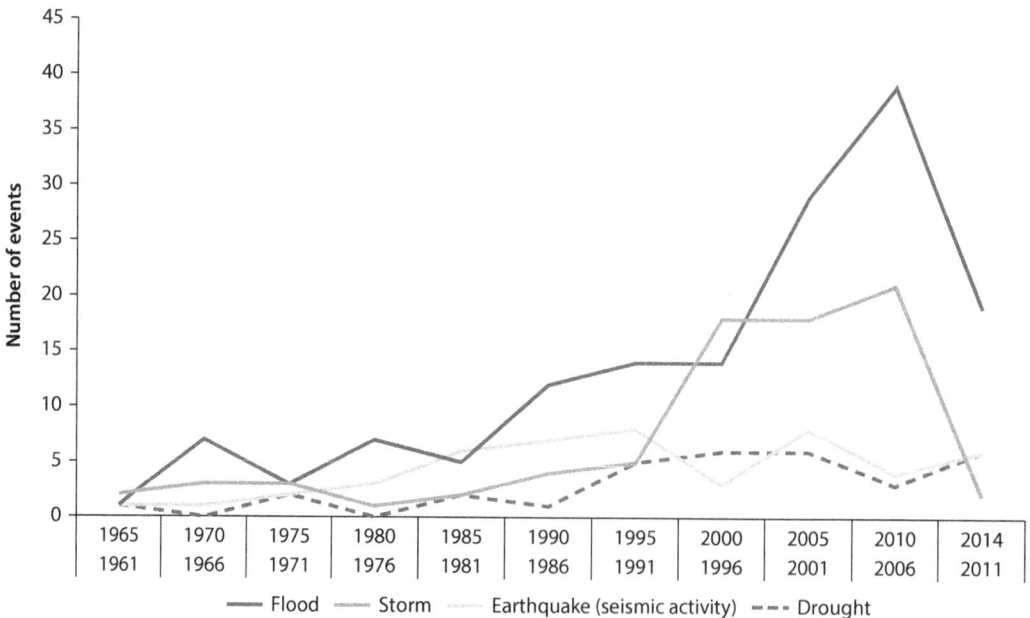

Source: Emergency Events Database (EM-DAT); The International Disaster Database.

countries with different impacts and hindering, in certain cases, their capacity to foster sustainable growth. Large-scale floods are the most recurrent disaster, with almost 40 events occurring throughout the region only between 2006 and 2010. Likewise, storms have repeatedly affected the region: in 1998, Hurricane Mitch directly affected around 6.7 million people, resulting in a death toll of 14,600 deaths, and causing more than US$8.5 billion in damages in El Salvador, Guatemala, Honduras, and Nicaragua. More recently, in October 2011, Tropical Depression 12-E hit the coasts of El Salvador and Guatemala and affected most of the countries in the region, with damages amounting to nearly US$1 billion.[2]

Over the period 1970–2010, major adverse natural events like earthquakes, hurricanes, and large floods have caused accumulated damages and losses that exceed US$80 billion.[3] Figure 4.2 presents how selected events drive the majority of damages and losses in the region, especially in urban areas given their accumulation of highly vulnerable structures in hazard-prone areas. While disasters originated by hydrometeorological hazards (including ENSO) are more frequent, their accumulated impact has represented US$22 billion. Seismic events are less frequent, but have had more devastating impacts and provoked damages and losses amounting to US$58 billion over the period (72 percent of the total damages and losses). On the other hand, long-term cyclical events such as droughts have an

Figure 4.2 Damages and Losses Provoked by Selected Floods, Tropical Storms (TS), and Earthquakes (EQ) in Central America

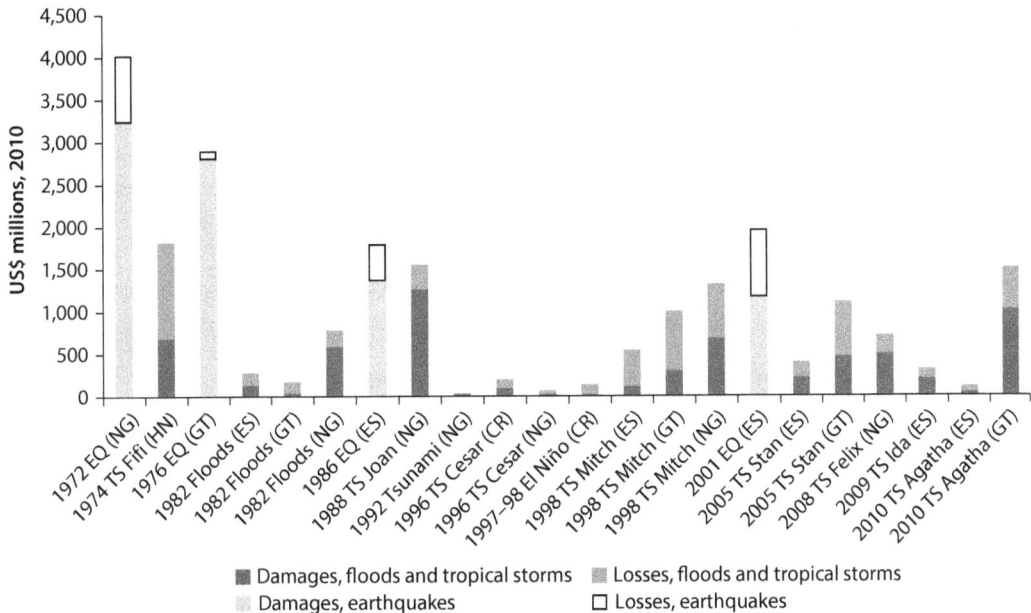

■ Damages, floods and tropical storms　▒ Losses, floods and tropical storms
▒ Damages, earthquakes　　　　　　　　□ Losses, earthquakes

Source: Calculations based on PDNA assessments; damages and losses associated with hydrometeorological events are pictured in blue/orange and those associated with geophysical events are pictured in green/white. To ensure legibility, only selected events are depicted here.
Note: NG = Nicaragua; HN = Honduras; GT = Guatemala; ES = El Salvador; CRI = Costa Rica.

impact in productive sectors, causing economic losses that could reduce the ability of urban areas to build resilience to disasters.

Moreover, climate change is expected to modify current weather patterns, which could translate into an increased frequency and intensity of extreme hydro-meteorological events in the region. More frequent and intense hurricanes, tropical storms, floods, and droughts could affect the provision of water (both in quantity and quality) and the alteration of ecosystem services within the impacted areas. While the increase of floods could have a larger direct impact in urban areas, droughts could also affect the urban population's food security.

What Is at Risk in Urban Areas in Central America?

Quantifying disaster risk is a first step toward understanding and better managing risks. Box 4.1 presents the Central America Country Disaster Risk Profile (CDRP) project,[4] which has the objective of contributing to this goal by assessing the potential direct economic losses from adverse natural events. A first step toward understanding what is at risk in Central America is assessing the building exposure.

Box 4.1 Building Risk Information for Decision Making: The Development of the Country Disaster Risk Profiles for Central America

What is a Country Disaster Risk Profile?

Probabilistic disaster risk profiles provide risk assessments and estimates of potential damage to property caused by severe natural hazards. These profiles outline a holistic view of financial risk due to natural hazards, assisting governments in long-term planning and preparedness. A Country Disaster Risk Profile (CDRP) presents a probabilistic estimate of risk aggregated at the national level.

The Country Disaster Risk Profile (CDRP) presents information on:

- Occurrence exceedance probability curve (OEP), which indicates the probability that the economic loss level indicated on the curve will be exceed by any event in any given year.
- Annual average loss (AAL) for both earthquake and windstorm risk, giving an estimation of the potential losses per year averaged over a number of years
- Probable maximum loss (PML) for a 250-year return period, estimating the potential losses for an event with a return period of 250 years, or a 1/250 annual probability of exceedance.

What is innovative in the CDRP for Central America?

The CDRP project gathered information to characterize and build an exposure model of the building stock in Central American countries using a top-down approach with a country-level resolution. This model consists of a building inventory stock model which captures important attributes such as geographical location, urban/rural classification, type of occupancy (for example, residential and nonresidential), building typology (for example, wood, concrete, masonry, and so on), and economic (replacement) value. This exposure model is developed using freely available (or available at minimum cost) datasets.

Source: CDRP for Central America and Gunasekera et al. 2015.

This means recognizing the elements that are exposed to adverse natural events by knowing the location of assets and their key characteristics, including the type of construction (material, age, and structural characteristics) and their value. On the basis of the results of the CDRP for Central America, we can conclude that cities concentrate the large majority of exposed assets and exposed value in the region. Map 4.1 shows the building exposure model for Panama City, where most of the value of building stock is concentrated in the downtown area. Table 4.1, which differentiates the building stock value between urban and rural areas for all Central American countries, shows that most of the building exposure is in urban areas, concentrating more than 70 percent of the total built-up area in the region. For example, almost 80 percent of the built-up area in El Salvador is urban, of which 42 percent is in San Salvador.

Certain building characteristics prevalent in Central America are highly vulnerable to major adverse natural events. Most of the external walls of dwellings in Central American countries are built with concrete block, brick, and stone—up to 84 percent in urban areas in El Salvador. Prefabricated concrete panels (and other

Map 4.1 Country Disaster Risk Profile Building Exposure Model for Panama City, Panama

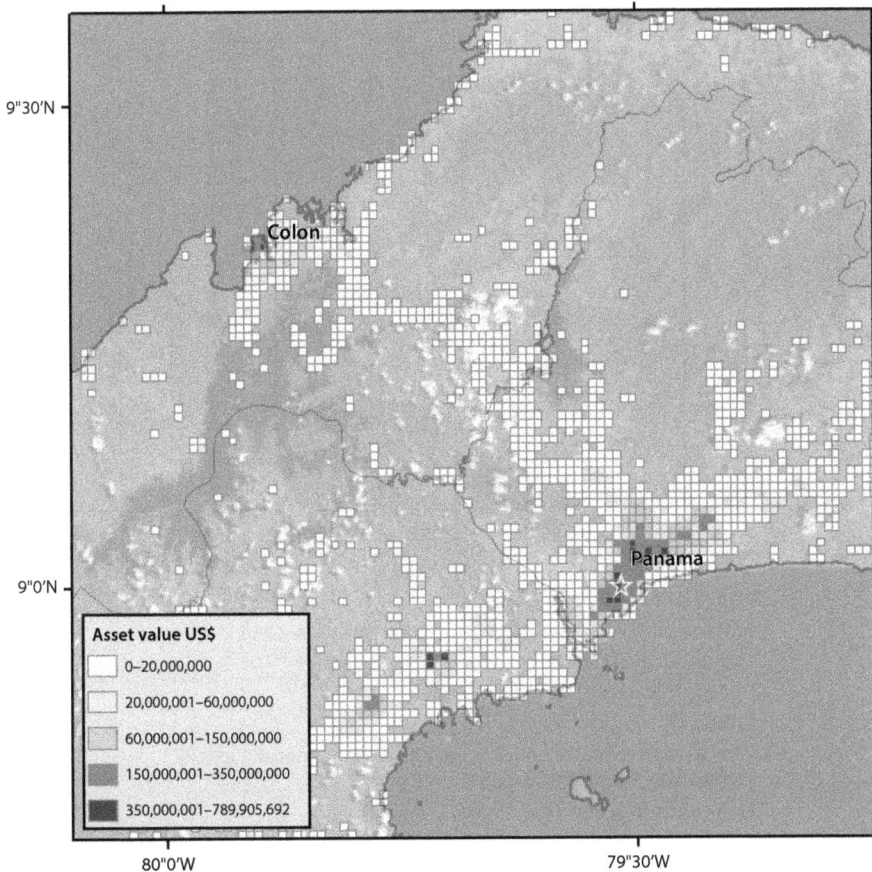

Source: CDRP (World Bank 2015).

Table 4.1 Exposed Asset Values of Central America Classified by Urban/Rural/Capital Areas
% total exposure

Country	Total (2005-US$ million)	Capital city	Urban	Total urban	Rural
Costa Rica	80,059	53.5	24.9	78.3	21.7
El Salvador	37,054	42.0	37.9	80.0	20.0
Guatemala	70,369	39.3	33.8	73.0	27.0
Honduras	27,565	21.0	50.2	71.2	28.8
Nicaragua	22,067	33.7	42.7	76.5	23.5
Panama	45,853	48.7	30.4	79.1	20.9

Source: CDRP (World Bank 2015).

Figure 4.3 Country Disaster Risk Profile Building Characteristics—External Wall Distribution of Dwellings in Central America

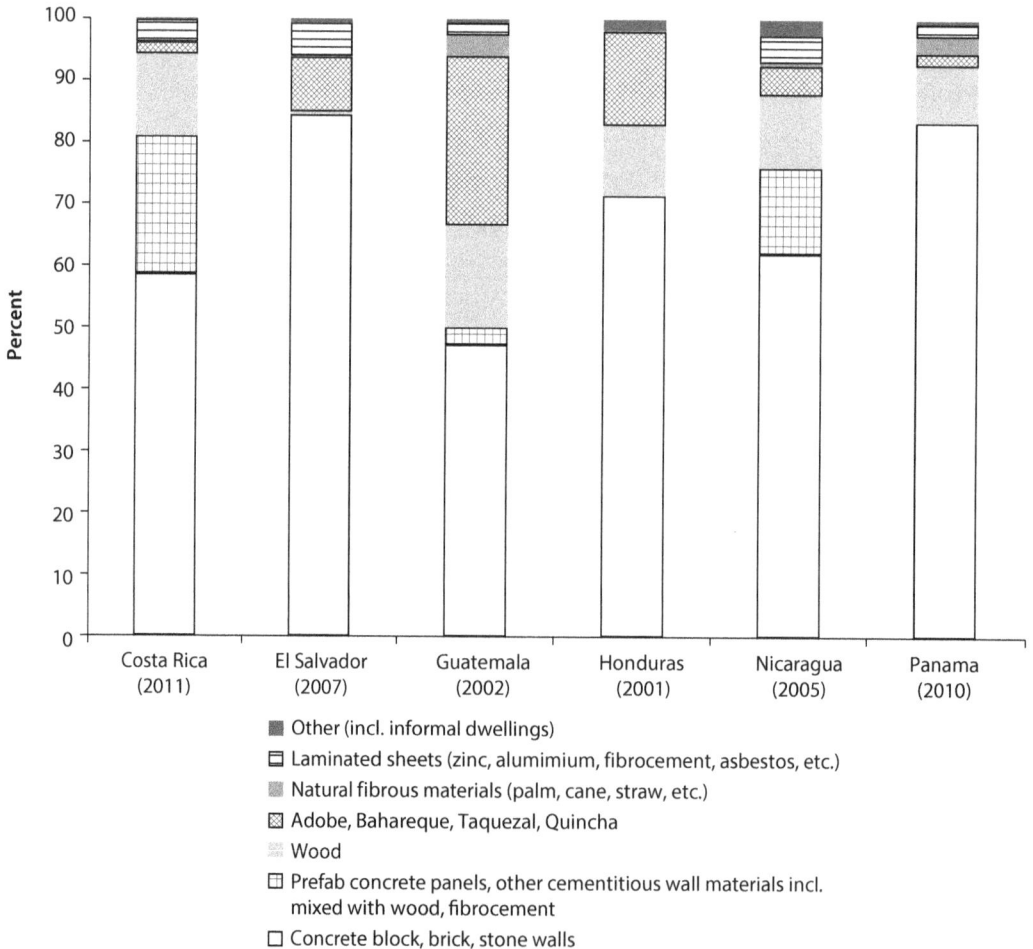

Legend:
- Other (incl. informal dwellings)
- Laminated sheets (zinc, alumimium, fibrocement, asbestos, etc.)
- Natural fibrous materials (palm, cane, straw, etc.)
- Adobe, Bahareque, Taquezal, Quincha
- Wood
- Prefab concrete panels, other cementitious wall materials incl. mixed with wood, fibrocement
- Concrete block, brick, stone walls

Source: CDRP (World Bank 2015).
Note: El Salvador, Honduras, and Nicaragua data refer to dwellings in urban areas, while Costa Rica, Guatemala, and Panama data refer to dwellings in the whole country.

cement wall materials) are the second-most-used material in Nicaragua's urban dwellings and Costa Rica's dwellings located throughout its territory. However, the presence of adobe, wood, and mud walled buildings in the region increase the risk of urban areas to disasters such as earthquakes and hurricanes. These building types are present in many urban areas of the region (see figure 4.3).

The largely unplanned and poorly managed urban growth over the past decades has resulted in a high share of urban population living in precarious settlements, contributing to the accumulation of highly vulnerable structures. Often located in hazard-prone areas and with limited access to basic services—such as adequate drainage—these settlements are the most vulnerable to disasters such as landslides and floods. This is particularly true for urban areas where most of the exposure value is located. CDRP results at the country level quantifying earthquake and hurricane risk, and differentiating them between urban and rural areas (Aubrecht et al. 2016) show that catastrophic risk is highly concentrated in urban areas in five out of the six countries (see figure 4.4). Map 4.2 provides an example of the concentration of earthquake risk in Managua represented by the annual average loss (AAL).[5] Honduras is the only country that concentrates most of its catastrophic risk in rural areas, and where hurricane risk is higher than earthquake risk. AAL from earthquake risk in urban areas is particularly high in Costa Rica and El Salvador, amounting to US$327 million and US$232 million, respectively. Overall, AAL in Central America resulting from earthquake risk in cities equals nearly US$800 million. Table 4.2 presents a

Figure 4.4 Urban and Rural Annual Average Loss in 2015 for Earthquakes (EQ) and Hurricanes (HU) in Central America
US$, millions

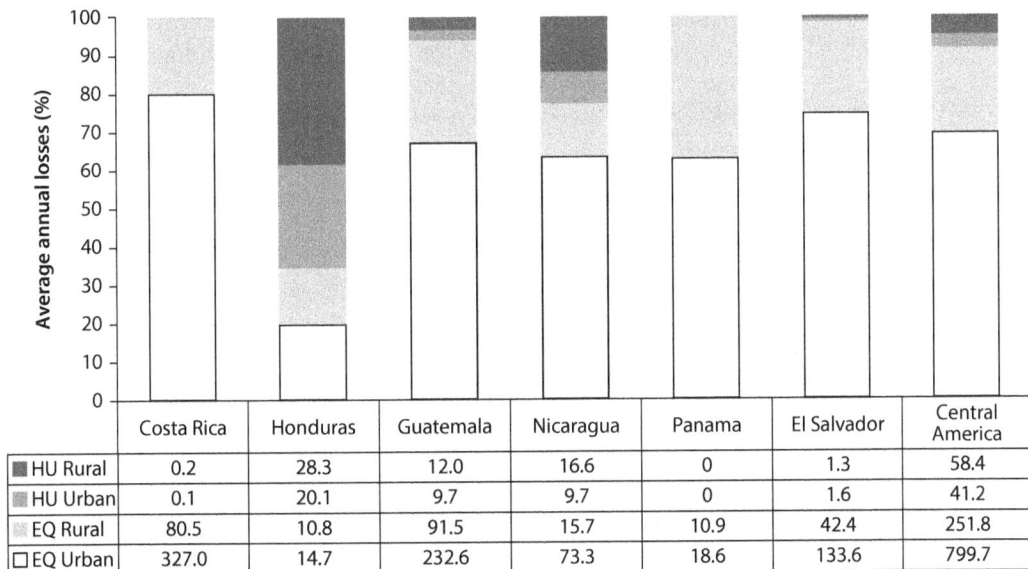

	Costa Rica	Honduras	Guatemala	Nicaragua	Panama	El Salvador	Central America
■ HU Rural	0.2	28.3	12.0	16.6	0	1.3	58.4
▨ HU Urban	0.1	20.1	9.7	9.7	0	1.6	41.2
▨ EQ Rural	80.5	10.8	91.5	15.7	10.9	42.4	251.8
□ EQ Urban	327.0	14.7	232.6	73.3	18.6	133.6	799.7

Source: CDRP (World Bank 2015).

Map 4.2 Annual Average Loss (AAL)—Estimation of Potential Losses per Year Averaged over Possible Hazard Scenarios

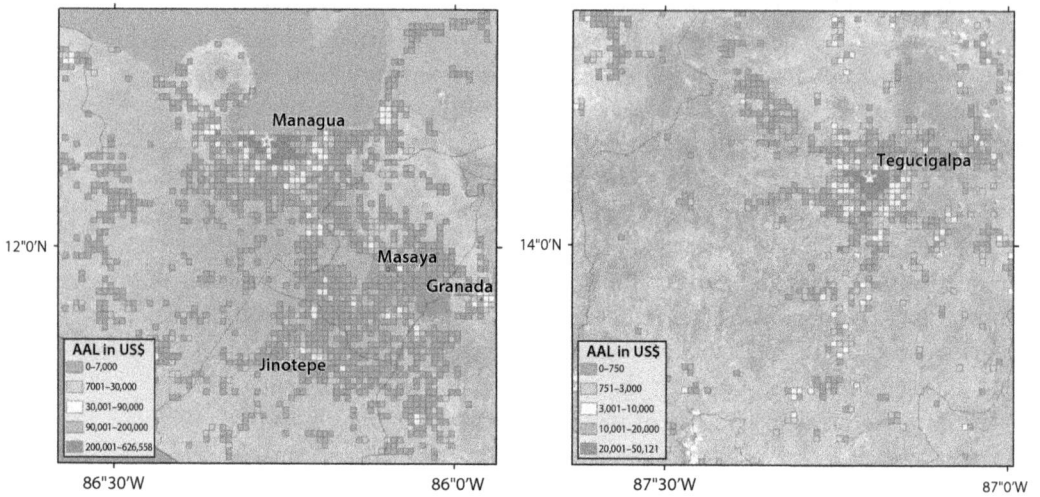

Source: CDRP (World Bank 2015).

Table 4.2 Historical Earthquakes in Central America, 1851–2001

Year	Magnitude	Location	Potential economic losses in 2015 (US$)
1851	6.2 earthquake	Honduras, not far from Tegucigalpa	490 million, 3 percent of GDP
1882	7.8 earthquake	Panama, northern coast	810 million, 1.8 percent of GDP (not considering potential losses to the Panama Canal)
1902	7.5 earthquake	Guatemala, near Quetzaltenango	3,000 million, 4.6 percent of GDP
1910	6.5 earthquake	Costa Rica, near Cartago	3,800 million, 8 percent of GDP
1972	6.2 earthquake	Nicaragua, near Managua	550 million, 5 percent of GDP
2001	7.6 earthquake	El Salvador, near San Salvador	1,810, 7 percent of GDP

Source: CDRP (World Bank 2015).

summary of major historical earthquakes that have impacted each country in the region, and estimates of the potential economic impact if similar events were to happen today.

Enabling Factors for DRM and Urban Resilience

An integrated approach to urban resilience, including how to avoid future risk, reduce existing risk, increase financial protection, and understand the trends and current patterns of risk, is key to build more resilient cities for the future. Today, DRM policy and regulatory frameworks in the region are in place at national levels, but the establishment of municipal and sectorial responsibilities for DRM remains underdeveloped. This opens an opportunity to tackle urban resilience with a more robust and comprehensive approach. First, avoiding generation of future disaster risks emerges as a central task for local governments, through the implementation of land use planning and building permits processes, responsibilities which are mostly decentralized across the region. Reducing existing disaster risk in urban environments in the region will require sectorial investment, channeled mainly through the central government. Resilient public investment requires coordinated efforts between the national investment systems and the urban planning units, thus ensuring the inclusion of disaster risk criteria in the investment cycle. At the same time, disaster financial protection becomes a critical aspect of economic resilience for countries and cities in the region, mostly managed from central governments, but with cities as main beneficiaries. Finally, understanding the levels of disaster risk faced by increasingly urban areas of the region remains the basic and fundamental enabling factor to manage the increasing disaster risk and thus strengthen urban resilience in Central America.

Avoiding Future Risk
A Strategic and Major Role for Cities and Local Governments in a Context of Ongoing Decentralization
In a context of rapid urbanization, where Central American cities are expected to host over 50 million people by 2050, land use planning, building regulations, and disaster risk–sensitive investments are key to build future urban resilience. Initial location of safe sites is inherently more economical than relocation of existing settlements. It is also recognized that disaster resistance can be achieved through new construction at a considerably lower cost than through retrofit of existing vulnerable construction. Moreover, implementation of risk-sensitive urban planning, building regulations, and strategic investments will be essential to prevent the expansion of settlements (formal and informal) in hazardous areas. New construction with appropriate design can be made disaster resistant for a small percentage of construction cost on the order of 5 to 10 percent, while the retrofit of existing vulnerable structures may require major expenditure, in the range of 10 to 50 percent of building value (World Bank and GFDRR 2015). While reducing the risk in existing buildings will be likely a long-term priority and focused on a few critical portfolios, the development of regulatory capacity for new construction will provide a foundation for the inspection and improvement of existing buildings.

Risk-Sensitive Land Use Planning
Urban and local development planning are under the domain of local governments and offer an important entry point to influence DRM and urban resilience. Most of the countries of the region have now decentralized responsibilities for urban development planning in the municipality's mandates. Among these responsibilities, the incorporation of disaster risk criteria in the elaboration of the urban and territorial plans is a concrete opportunity for local governments to

contribute to build more resilient cities. This will require the strengthening of local planning capacities of the municipal teams with technical support from technical and research institutions, as well as availability of disaster risk data in adequate formats to support the decision-making process.

DRM is an essential part of comprehensive urban development planning. The process of generating local DRM plans is becoming an important tool to raise awareness among local authorities and communities. However, it is still somehow detached from other relevant planning processes currently undertaken by municipalities. This is also compounded by the fact that most of the municipalities currently do not follow standardized mechanisms to ensure that small DRM investment projects are prioritized to support community development plans. In this context, DRM plans need thus to be included and inform the set of planning instruments that are guiding municipal local development, rather than become an isolated and specific plan. The experience of the El Salvador Local Government Strengthening Project (PFGL) provides valuable insights into the need to articulate local DRM plans within other broader and relevant planning tools for local development (see box 4.2).

Local-level hazard information needs to be developed for effective inclusion of disaster risk criteria in land use planning. The incorporation of hazard zoning, as a criteria for defining land use planning in cities, is a concrete prospective disaster risk reduction (DRR) tool for building urban resilience in the region. Hazard maps are mostly available at low-resolution national scales, and therefore not adequate to inform the diagnostic stages of local land use plans, especially for small and medium-size cities. A range of methodological approaches that suits different

---

Box 4.2 El Salvador: Linking Local Development and Disaster Risk Planning Tools

One of the lessons learned of the World Bank's technical assistance El Salvador Local Government Strengthening Project (PFGL) is the need to articulate the DRM plans within the various local planning instruments. One of the components of the PFGL supports the development of Municipal Development Plans (MDPs), focusing on local economic development and articulating it within the regional and national economic context, including key investments that both communities and municipal leaders have identified and have agreed upon as priority investments. The other component supports the development of DRM Municipal Plans in the 262 municipalities of the country. During the initial stages of these MDPs and the DRM plans, the need to ensure an integrated approach for the methodological development of both instruments became evident. Under this approach the disaster risk scenarios identified for the DRM plans could inform the diagnostic and prioritizing of investment in the MDPs. This new approach has helped to capitalize the participatory planning process for both tools in many municipalities in El Salvador, factoring disaster risk into the vision of local development and prioritization of municipal economic activities.

---

levels—from realized risk maps, based on historical impacts, to probabilistic risk assessments—needs to be considered to materialize the inclusion of risk identification in land use planning and spatial zoning.

Local capacity needs to be developed for effective DRR through land use planning. The challenge is how to promote systematic improvement of spatial planning that includes disaster risk information to reduce future exposure to hazards and future risks. There is recent progress in policy frameworks in terms of including risk analysis in land use planning regulations (see box 4.3), but capacity building is needed to implement these reforms at the local level. In that sense, human resources in central planning offices should gradually support and translate these knowledge and capacities to local governments, especially in small and medium size municipalities. A similar effort

---

Box 4.3 Updating the Regulatory and Methodological Frameworks for Implementation of Risk-Sensitive Local Land Use Plans in Panama

In Panama, the national regulatory framework and guidelines for elaboration of local land use plans only integrated DRM criteria beginning in 2010, and did so only nominally, without any practical content or methodological references on how to factor risk identification and reduction criteria in the plans. With support of a Global Facility for Disaster Reduction and Recovery (GFDRR) grant, the regulatory framework was updated in 2015 by means a of a new Resolution enacted by the Ministry of Housing and Land Use Planning (MIVIOT), which is applicable to all local, regional, and sublocal land use plans in the country. A new section was included with explicit guidelines for including risk identification during the diagnostic stage.

Whether based on historical disaster occurrence databases or more sophisticated probabilistic studies, when available, the plans require now the identification of hazards, as well as exposed assets in terms of buildings, heritage, natural conservation, and critical infrastructure. The concepts of "non-mitigable risk zones" (where risk reduction measures for an existing population are not viable) and "high-hazard exclusion zones" (where construction may not be permitted) are incorporated as part of the zoning criteria. Concurrently with the new ministerial resolution, the implementation of a gradual administrative decentralization has begun recently in the country.

For example, the district of Boquete, located in the volcanic and agricultural highlands of Panama, has been hit many times by destructive floods. Under the leadership of its municipality, Boquete is undertaking measures for risk identification and reduction through a local ordinance drafted according to the criteria set in the new DRM resolution for local and regional plans. The ordinance establishes economic incentives for development in low gradient zones outside of river flood plains and restrains land uses and new construction on zones know to be prone to floods and landslides. Both MIVIOT and Boquete's initiatives illustrate the complementary and differentiated central and local government roles in promoting DRR from national regulation to local application on the ground.

Source: World Bank and GFDRR 2016a.

can be made to build the capacity of technical teams of main municipalities, which are in better position to undertake the implementation of these planning tools alone.

Building Codes and Regulation

Postdisaster experience provides the awareness levels for updating and strengthening building regulatory mechanisms. These efforts are often driven and delivered by a wide range of stakeholders and specialized nongovernmental organizations (NGOs). Such initiatives should be considerably expanded, coordinated, and institutionalized in predisaster scenarios. They should aim at demonstrating the benefits of meeting safe building practices and creating the buy-in for a wider culture of code compliance. In the aftermath of a major disaster, there is broad recognition of the necessity of construction quality improvement and the implementation of effective building regulatory mechanisms. Often, as a component of reconstruction funded by external agencies, some building standards are directed, as a precondition of funding. There is also sporadic training of local construction workers in improved resilient construction. However, these measures are short lived without the institutionalization of a permanent building regulatory authority with capacity for effective code implementation and maintenance.

There is a need for further funding, staffing, and execution to implement building regulation at the local level. While most of the countries have national building codes that include disaster risk criteria, one of the generalized problems is the lack of funding and support for the implementation and supervision of building regulation at the local level.[6] Permit-related and inspection services are usually expensive, and inefficient, sometimes acting as a deterrent to meeting code requirements. This can actually encourage building informality, thus increasing the vulnerability of the local urban population in the context of significant seismic risks. Nicaragua, where obtaining a construction permit took 189 days in 2005, has tackled this problem through the implementation of "municipal simplification projects" in three pilot municipalities.[7] This reduced compliance costs of operating and construction permits by 30 percent on average, and increased business formalization sevenfold. Building permits and inspections can be major enabling factors for urban resilience but require specific support in terms of training of building officials, as well as funding mechanisms for appropriate compensation for those adhering to the codes.

Disaster Risk–Sensitive Investments

Promoting resilient investments in cities will require coordinated efforts between national investments systems and municipal planning units. Inclusion of disaster risk analysis, as part of the project investment cycle, is a key aspect toward building resilient investment strategies. Conceptual and methodological frameworks aimed at integrating disaster risk considerations into public investment have been developed and promoted in the region, mostly for the process of preinvestment disaster risk and cost-benefit and cost-efficiency analysis. These efforts have been promoted by intergovernmental organizations (such as CEPREDENAC) and

United Nations agencies, within the national public investments systems, but without major involvement of planning units of municipalities at this stage. For instance, in Costa Rica, these developments have crystallized in regulatory reform, making risk analysis a mandatory aspect of the public investments processes (see box 4.4). However, for the rest of the region, they are still part of general methodological guidelines.

Beyond the important advocacy work done in the region with the public investments systems, there remain some methodological challenges for effective inclusion of DRM criteria in the formulation of public investment projects. Including specific risk-sensitive criteria into preinvestment assessments will require a different set of sectorial and hazard-specific guidelines which need to be developed and tested. Additionally, current timings for formulation of public investment projects do not factor the need for incorporating disaster risk analysis (IDB 2013). Major work to build capacities and socialize these methodological guidelines needs to be undertaken before it can be materialized in resilient investment in cities.

Effective resilient investments at the local level also require coordination and planning at the supramunicipal level. One of the attributes contemplated in the decentralization frameworks in the region is the faculty of the municipalities to conform intermunicipal associations with other neighboring municipalities (*mancomunidades*). This is particularly important to manage hazards such as floods, landslides, forest fires, and others, which can be triggered in a municipal jurisdiction but manifested with adverse impacts in others. A clear example is when deforestation and environmental degradation processes in high river basins exacerbate floods in medium and low river basins. Disaster risk information

---

Box 4.4 Integrating DRM Considerations into the Review Process of Investment Projects in Costa Rica

Costa Rica has integrated risk management considerations into the review process of all investment projects for the country. The Ministry of National Planning and Economic Policy (MIDEPLAN) recently added a disaster risk review in the project proposal format for national investments, through Executive Orders 34 694-PLAN-H of August 2008 (Public National Investment System), 35 098-PLAN of March 2009 (National Public Investment Plan), and 35 374-PLAN of July 2009 (Technical Standards, Guidelines and Procedures for Public Investment). Under this measure, government agencies submitting investment projects for approval by MIDEPLAN are now required to conduct a disaster risk assessment of the proposed investment and include mitigation measures in case the project is exposed to adverse natural events. The country is currently assessing systems that could assist public officials in the decision-making process by evaluating the disaster risk of planned investment projects. Additionally, MIDEPLAN implemented an ambitious training program, which includes risk assessment, for public functionaries involved in the public investment process.

Source: World Bank and GFDRR 2016b.

Box 4.5 Disaster Risks as a Planning Tool to Support Development Planning in *Mancomunidad del Sur* in Guatemala

The Guatemala City Metropolitan Area (GCMA) is the most important urban concentration in Guatemala with an estimated population of 2.7 million, or 20 percent of the total. Estimates from the National Institute of Statistics (INE) suggest that by 2020 six of its municipalities (Mixco, Amatitlán, Villa Nueva, San Miguel Petapa, Santa Catarina Pinula, and Villa Canales), will house around 1.7 million people, or 10 percent of the national population. These six municipalities located in the south of the GCMA have recently created a metropolitan association—the *Mancomunidad del Sur*—with the main goal of developing a common regional planning strategy (*Gran Ciudad Del Sur: Vision 2022*). The strategy consists of moving away from a monocentric spatial development toward a multicentric metropolitan region, while addressing common problems and taking advantage of possible synergies. To support this effort, a project supported by the World Bank will address an important limitation: the lack of updated geo-referenced spatial information on land use, infrastructure, and risk, as well as socioeconomic, housing, and mobility data, to inform metropolitan planning and investment programs in the GCMA. This effort in metropolitan planning is unprecedented in Guatemala and is expected to set the basis for future efforts in regional and spatial integration.

Source: World Bank and GFDRR 2016.

---

should be part of the planning tools to support the work of "supramunicipal coordinating bodies," and thus contribute to improved overall governance and resilient investments in urban areas, particularly in a context where subnational/provincial levels are weak. The case of the *Mancomunidad del Sur* represents one of a few, but very inspiring, examples in that direction (see box 4.5).

Budget allocation tracking, or systematic tracking of DRR spending, is an important step toward effective disaster risk–sensitive investments. Currently, it remains very difficult to assess the resources allocated to DRR investments and correlate them with public reforms and monitoring of DRR policies. Such tracking must also compare budget allocations with actual expenditures, and against targets and actual accomplishments. Guatemala and Panama have developed budget allocation tracking systems that are providing valuable lessons learned to inform similar developments in other countries. While still premature, future consideration must also be given to replicating budget allocation tracking systems at the local level to examine DRR resource availability and use.

Reducing Existing Risk

Challenges and Opportunities for Urban Risk Reduction in the Region

Reducing existing risk requires addressing the historical construction of vulnerability in the region, and could be achieved by developing effective systems to prioritize infrastructure correction, retrofitting, and, in extreme cases, promoting preventive resettlements. Urban disasters are manifestations of existing levels of risk accumulated in urban contexts. Additionally, rapid urbanization is often associated with environmental degradation, which exacerbates disaster impact in cities. For instance, deforestation and wetlands damage are among the underlying factors that explain historical construction of disaster risk levels in Central American cities today, while recent natural hazards, such as earthquakes, cyclones, and floods, have revealed different vulnerability levels of the built environment. Effective tools to identify and prioritize infrastructure correction, retrofitting, and conducting preventing resettlements are key to reduce existing vulnerability.

Prioritization of Infrastructure Correction and Retrofitting

In a context of limited resources available to local governments, major corrective DRR measures prioritized in DRM municipal plans need to be negotiated and supported by central governments. As mentioned in the previous section, most of the DRM municipal plans are somehow detached from other planning instruments. At the same time, since local governments can only assign limited resources to implement corrective measures, these remain mostly diagnosis tools rather than operational plans that can guide and support major initiatives to reduce existing levels of disaster risk, unless they are backed by resources provided by the central government. Local governments can play an important role in fostering the participatory processes through DRM planning exercises, but coordinated action with the central government is required to undertake major risk reduction measures.

The central government will continue playing a major role in reducing disaster risk of local public services provision. In addition to local government commitment, engagement by the central government and ministries remains critical to support financing disaster reduction plans, as part of a broader DRR strategy of the country. The limited penetration of DRM responsibilities in sectorial regulatory frameworks, compounded by the slow decentralization of public services (as presented in chapter 2), results in low capacity of local governments to develop disaster-resilient public services. In this context, there is work to be done within the ministries in line and central entities providing public services to update their sectorial regulatory frameworks so they include explicit responsibilities to identify and reduce disaster risks.

Reducing existing urban risk also requires the availability of local risk assessments along with political commitment for public investments. In a context of other pressing socioeconomic priorities for local authorities, the decision of undertaking corrective DRR measures needs to be supported by a robust disaster risk assessment, providing the social, economic and political elements to make the case for action of the local and national authorities. As adaptation to climate change and strengthening of urban resilience are emerging as relevant policy aspects within political agendas of the cities, corrective disaster risk measures can provide concrete means to achieve those comprehensive goals, at least in the short and medium term.

Retrofitting existing infrastructure to reduce vulnerability is of critical importance. Most of the major urban agglomerations in Central America are located in seismic-prone areas, including all the capitals, which all have been affected by destructive earthquakes at different times in history. In that context, removal, replacement, and retrofit of existing unregulated and unsafe buildings require an incremental approach that can reduce disaster risk over a reasonable period of time. Focusing on critical infrastructures, such as schools, hospitals, potable water treatment plants, bridges, and drainage systems, as a prioritization strategy for identification of opportunities for retrofitting infrastructure, can facilitate the engagement of local and national governments. Recent seismic risk assessment studies have been undertaken for a group of major cities in the region and there is a critical mass of local technical capacity and expertise that could help to inform retrofitting plans.

Preventive Resettlements

Addressing preventive resettlements is a DRR opportunity for local authorities. Given the social, legal, and political implications of resettlements, implementing a planned relocalization as a DRR measure is a step that governments usually take only after assessing the feasibility of other risk management options. But as a result of increasing levels of exposure of vulnerable human settlements to localized hazards (such as landslides), where risk mitigation is technically not feasible or the risk levels are beyond thresholds of "acceptable risk," preventive resettlement or planned relocalization is increasingly becoming an option assessed by local authorities. There are some experiences of preventive resettlement in Central America, which underscore that resettlements should be incorporated into comprehensive DRR policies and plans, and institutional capacity should be built. Box 4.6 presents such an experience in Guatemala.

Box 4.6 The First Mayan City in the 21st Century: A Preventive Resettlement Experience in Guatemala

As a result of the tropical storm Stan in 2005, 17,000 homes were either totally destroyed or rendered uninhabitable. In response to the disaster, the government launched the National Reconstruction Plan to reconstruct the economic and social infrastructure destroyed, and to create 80 new urban centers.

The government used this opportunity not only to provide houses to the affected population but also to resettle nonaffected residents who lived in disaster-prone areas. One of these cases was documented as a case study from Latin America on preventive resettlement, which was published by the World Bank in 2011. Even though the experiences analyzed belong to the rural districts of Panajab and Tz'anchaj of the department of Solola, the case showed important lessons that could be applied to preventive resettlement in urban areas, such as the importance of (i) coordination of national, departmental, and municipal levels; (ii) incorporation of the resettlement plans into the land use plans; (iii) incorporation of social and cultural dimensions in the formulation and implementation of resettlement plans; (iv) participation and community organization; and (v) accountability mechanisms, among others.

Source: World Bank and GFDRR 2011.

Financing Inevitable Risk
Increased Financial Resilience of Governments, Private Sector, and Households through Financial Protection Is Key for Urban Resilience

In a context of rapid concentration of population and assets in Central American cities, financial resilience is key to protect people and assets from existing and future disaster risks. Increased financial resilience of governments, private sector, and households through disaster risk financial protection is an inherent component of urban resilience. Potential disaster impacts in main urban centers of the region (as has happened with all capitals of Central America at different times in history), will directly and indirectly affect the financial and development stability of these countries. As mentioned in section 1, over the period 1970–2010, major adverse natural events like earthquakes, hurricanes, and large floods have caused accumulated damages and losses that exceed US$80 billion. In this context, actions to reduce the negative financial effects of disasters in a way that protects both people and assets are becoming an important DRM strategy for governments.

Local governments are among the main beneficiaries of financial protection, but the task for promoting and ensuring disaster financial protection remains a central government's responsibility. The central government has a major role in disaster emergency relief, recovery, and reconstruction in Central American countries and, thus, in addressing disaster risk financial protection and insurance concerns. Reconstruction of uninsured or underinsured public infrastructure in cities—including low-income housing—typically accounts for the majority of public spending following disasters. Whether or not the government is legally required to provide this support, social and political pressure can make such support an implicit contingent liability (World Bank and GFDRR 2015a). Because of the lack of clear cost-sharing rules between local and national governments, the national government is de facto called to act as the lender of last resort in case of disasters.

Noteworthy progress in risk retention mechanisms in recent years in the region has allowed for a more efficient response to urban disasters. The governments of the region have strengthened the financial mechanisms to manage disaster risk. Contingent credit is a financial instrument that allows governments to secure funds in advance of disasters to be available immediately in case of emergency. The World Bank launched in 2008 the first loan of this kind, called the Catastrophe Deferred Drawdown Option (CAT-DDO), and Costa Rica became the first country to obtain such loan. From that year onward, the remaining Central American countries had access to different contingent credit facilities, as shown in table 4.3. Contingent credits complement other funding lines such as national reserves to finance high frequency, low severity events. Panama established a sovereign wealth fund in 2012 (Panama Savings Fund, FAP), and designated disaster losses larger than 0.5 percent of GDP (excluding insurance coverage and the amount of contingent credit lines), as one of the three triggers for a payout.

In contrast, little progress has been made in risk transfer mechanisms to protect public assets in cities. The domestic insurance market and insurance solutions for

Table 4.3 Risk Financing Mechanisms in Central America

Country	Contingency loan (IDB) US$ millions	Contingency loan (CAT-DDO–BM) US$ millions	Emergency fund
Costa Rica	—	US$65	✓
El Salvador	—	—	✓
Guatemala	—	US$85	✓
Honduras	US$100	—	—
Nicaragua	US$186	—	✓
Panama	US$100	US$66	✓

Sources: World Bank, IDB.
Note: — = not available.

the agricultural sector are part of the risk transfer mechanisms in the region. However, only a small percentage of public assets in cities are insured against disasters, and the quality of the insurance coverage is uncertain. Costa Rica has made progress in terms of developing insurance requirements for social housing programs (*Bonos de Vivienda Social*). Another example is Panama, which has developed a co-insurance scheme to transfer the risk of public assets, where all state institutions must have a risk management system that treats the government as a single client, thereby ensuring that a standardized, collective, and centralized scheme exists. Specific catastrophic insurance and market-based transfer mechanisms are not yet developed, but the region is currently taking on opportunities for regional risk pooling. Central America committed in 2014 to join a Caribbean Catastrophe Risk Insurance Facility (CCRIF), which will allow aggregating the risk into larger and more diversified portfolios between Central American countries, to reduce the cost of accessing international insurance markets.

Progress in financial protection has not been informed by a comprehensive strategic approach to financial disaster risk and insurance. Despite recent advancements in adopting financial protection tools in the region, governments still address financial effects of disasters on an ad hoc basis following the events. The establishment of financial protection tools has not been guided by a strategic view to optimize risk transfer and risk retention mechanisms, based on the countries' risk profiles. So far, only Panama has adopted a Strategic Framework for Disaster Risk Financing and Insurance, which was recently developed with the support of regional and international entities, including the Centre for the Coordination and Prevention of Natural Disasters in Central America (CEPREDENAC), the World Bank, the Inter-American Development Bank, and the Global Facility for Disaster Reduction and Recovery (GFDRR) (see box 4.7).

Understanding Disaster Risk
Managing Disaster Risk and Building Urban Resilience Require a Clear Understanding of the Urban Patterns and Disaster Risks
Improving the knowledge base of vulnerability exposure and hazard profiles at local levels is a basic condition to implement policies and measures to reduce disaster risk and improve urban resilience. Understanding disaster risk

Box 4.7 Panama Leads the Way in the Region toward an Integral DRFI Strategy

With the promulgation of Decree 578 (2014) the government of Panama formalized its guiding framework to manage fiscal risk in the event of natural disasters, making Panama the first country in the region to implement such a framework. The Panama DRFI (Disaster Risk Financing and Insurance) Strategy represents the culmination of a series of public reforms, consultations, and studies undertaken by the government in recent years, which includes the updated mandates on disaster risk protection conferred to the Directorate of Investment, Concessions and Risk of the Ministry of Finances (DICRE). These efforts have created a strong legal mandate in Panama for establishing a financial management strategy (see figure B4.7.1) that addresses disaster risks. The document incorporates important lessons from international experience, such as the following: (i) include disaster risk as part of an integrated framework of fiscal risk management; (ii) ensure that governments have access to immediate funds following a disaster; (iii) consider the creation of a national disaster fund; and (iv) reduce the government's contingent liabilities against disasters associated with the impact of natural hazards by insuring critical public assets and promoting the private insurance market for catastrophic risks.

Figure B4.7.1 Layered Financing Strategy for Disasters Associated with the Impact of Natural Hazards

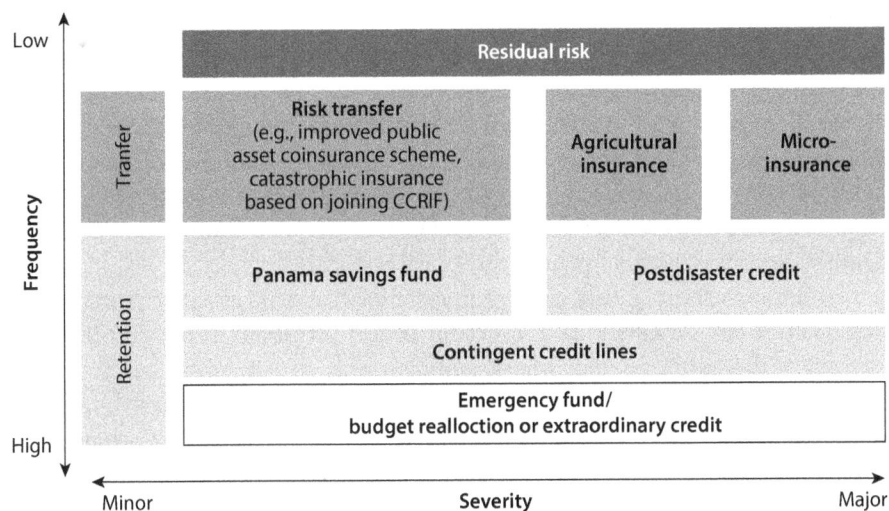

Source: World Bank and GFDRR 2015b.

implies in the first place a comprehensive knowledge of the natural events that could have a negative impact on people and assets in the territory, including attributes such as occurrence frequency, returning periods, probabilities, and intensities (understanding the hazard). Second, it is necessary to identify people and assets that are exposed to those hazards (understanding exposure), which is a very dynamic aspect in a context of rapid urbanization processes. Third, once the exposed segment of population and assets are identified, their vulnerability to specific hazards must be determined (understanding vulnerability), to finally assess the likelihood of a negative impact (understanding disaster risk).

Institutional arrangements for generating hazard information are diverse in the region. Some countries such as El Salvador, Guatemala, and Nicaragua have centralized technical institutions that generate primary information on geological and hydrometeorological hazards, with different degrees of autonomy and without an explicit mandate to assist in the generation of territorial and sectorial risk assessments. Panama lacks a national hydrometeorological service, and relevant information on geological hazards is produced by a geosciences institute belonging to the University of Panama. In Costa Rica, there are two technical centers providing seismic and volcano monitoring services. Only El Salvador, following the earthquake that struck the country in 2010, created a specialized institution (SNET, now the Environmental Observatory), based on the CENAPRED[8] model of Mexico. In most cases, these institutions lack clear mandates to provide technical assistance for disaster risk assessment to local governments.

Sound disaster risk assessments for cities need modeling and monitoring of natural hazards supported by strengthened national networks. To provide information services, national networks of hydrometeorological and geological monitoring stations need to be strengthened to generate baseline data for risk studies. The strengthening of the climate services is crucially important in a context of changing climate and the need to inform locally designed disaster risk and adaption measures. All national hydrometeorological monitoring networks in Central America are below the density coverage ratio established by the World Meteorological Organization (WMO) and lack the required human and financial resources to be adequately maintained (CRRH-SICA 2015).

Developing robust "public assets exposure databases" is key to support exposure analysis and vulnerability profiles for public portfolios at the city level. In the case of the housing sector, physical attributes such as the construction type, occupancy, or age of the building are essential to assess the vulnerability and potential losses (as replacement values) in case of disaster occurrence. At the national level, public assets databases are deficient and incomplete in the region, so the situation is even weaker for cities and municipalities, compounded by the needs of the exposed infrastructure in geospatial data format. Usually when the hazard information is available, assessing the exposure and vulnerability becomes a limiting factor to conduct risk assessments for specific sectorial portfolios.

Probabilistic Risk Assessments

Probabilistic risk assessment studies have been conducted in a number of cities in Central America, yet only as pilot initiatives. Seismic risk assessments using the Central American Probabilistic Risk Assessment (CAPRA) platform (see box 4.8) were implemented in David (Panama), Guatemala City, Managua, Panama City, San José, San Salvador, and Tegucigalpa. Most of these studies assessed the disaster risk for the housing, education (schools), and health (hospitals) portfolios, and involved an interinstitutional coordinated effort, involving the work of technical institutions and line ministries. Beyond the results of these studies, their implementation was focused on building the capacities of a network of practitioners and researchers from the public sector in probabilistic risk assessments, setting the basis for a regional network on DRM.

The experience from implementing the pilot studies so far confirms some perceptions mentioned previously about the risk assessment processes in the region. These are (i) the studies required the set-up of ad hoc multisectorial and multidisciplinary teams, as well as finding an institutional champion (which varied for every study) to coordinate and steer the entire process; (ii) building the exposure data to assess the vulnerability component proved to be among the most challenging tasks, revealing the lack of good public assets databases and updated infrastructure geo-referenced information in key sectors; (iii) while there are good technical capacities in technical institutions and universities,

---

Box 4.8 Central American Probabilistic Risk Assessment Program

The CAPRA Program was created in 2008 as a collaborative initiative between CEPREDENAC, the United Nations International Strategy for Disaster Risk Reduction (UNISDR), the Inter-American Development Bank, the World Bank, GFDRR, and the Australian Development Agency (AusAID).

From its inception, CAPRA has sought to strengthen the institutional capacity to assess, understand, and communicate disaster risk, aiming to generate relevant information to be incorporated into development programs and decision-making strategies. At the operational level, CAPRA utilizes a modular freeware environment which enables technical professionals from different disciplines to carry out probabilistic Disaster Risk Assessments.

The hazard modules constituting CAPRA's freeware—which can be used to assess earthquakes, hurricanes, rainfall, volcanoes, floods, landslides, and tsunamis—are based on sound peer-reviewed databases of hundreds of historical and simulated events. The information generated from those hazards' assessment is then combined with (i) the exposure databases, including assets-at-risk (infrastructure and population), and (ii) the vulnerability associated to those assets-at-risk. Finally, the main module, CAPRA-SIG, combines the hazards' scenarios, the exposure databases, and the vulnerability information and estimates the loss exceedance curves (both for economic and human losses).

box continues next page

Box 4.8 Central American Probabilistic Risk Assessment Program *(continued)*

Graphically, one of the main outputs is a set of risk maps that could potentially turn into a useful asset to provide essential information for future preventive management of disaster risk. Map B4.8.1 presents a probabilistic earthquake risk damage distribution map of the city of Santa Tecla, El Salvador, for the housing and commercial sector—expressed in terms of annual average losses.

Map B4.8.1 Probabilistic Earthquake Risk Damage Distribution Map, Santa Tecla, El Salvador, 2016

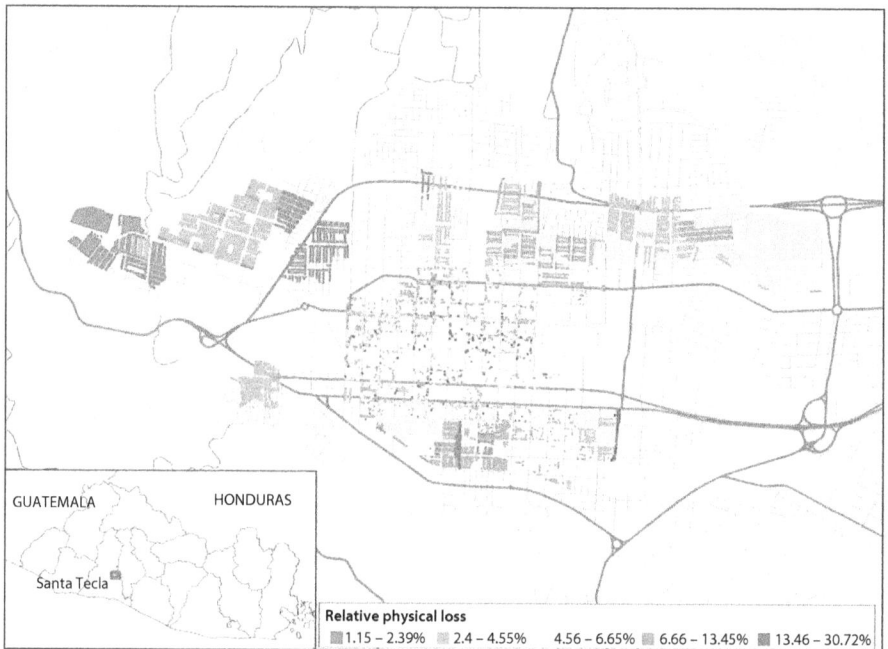

Source: CAPRA team, World Bank 2016b.

---

risk assessments are not part of the regular institutional mandates; (iv) even though the results were focused on cities, it was difficult to raise awareness and engage local government authorities; and (v) in most cases, the results of the studies have not influenced decision making, or led immediately to DRR plans or strategies for the sectorial portfolios assessed in the study.

Comprehensive risk assessment studies at the urban level are gradually incorporating probabilistic approaches, but greater articulation with the decision-making process is needed. The ultimate benefit of risk modeling and hazard mapping initiatives, such as CAPRA, cannot be realized without effective mechanisms to ensure application of hazard information to safe siting and improved construction for urban development. There is still a major challenge to improve the ways to communicate the technical outputs of disaster risk assessments to local and national authorities so they can lead to concrete DRR measures.

Ideally, a combination of probabilistic risk assessments and participatory risk assessment processes, involving risk perception and the determination of the politically and socially accepted level of risk, can lead to an investment in DRR measures in urban contexts.

There is also a need to match increased demand on risk assessments associated to hydrometeorological hazards. There has been a major development and focus research in the region on tools to assess seismic risk. However, the most frequent events in Central America are those associated with hydrometeorological hazards. Modeling these risks for localized scenarios entails significant methodological challenges and access to information that is not easily available, mostly because of a historical lack of systematic collection of data and deficient monitoring. There is growing interest in integrating climate scenarios as part of the climate risk assessment processes, which also represent major methodological challenges. In a context of relatively small countries, regional cooperation still plays an important role, through initiatives such as the Central American Climate Forum, championed by the Central American Hydraulic Resources Committee.

Geospatial Data

As tools and platforms for probabilistic risk assessments, previously under the domain of insurance companies, become increasingly available publicly, opportunities for improved geospatial data widen. There is also an increasing offer of open-source geospatial data platforms that can help to overcome some of the above-mentioned difficulties with the lack of institutional drivers for risk assessments and risk mapping. These open-source platforms can promote data sharing and collaboration between diverse actors such as government agencies, the private sector, academia, and civil society. One example is found in Panama, where a few institutions, guided by the World Bank Open Data for Resilience Initiative team (OpenDRI) and its broader Open Data Initiative, have developed a DRM GeoNode (see box 4.9).

These kinds of initiatives are particularly important in contexts where disaster risk data is dispersed and atomized in various institutions, with absence of spatial data interoperability and institutional exchange protocols. These promote the identification of existing risk data that represent relevant exposure, hazard, and vulnerability data at local levels. Given the relatively high penetration of Internet and mobile cellular coverage in Central American countries, there is a high potential to capitalize on crowdsourced disaster risk mapping initiatives, adding to what should be an increasing trend of using these open-source tools for urban resilience.

Developing cities' disaster risk exposure databases is also fundamental for furthering financial risk protection strategies. Lacking knowledge about cities' exposure to risk—and cost of this risk—can lead to suboptimal investment decisions to protect welfare. Historical records on how disasters affected public finances and information on probabilistic financial and actuarial analysis such as modeled disaster losses are key inputs for evidence-based decision making in

---

Box 4.9 Promoting Data Sharing and Interinstitutional Collaboration: The Case of the DRM GeoNode in Panama

Recognizing factors that were limiting the sharing of disaster risk–related geospatial information in Panama, the Ministry of Finance (MEF) and the Ministry of Housing and Land Use Planning (MIVIOT), with support of GFDRR, led the development of a GeoNode, an open-source web-based application and platform for developing and sharing geospatial information. So far the GeoNode has helped to gather in an open repository existing basic cartography, hazard mapping and catalogues of earthquakes, data from the Panama DesInventar disaster database, mapping of development indicators, and results of the probabilistic disaster risk assessments that have been undertaken in last few years (CAPRA studies in David, Panama City, and Boquete).

MEF is gradually feeding into the GeoNode public assets information toward the building of a public assets exposure layer, while MIVIOT has provided recently developed spatial information on urban and land use plans. Inspired by this overture, the municipality of Panama has implemented a GeoNode that includes the original inventory and repository of data. It has been expanded with a wide range of urban planning and DRM-related information, including the cadaster. In a context of dispersed and not easily accessible disaster risk information, the DRM GeoNode has proven to be an effective tool to share relevant existing disaster risk information and engage institutions and local governments, which become providers and users of DRM information.

---

financial protection that can affect urban resilience. The capacity-building process on risk assessment, particularly on probabilistic methods and tools, as well as the development of public assets exposure databases of main cities in the region, are essential to inform the development of sound disaster risk financing strategies that ultimately build economic resilience in an increasingly urbanized Central America.

Moving Forward in Building Resilient Cities

Modern and comprehensive regional and national policies for DRM have been developed in the last five years. After a long and comprehensive consultative process, countries adopted the Central America Comprehensive Policy for Disaster Risk Management in August 2010 (known by its Spanish acronym PCGIR), which sets policy guidelines for the governments to further update and establish modern policy and strategic frameworks for DRM. Since then, Costa Rica, Guatemala, Honduras, Nicaragua, and Panama have adopted new national policy and planning frameworks informed by the PCGIR and that address the different DRM processes.

Despite regional and national progress, legislative development of DRM responsibilities at subnational and local levels is needed. While the national DRM frameworks identify the role and promote local responsibilities for DRM, this is not yet reflected in the diverse policy decentralization frameworks in Central America. Only Panama's decentralization framework, which was enacted in 2009 and entered in force in 2015, establishes "…the integral DRM for protection of the population and implementation of national policies on disaster prevention and mitigation" as a municipal-level responsibility. Thus the work of the municipalities in DRR is not yet inscribed in their own regulatory frameworks, and it is mostly promoted as a new task from national DRM frameworks.

Measuring risk, seen as a basis for intervention, is relevant when the population recognizes and understands that risk. Despite recent progress at a national level, most Central American cities do not have sufficient technical and financial resources for measuring and representing local risk. Models, maps, and indexes at a local-urban level are lacking. The evaluation of risk that is needed would include the evaluation of hazards, the different aspects of vulnerability when faced with these hazards, and estimations regarding the occurrence of possible consequences during a particular exposure time.

Financial protection is fundamental for the sustainability of development and economic growth in Central America. This implies an adequate allocation and use of financial resources to manage and implement appropriate strategies to retain and transfer disaster losses. Most countries in the region have created reserve funds or budget procedures when facing natural-triggered disasters; nevertheless at a local-urban level, there is a lack of resources for designing comprehensive financial protection strategies based on probabilistic estimates of risk.

Main Areas of Focus
- Identifying urban vulnerability and resilience drivers; lack of, and opportunities for, increased capacity/resources; and barriers and opportunities to implement urban-centered and national-level disaster risk resilient investments.
- Implementing decentralization reform to strengthen DRM responsibilities within the regulatory frameworks of territorial entities and sectors.
- Developing and integrating DRM planning tools at the local level as part of the broader local development planning of municipalities, with a focus on land use planning and building permits.
- Local governments can promote dedicated building-resilience standards and certification systems, as supporting mechanisms for risk reduction, by providing incentives, especially nonfinancial incentives.
- Ensuring that specific infrastructure investments incorporate measures to manage disaster risk impacts across the lifetime of the investment, from design through construction, maintenance, and contingency planning.
- Implementing targeted interventions in vulnerable communities to effectively minimize physical, social, and financial disaster and climate risk.
- Delivering technical assistance to facilitate specific infrastructure investments and a sector-wide approach that values extending the lifetime of public infrastructure.

- Focusing on maintaining the quality and functionality of assets to reduce average annual losses resulting from disaster risk and caused by growing vulnerability of infrastructure due to poor upkeep.
- Developing comprehensive disaster risk financing strategies by quantifying the financial value of disaster reserve fund needs. This is done by assessing explicit and implicit contingent liabilities, identifying opportunities to streamline post-disaster budget execution, and exploring opportunities to grow the non-life insurance market.

Notes

1. To be included in EM-DAT, a disaster must meet at least one of the following criteria: 10 or more people reported killed; 100 or more people reported affected; declaration of a state of emergency; or call for international assistance.
2. ECLAC 2011, "Regional Assessment of the impacts of Tropical Depression 12E in Central America."
3. US$2,000. The data presented here on the economic impact of historic events are based on the Post Disaster Need Assessments (PDNA), which account for direct damages to assets and buildings (that is, damages) and indirect losses due to variation in prices or revenues (that is, losses). This methodology is very different from the one presented in the subsection "What is at risk in urban areas in Central America?" and results cannot be compared. Data on the historic impact of disasters have been compiled by CEPAL (2014), *La estimación de los efectos de los desastres en América Latina,* Serie Medio Ambiente y Desarrollo 157.
4. This project has been funded by the World Bank through a Global Facility for Disaster Reduction and Recovery (GFDRR) grant (TF014499) from the government of Australia (AusAid) under the CAPRA Probabilistic Risk Assessment program (P144982).
5. The AAL is a risk metric commonly used that represents the mean value of a loss exceedance probability (EP) distribution.
6. A recent World Bank and GFDRR (2015a) publication *Building Regulation for Resilience: Managing Risk for Safer Cities* explores and documents the factors that have limited the incidence on effective disaster risk reduction of land use and building regulations in low- and middle-income countries.
7. This case is profiled in Strategic Communications for Business Environment Reforms, IFC, 2007.
8. CENAPRED was established following the earthquake of 1976 in Mexico City, with a robust mandate and technical capacities to generate the risk information to all territorial levels in Mexico.

Bibliography

Aubrecht, C., R. Gunasekera, J. Ungar, and O. Ishizawa. 2016. "Consistent Yet Adaptive Global Geospatial Identification of Urban-Rural Patterns: The iURBAN model." Proceedings of the National Academy of Sciences (PNAS), in preparation.

CRRH-SICA (Comité Regional de Recursos Hidráulicos y Sistema de la Integración Centroamericana). 2015. "Diagnóstico de capacidades, umbrales de referencia para el monitoreo y lineamientos de SAT en sequía para Centroamérica." CRRH-SICA.

Gunasekera, R., O. Ishizawa, C. Aubrecht, B. Blankespoor, S. Murray, A. Pomonis, and J. Daniell. 2015. "Developing an Adaptive Global Exposure Model to Support the Generation of Country Disaster Risk Profiles." *Earth-Science Reviews* 150: 594–608.

IDB (Inter-American Development Bank). 2013. "Integración de la Gestión de Riesgo de Desastres y la Adaptación al Cambio Climático en la Inversión Pública Centroamérica." NOTA TÉCNICA IDB -TN-509.

Socio-Economic Database for Latin America and the Caribbean (SEDLAC), Center for Distributive, Labor and Social Studies (CEDLAS). http://sedlac.econo.unlp.edu.ar/eng/statistics-detalle.php?idE=35.

World Bank. 2007. "Strategic Communications for Business Environment Reforms: A Guideline for Stakeholder Engagement and Reform Promotion." International Finance Corporation.

———. 2015. "Country Disaster Risk Profiles for Costa Rica, El Salvador, Guatemala, Honduras, Nicaragua and Panama." World Bank.

World Bank and GFDRR (Global Facility for Disaster Reduction and Recovery). 2011. "Preventive Resettlement of Populations at Risk of Disaster: Experiences from Latin America." World Bank and GFDRR.

———. 2015a. "Building Regulation for Resilience: Managing Risk for Safer Cities." World Bank and GFDRR.

———. 2015b. "Strategic Framework for the Financial Management of Disaster Risk." World Bank and GFDRR.

———. 2016a. "Experiencias en la inclusión de la Gestión de Riesgo de Desastres en el Ordenamiento Territorial en Panamá: desde la implementación del marco normativo nacional a su implementación a nivel local." World Bank and GFDRR.

———. 2016b. "Disaster Risk Management in the Latin American Region—Country Notes, Costa Rica." World Bank and GFDRR.

CHAPTER 5

Making Cities Competitive to Create More and Better Jobs

Albert Solé

Overview

Central American cities have a central role in boosting economic growth and generating employment opportunities for their residents. As urbanization leads to an increasing concentration of economic activity in cities, improving competitiveness at the city level becomes increasingly important, and international experience shows that a subnational lens to economic development can make a significant impact. Competitive cities are able to sustain economic success by engaging in proactive local economic development (LED) policies to support the growth of existing firms, attract outside investors, and stimulate the creation of new businesses.

This chapter discusses how effective LED can contribute to raising competitiveness in Central America. Section 1 analyzes the different growth models at play in the region and explains why improving competitiveness is critical to sustain economic growth in the region. Section 2 presents lessons learned from global competitive cities, which illustrate how local policies can support competitiveness. Section 3 identifies specific examples and areas of opportunity for Central American cities. Last, section 4 presents a set of policy recommendations on how to go about developing and implementing effective economic development strategies at the local level.

Key Messages
- Through effective LED policies, Central American cities can improve their competitiveness and facilitate economic growth and job creation in their territories.

- Critical success factors for LED are a clear understanding of local economic advantages, the development of a strong public-private dialogue (PPD) at the local level, and the development of local capacity at the appropriate geographical scale.

Why Local Economic Development Matters for Central America

The region must continue to expand sources of inclusive growth in order to reverse widespread inequality and poverty. Taking full advantage of a massive demographic dividend[1] will require increased efforts from Central American countries to accelerate the shift toward higher-value-added production activities. The extent to which an economy competes in a globalized environment is defined by how the productivity of firms and workers compares to others. *Productivity-led growth* refers to improving the efficiency by which the private sector uses an economy's human, capital, and natural resources. This path involves consistent efforts by national governments toward macroeconomic stability, but there are additional policies to promote private sector development (PSD). Examples range from enhancing productive capacities and improving investment climate conditions, to more outward-oriented policies such as expanding and diversifying exports markets and supporting the integration of local businesses into global value chains (GVCs). The policies that governments design and implement can be categorized according to the scope and the type of intervention. PSD policies can apply to businesses in specific industries (vertical) or to all firms irrespective of the industry they belong to (horizontal), while instruments, whether a market intervention or a public input, are based on the market failures being addressed (Fernández-Arias, Agosin, and Sabel 2010).

A subnational lens to economic development provides Central American countries with new avenues for policy making in supporting the region's economic transition. Economic development efforts in the region are led by central governments—despite cities generating two-thirds of the region's gross domestic product (GDP)—and have gravitated primarily around investment climate regulation. Zooming in at the subnational tier of economic development policy provides unique opportunities for policy makers to unleash transformative and high productivity-led growth by strengthening local and regional competitiveness factors. Multiple reasons make cities and regions particularly well suited to facilitate and implement PSD support mechanisms. The geographic scale of cities and regions can match the spatial agglomeration of firms around networks of suppliers, producers, and buyers sharing similar needs in hard infrastructure, or access to knowledge or a talent pool. This scale makes it easier to convene a range of local stakeholders and facilitate inclusive consultation processes.

By developing LED policies, Central American countries can leverage the potential of cities to contribute to long-term economic growth. LED is an approach to economic development that involves strategies through which cities or regions can support economic activity and employment creation at their territorial scale. Policy interventions are generally categorized within one or more of these four areas: (i) institutions and regulations that improve the business environment, (ii) provision of adequate infrastructure and land for economic activities, (iii) programs and policies aimed at developing skills and innovation, and (iv) enterprise support and finance. A World Bank global analysis on competitiveness shows that cities that are fostering economic growth and job creation are able to build effective partnerships between public and private actors (growth coalition) and to implement strategies that combine actions across the four areas mentioned above. The emergence of LED, irrespective of the existing local capabilities, provides important lessons that can be leveraged by subnational actors aiming to mainstream spatial economics considerations into their local development plans.

Improving Competitiveness Is Critical to Sustain Economic Growth in Central America

Moderate performance of Central American economies has been driven by consistent trade reform and favorable external conditions. During Latin America's foreign debt crisis in the 1980s known as the "lost decade," compound annual growth in Central America averaged 1.1 percent (Porter 2013). Later during the 1990s, the regional economies flourished as the consolidation of peace,[2] sound macroeconomic policies and pro-trade reform, expanded foreign investment and positioned the region to take full advantage of the commodity boom. More recently, the region suffered the effects of the last global debt crisis indirectly through the United States, because of the country's importance as the region's major trade partner, investor, and source of remittances (Guillén 2011). Partly explained by sound macroeconomic policies, the crisis has not eroded financial markets in Central America as much as in other regions, but fiscal deficits and public debt have remained high since its outset in 2008 (IMF 2012). Mid-term growth projections remain stable, positively influenced by low oil prices[3] and a sooner-than-expected recovery of the U.S. economy. The International Monetary Fund (IMF) forecasts indicate that Panama could be the best performer in Latin America with 6 percent average growth during the next 3 years, followed by Costa Rica and Nicaragua with 4 percent. El Salvador, Guatemala, and Honduras will remain stagnant at a band of 1 to 3 percent growth.

However, most Central American countries would need a per capita growth of real income of between 6 and 14 percent to close the gap with the world's most prosperous countries by 2030 (figure 5.1). Latin America, as a whole, would need a per capita growth of real income of 7.5 percent annually, keeping the same pace of inequality reduction observed in recent years. That is more than twice the 3.1 percent achieved between 2003 and 2011, the period of higher growth in the region. Assuming a continuation of the 3.1 percent rate and the same pace of inequality reduction, Latin America would need 41 years to close the gap with global top performers, while it would take 51 years if inequality were to remain constant at the 2011 level (World Bank 2013a). For Central American economies, the needed growth is even higher.

Other indicators portray a region with profound socioeconomic drawbacks, and that is not well-equipped to create the necessary jobs for a booming young demographic. GDP per capita in the region has increased well below the global average of middle-income economies and, compared to the rest of Latin America, the region has underperformed in poverty reduction.[4] Central America's pace of decline in income inequality has been largely stagnant over the last decade, hindering the region's capacity to lift people out of vulnerability and into middle-class layers of society. In Costa Rica and Panama, where economic growth has been highest, inequality remains flat or even widens.[5] By the mid-2000s, countries in the Northern Triangle—El Salvador, Guatemala, and Honduras—suffered mounting crime and emigration to other countries, especially to the United States.

Figure 5.1 Growth Rates Needed to Achieve the Benchmark in GDP per Capita and Gini in 2030 for Latin American Countries

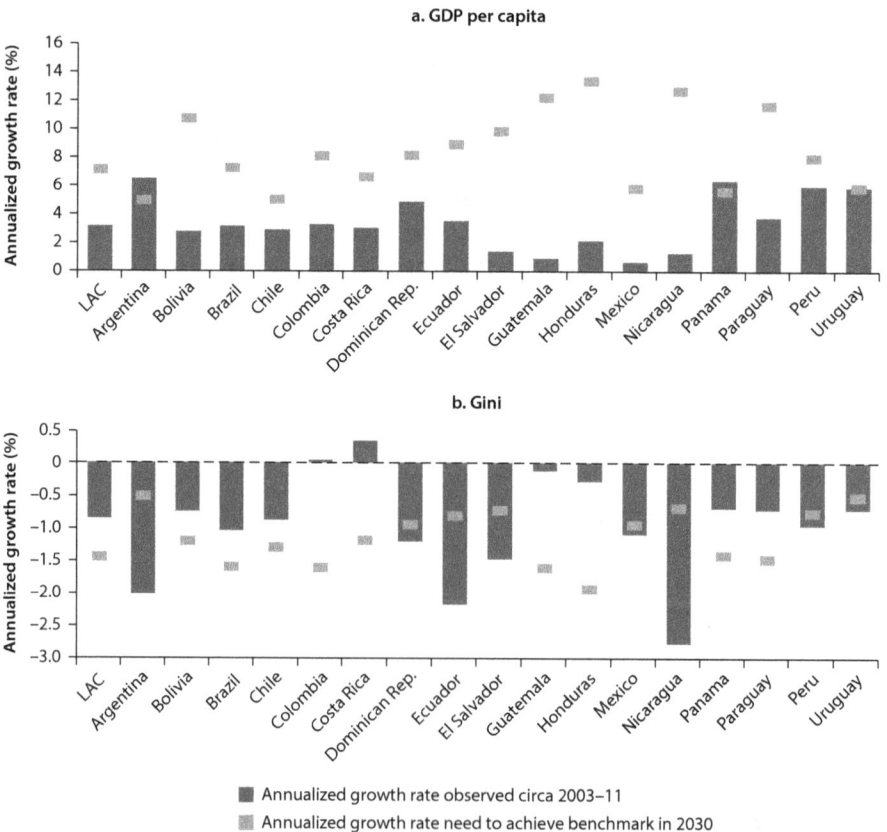

a. GDP per capita

b. Gini

■ Annualized growth rate observed circa 2003–11
▨ Annualized growth rate need to achieve benchmark in 2030

Source: World Bank 2013b.
Note: LAC = Latin America and the Caribbean.

Out of the 3 million Central American immigrants living in the United States, 90 percent relocated from these countries (MPI 2013). Factors such as outbound migration and the weight of the informal economy continue to distort unemployment data, which ranges between 4 and 6 percent, except in Costa Rica where unemployment hit 8 percent in 2014. Underemployment, however, remains high,[6] at 63 percent for the population under 30 years of age.

Central American economies showcase different growth trajectories, but on average, their competitive advantage has relied on the region's natural endowments and proximity to the United States. Recent economic history in Central America is explained, to an extent, by the ability of each country to capitalize on these two factors. A combination of favorable climate and ecological diversity facilitated agricultural development and a competitive tourism industry, while foreign investment boomed in sectors where rapid response through shorter lead times and lower labor costs constituted key success factors to serve the U.S. market. The economies of El Salvador, Guatemala, Honduras, and Nicaragua are still relying heavily on these economic drivers, while Costa Rica and Panama have managed to diversify their economies and transition to more productive sectors.

Although production in most Central American countries has been increasingly moving to manufacturing, jobs are still concentrated in low-skill productive sectors that are exposed to external shocks. It is estimated that in countries such as El Salvador, Guatemala, Honduras, and Nicaragua, more than 50 percent of the workforce is concentrated in low-skill activities related to commerce and agriculture, while only 15 percent is employed in manufacturing. The region's natural endowments, such as favorable climate for year-round production, competitive hours of sunlight per day, and the quality of soil, constitute strong comparative advantages for the production of coffee, sugar, and fruits. However, these are extremely vulnerable to natural disasters, price volatility, and other shocks. On the other hand, the textile and apparel *Maquila* industry is linked to free trade zones, or *zonas francas*, given the existence of lower import and export duties, and, in the case of Honduras, is the second-largest GDP contributor after remittances. However, *Maquilas* are exposed to the price of commodity inputs and the volatility of foreign direct investment (FDI).

Services account for a growing share of GDP across the region, ranging from 52 percent in Nicaragua to 75 percent in Panama. Broadly defined, the *services* category includes nontraded business activities such as commerce or retail, consolidated industries like tourism, as well as emerging ones like business process outsourcing (BPO). Following the expansion of cloud-based business models and consequent demand for outsourced sales, the reduction in telecom rates and a considerable pool of bilingual labor force have positioned Central America as a competitive location for the call center industry. Although the aggregated industry turnover is still low, it is growing at an impressive pace. Likewise, tourism is a major source of income for countries in the region, ranging from 5 to 10 percent of GDP. International tourism amounts to 7.6 percent of the GDP in Costa Rica and 4.3 percent in El Salvador.

The exports basket in Costa Rica is dominated by high technology-based exports and knowledge-intensive services. A sound trade liberalization reform and a relatively high-skilled labor pool allowed Costa Rica to nurture a vibrant exports sector. Today the country is globally recognized for its success stories in FDI. Exports account for 55 percent of GDP, up from 27 percent in 1980, and the share of high-tech products and information and communications technology (ICT) is one of the highest when compared to upper-middle-income peers. Agricultural production declined from 13 percent of GDP in the early 1980s to 5 percent today, while the manufacturing sector has stagnated at a 20–22 percent GDP contribution for the past 25 years and decreased in terms of employment (from 25 to 12 percent).

Panama's growth is heavily influenced by the operation and consecutive renovation phases of the Panama Canal. This emblematic infrastructure positions Panama as a transport hub and unique economy when compared to other Central American countries. It explains the country's specialization in logistics and distribution services and makes more difficult any comparison on sources of economic growth with other countries in the region. The Colon Free Trade Zone is home to 2,000 enterprises and 15,000 jobs. In 2014, Panama surpassed the US$10 billion mark in export of services, led by canal-related transport services (US$5.4 billion), tourism (US$3.4 billion), and financial, insurance, and business services (collectively, US$1.2 billion) (ITC 2014).

To create more and better jobs, Central American countries must strengthen the competitiveness of the private sector. Successful economic development, capable of raising income and living standards simultaneously, is ultimately driven by improved firm-level competitiveness. Governments around the world have different levers to improve the context in which firms expand and innovate. They exercise monetary and fiscal powers to foster macroeconomic stability, but they also apply innovative policy tools to promote PSD by improving the business environment in which firms operate. Traditionally in Central America, these measures have been led mostly by national government agencies, and have geared toward improving the investment climate. Notwithstanding the success of these policies, concentrating economic development policies to the work of national investment promotion agencies (IPAs) is in fact a missed opportunity. The impact of top-down PSD initiatives is not maximized when these work in isolation. It is the lack of a more comprehensive policy framework to address the challenges of the local business fabric that limits the capacity of Central American governments to strengthen the business environment and country competitiveness through alternative policy innovations.

Building on Local Economic Development: Lessons from Global Competitive Cities

Global interest in LED policies has grown parallel to rapid urbanization patterns. As city leaders are increasingly posed with significant socioeconomic challenges, job creation in urban areas has become a priority in global economic development (World Bank 2012). A thriving economy creates conditions for prosperity in the form of higher incomes and widespread improvements in the standard of living. The international community is coming to realize that LED policies can have considerable impact in a local economy. A recent World Bank study benchmarking the world's largest 750 cities identifies a set of common principles applied by cities showing outstanding economic performance (see box 5.1): above-average growth in private sector job creation, disposable incomes, and labor productivity. Acknowledging that city-level policies can make a difference in the competitiveness of the local private sector, which generates 75 percent of all jobs and 80 percent of gross value added in cities worldwide, has important policy ramifications. Understanding what makes these cities succeed, as well as the subsequent analysis of best practices, will inform the discussion on potential LED policies in Central America.

There is a link between LED policies and a city's income level and economic structure. As figure 5.2 shows, local economies generating US$2,500 per capita, or less, are driven primarily by business activities such as consumer services, wholesale and retail. These can be labeled "market towns." Industrial activity tends to dominate in lower-to-middle-income "production centers" with levels of per capita GDP between US$2,500 and US$20,000. When cities graduate from this category they tend to transition toward creative and financial centers. The analysis concluded that, in navigating this economic transformation, cities use similar or differentiated policy *levers* to maximize the outcomes of their LED interventions. At lower levels of income, policies emphasize structural transformation, namely building institutional capacity,

---

Box 5.1 Competitive Cities Drive Job Growth and Increase Income and Productivity

Competitive cities sustain economic success by engaging in action-oriented policies across three channels of firm-level growth: the growth of existing firms, the attraction of outside investors, and the creation of new businesses. In addition to attracting outside investment, successful cities assist existing firms in addressing different constraints to growth, and support the formation of new businesses. Competitive cities are characterized by above-average economic performance measured through specific indicators:

- *Accelerated economic growth:* The top 10 percent of cities achieved 13.5 percent annual GDP per capita growth, compared to 4.7 percent in an average city.
- *Outstanding job growth:* The top 10 percent of cities achieved 9.2 percent annual jobs growth, compared to 1.9 percent in the remaining 90 percent.
- *Increased incomes and productivity:* The top 10 percent of cities increased the average disposable income of their households by 9.8 percent annually.
- *Magnets for FDI:* The top 5 percent of cities obtained as much FDI as the bottom 95 percent of cities combined.

Figure 5.2 The Different Economic Structures and Needs of Cities at Different Levels of Income

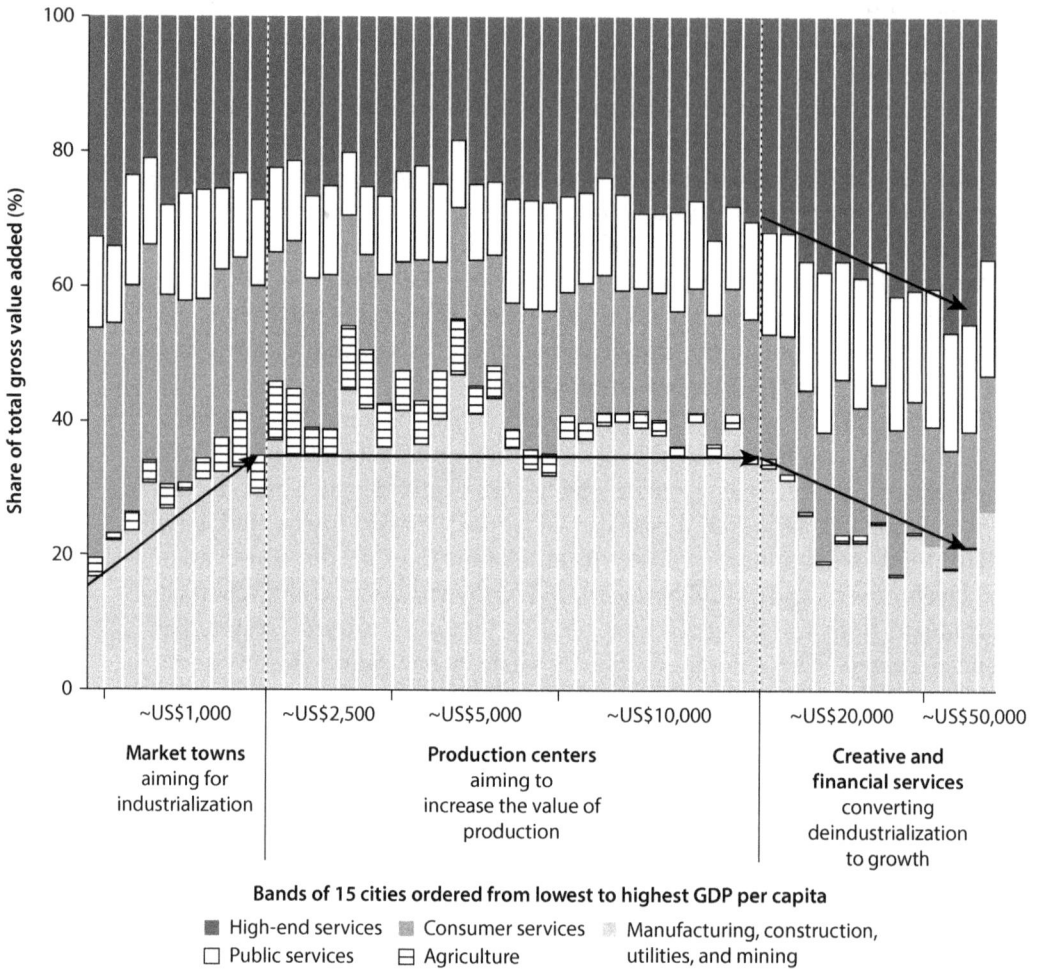

Source: World Bank 2015a.

pushing regulatory reform, and investing in basic infrastructure. As the city develops, the focus shifts to scaling up productive output by improving the efficient use of the resources in the economy, for instance through high-end services. Improving human capital tends to be a permanent goal in the economic development agenda, but cities may often need to choose between more jobs or better jobs, depending on their stage in the economic transformation cycle.

Competitive cities focus their interventions across four broad policy levers, or tools, to influence local determinants of competitiveness. These levers are strongly intertwined, and together provide a comprehensive framework to assess what policy options LED practitioners can deploy to create jobs while raising incomes and productivity. Subnational tools for policy action can be summarized in four categories:

- *Institutions and regulations:* taxes, licenses, duties, legal regulation, promotion and branding
- *Infrastructure and land:* roads, electricity, water, sanitation, transport, communications, and land (including colocation arrangements for similar firms)
- *Skills and innovation:* basic education, vocational training and workforce development, and innovation networks
- *Enterprise support and finance:* access to capital, subsidies, incentives, export assistance, and capacity development for operational activities (legal, financial, administrative)

Success in LED is largely based on the convergence of proactive city leadership and adequate policy capabilities to facilitate action in several competitiveness areas. City leaders generally have different avenues to push for the implementation of economic development initiatives. Figure 5.3 lists some of the competencies usually available to a city's government (or "Mayor's wedge"). Bringing these initiatives to fruition will require collaborating with other stakeholders through permanent or temporary "growth coalitions" of public

Figure 5.3 Competitive Cities Know Their Own Competencies Relative to Other Stakeholders, and Prioritize Their Efforts Accordingly

	Institutions and regulations	Infrastructure and land	Skills and innovation	Enterprise support and finance
National government	Macroeconomic management National investment and trade policy Legal framework and property protection Industry-specific taxes and regulations	Highways, roads airports, ports Power grid Regulations for infrastructure provision, such as PPP laws	Public education system Immigration policies to attract talent Research and development funding, support schemes Healthcare	Export and trade facilitation Access to finance support schemes
Mayor's wedge City government	Municipal taxes and incentives Zoning and land use policies Construction permits; business licenses Public safety and law enforcement	City roads and public transportation Water and sanitation Public safety Housing/slum upgrading	Talent attraction programs Cluster development support Linking firms with academia	Business support services Investment policies, promotion, and aftercare Facilitation of seed, catalyst, and risk capital
Private sector	Standards and certification associations	Additional infrastructure and shared services	Vocational training programs Research and development	Business associations and support networks Market intelligence and business information Equity and debt

Source: World Bank 2015a.
Note: PPP = public-private partnership.

and private stakeholders, in addition to pushing for intergovernmental coordination. While personal leadership and trust among different stakeholders is essential, the establishment of facilitating institutions and assignation of responsibilities for implementation prove to be more effective forces in driving sustainable LED. These structures can emerge for the implementation of a single action or become permanent.

What Central American Cities Can Do

An overview of LED opportunities in the region unveils specific areas of opportunities for Central American cities to improve their performance across the different key areas of local competitiveness:

- *Institutions and regulations*: Local governments can learn from each other to further improve the business environment at the local level.
- *Infrastructure and land*: The impact of local territorial development plans and investment in LED can be improved by bringing an economic development lens into the territorial and investment planning processes.
- *Skills and innovation*: Local partnerships can help bridge the region's skills gap by helping match the supply and demand for specific skills.
- *Enterprise support*: The effectiveness of existing enterprise support services can be improved by developing a more strategic approach to investment promotion and improving local firms' access to business support services.

Institutions and Regulations
Learning from Each Other to Further Improve the Business Environment at the Local Level

Local institutions and regulations shape an important part of the business environment at the city level. For example, they often determine how easy it is for firms and entrepreneurs to start a new business, obtain a construction permit, or register a property. The regional Doing Business for Central America (World Bank 2015b) compared business regulations at the local level in the six Central American countries and the Dominican Republic. It found substantial variations in business regulations and their implementation across the countries, and also among cities within the same country. Figure 5.4 below presents the performance of several cities across the three areas surveyed (starting a business, obtaining a construction permit, and registering a property), and reveals opportunities for reform and exchange of good practices.

Central and local governments in Central America are working on improving the ease of doing business at the local level. In Costa Rica, municipalities in the San José metropolitan area compete in attracting investment by establishing one-stop shops or "single window" systems to expedite business registration procedures and construction permits, making city regulations easier to navigate for businesses and entrepreneurs. As noted in chapter 2, this type of initiatives

Figure 5.4 Ease of Doing Business in Central America

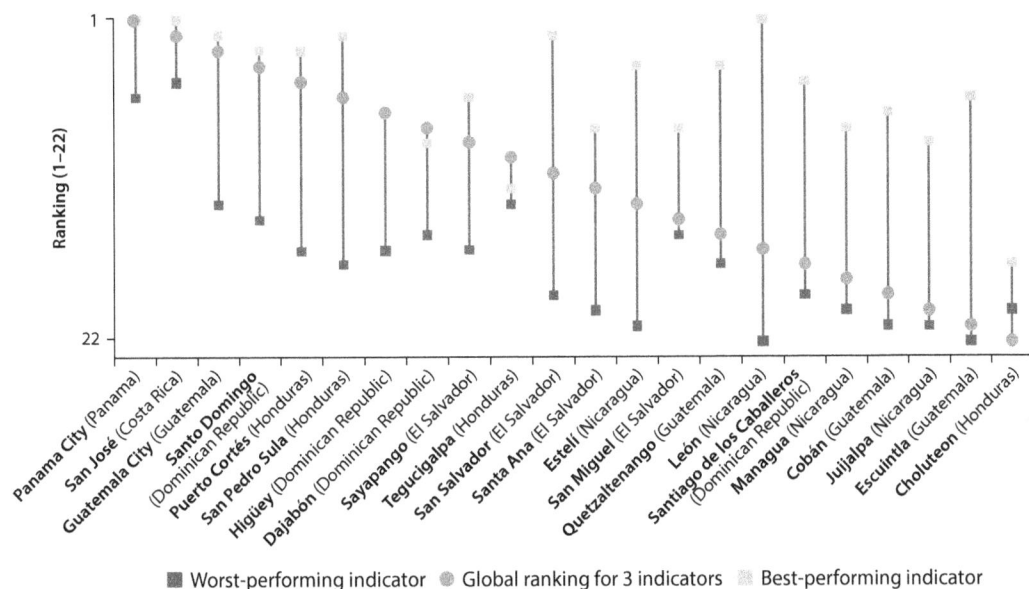

Worst-performing indicator   ● Global ranking for 3 indicators   Best-performing indicator

Source: World Bank 2015b.

relies on increased capacity at the local level and coordination between central and municipal governments, and can benefit from cooperation between municipalities. Panama City has created a single window for processing construction permits that is overseen by the Ministry of Housing and Territorial Development (MIVIOT) based in the municipality's office. In El Salvador, building on the experience of the Planning Office of the Metropolitan Area of San Salvador (OPAMSS), the Vice Ministry of Housing has created Territorial Planning and Management Offices (*Oficinas de Planificacion y Gestion Territorial*). These technical units are set up at the level of associations of municipalities (*mancomunidades*), which gain from the economies of scale required to make them sustainable at the local level.

Infrastructure and Land
Bringing an Economic Development Lens to Local Development Plans
International experience shows how competitive cities are able to identify and deliver infrastructure investments through effective partnerships between the public and private sectors, and between different levels of governments. Central American cities can improve the impact of infrastructure investments on LED through greater involvement of local governments and local economic actors in the planning process. As noted in chapter 2, city development plans are often prepared with limited involvement and ownership of local governments. Greater involvement of local governments in the preparation of local development plans

could not only improve the coordination between spatial planning and infrastructure investment at the city level, but it can also ensure the involvement of local economic actors in the process.

Local "growth coalitions" can help cities identify key priorities and leverage investments from the national government. For example, Bucaramanga, in Colombia, was able to successfully lobby the central government for infrastructure upgrades that were most needed for the city's economy. A partnership between the city government and the local private sector led to the identification of transportation as a key constraint to the growth of local firms. The city government used a study prepared by the city chamber of commerce to persuade the national government to fund specific infrastructure investments. Tangier, in Morocco, leveraged national investments in a new port to attract foreign investments through coordinated efforts from the national and local IPAs.

Connectivity infrastructure is an example of national investments that can be leveraged at the local level. An analysis of logistics bottlenecks in Central America (World Bank 2012a) identified urban congestion, along with border wait times, as one of the main causes of delays in the shipping of goods in the region. The absence of bypassing routes accounts for approximately 12 percent of transit time on routes passing through Guatemala City and Panama City. Urban bypass roads are an example of a major investment requiring the financial support of the central government, but with potentially large impacts on a city's spatial and economic development. Investing in this type of infrastructure opens up new areas for development to be planned in connection with a citywide spatial development strategy, enabling new economic activities and contributing to a more sustainable urban development. The introduction of bypass routes can also significantly improve livability in the city itself by relieving traffic congestion and air pollution associated with freight traffic passing through the city.

Efforts to improve infrastructure for economic activity have mainly focused on specific areas with limited connection to citywide development strategies. Through the creation of special economic zones (SEZs), Central America countries have been offering improved infrastructure along with favorable fiscal conditions in order to attract investments in targeted export-oriented sectors. The section below on enterprise support discusses how Central American countries can improve the long-term impact of these initiatives by having a more strategic approach to investment promotion and aligning it with local territorial development strategies.

Skills and Innovation
Bridging the Skills Gap by Matching Supply and Demand
Subnational actors are ideally positioned to match supply and demand of human capital. Recent World Bank analysis[7] concluded that improving human capital is imperative to address the jobs challenge in Central America, considering the region's poor record in educational and skills development indicators.[8] An unskilled workforce hinders economic development and ties an economy to

low-wage industries, as is the case in the Northern Triangle and Nicaragua, making it more difficult to break the vicious circle of inequality, youth unemployment, and migration. Broad government efforts to overhaul the educational system must be coupled with pragmatic policies to bring these skills closer to firms, through a demand-driven approach to secondary and post-secondary education in order to improve the rates at which graduates enter the labor market. City managers have an advantage when it comes to facilitating these linkages between firms and universities and training institutions.

There are examples of Central American cities taking one step forward in aligning education and training providers with the skills required by a specific industry or investor. Cartago, a city of half a million people in Costa Rica, and home to the largest campus of the Costa Rica Institute of Technology (TEC), worked with the Costa Rican Investment Promotion Agency (CINDE) to establish the technical curricula needed to prepare a pool of skilled workers demanded by medical device multinationals. Since the local university was not able to provide this training at that point, CINDE and the city of Cartago facilitated a collaboration with the University of Minnesota. Today there are 52 students enrolled in an engineering master's program tailored to the needs of the medical device industry, the first of its kind in Latin America. Attracting foreign universities to establish branch campuses and expand the offer in graduate level programs can also help strengthen and improve the programs offered by universities in the region. Cities can also run programs designed to reintegrate returning migrants,[9] providing local economies with workers with a differentiated experience and skill set. This link between local supply and demand of skills can be driven either by a joint initiative between central and local governments like in Cartago or through private businesses as depicted in box 5.2, which describes the case of Aeroman, a top employer in El Salvador. Aeroman's collaboration with a local university helped the firm build a successful business strategy around human capital.

Box 5.2 The Case of Aeroman: Local Partnership for Skills Improvement

Commitment to Quality through Improved Technical Skills

Established in 1983 as the maintenance and engineering division of TACA Airlines, Aeroman became a top provider in maintenance, repair and overhaul (MRO) services for narrow body airplanes in America. Since its beginnings, the firm has shown a clear commitment to the continued upgrading of technical skills in order to sustain high levels of quality and achieve competitive turnaround times. Combined with its cost advantage and its strategic geographic position connecting South and North America, these factors have been pivotal in the success of the business.

box continues next page

Box 5.2 The Case of Aeroman: Local Partnership for Skills Improvement (continued)

When Private, Public, and Education Actors Intersect

Through collaboration with the Don Bosco University, a course for aircraft maintenance technicians was developed in 2005. Currently 300 students are enrolled in the program and 237 have graduated from it, many of them employed at Aeroman. The curricula will soon expand to also include engineering courses. According to Aeroman's chairman, a new mechanic must undergo two years of training before working in the production lines. Such investment per worker demonstrates the company's commitment to continued upgrading of the technical capabilities of Aeroman's workforce.

Promising Outlook

Today, Aeroman is the only member of the Airbus MRO network in Latin America and services several commercial airlines. It has recently reached its 1,000th heavy maintenance check (performs around 150 annually), the vast majority of which have been to U.S. airlines such as US Airways or Jet Blue. Aeroman has 12 lines for Boeing and Airbus narrow bodies and plans to add capabilities for Embraer in 2016. The firm is expected to add 6 new lines and create 3,500 new jobs in the next seven years. A new hangar will enable Aeroman to pursue widebody MRO and it will include a dedicated training building.

Enterprise Support

Developing a More Strategic Approach to Investment Promotion and Improving Local Firms' Access to Business Support Services

Leveraging Special Economic Zones

Central American countries have relied heavily on SEZs to promote export-oriented activities. The region was an early adopter of export processing zones (EPZ), or *zonas francas*, along with Colombia, the Dominican Republic, and Mexico. Often viewed as quick fixes to boost exports, *zonas francas* were public-driven at first and applied similar sets of incentives[10] to jockey for investors through reduced production costs, trade tariffs, and corporate taxes. However, limited long-term social benefits, measured by increased wages, knowledge spillovers, and improved working conditions, did not always outweigh their costs. Over time, the tool evolved into the SEZs, which now account for a large share of light manufacturing jobs in El Salvador, Guatemala, Honduras, and Nicaragua. Although SEZs have contributed to attracting FDI, many of the firms that invest in them rely heavily on continued access to low wages, affordable electricity, and fiscal incentives. International evidence suggests that attracting cost-based production without capitalizing on local spillovers limits the sustainability of the economic gains.

Examples in the region show how countries can develop a more strategic approach to investment promotion. With a 5–10 year lead time over most Central American countries, the Dominican Republic represents a good benchmark for countries that managed to shift investment from sectors intensive in unskilled labor to higher-value-added sectors with stronger links to local suppliers. In 2003, textile and apparel firms accounted for more than 50 percent of all companies operating out of the SEZs in the Dominican Republic. They accounted for an even larger majority of exports and employment. By the end of 2010, textiles and apparel accounted for only 22 percent of SEZ companies, as promotion efforts were actively oriented toward other economic sectors such as services, tobacco, agribusinesses, pharmaceuticals, and electronics. The region is also home to very renowned success stories and emerging cases in FDI, such as the establishment of microchips manufacturer, Intel, in Costa Rica in 1996. In Honduras, the textile cluster underwent a remarkable evolution from low-skill, low-value productive stages to more capital-intensive ones.

With the guidance of world-class investment promotion organizations (IPOs) based in the region, local authorities can tie strategic investments to both existing and new SEZs. In El Salvador, Guatemala, Honduras, and Nicaragua, SEZs constitute an important source of light manufacturing jobs, primarily in textile and apparel industries. In Nicaragua, SEZs accounted for 80 percent of exports in 2005, compared to 67 percent in Panama. Textile exports originating from SEZs in El Salvador account for nearly half of national exports, representing US$2.4 billion. This economic scenario is an opportunity for subnational agents to leverage their precise understanding of the region's assets and productive specialization in encouraging technology and know-how transfer from lead firms in existing SEZs and informing the planning of new ones.

Large and mid-size cities in Central America collaborate with their respective IPOs to guarantee that the mix of incentives promoting upstream and downstream linkages is aligned with the transitional steps toward trade liberalization. Countries like Nicaragua and Costa Rica have globally renowned institutions in this arena. While Nicaragua's PRONICARAGUA is recognized by its efficiency and celerity in responding to the requests of international investors, CINDE has particularly excelled in the after care services aimed at consolidating and expanding the operations of established multinational corporations (MNCs). As opposed to the "build it and they will come" approach, CINDE dedicates half of its 40-person team to business promotion, including a team of "investment intelligence" experts to anticipate global demand in the countries with strategic knowledge-based sectors. Encouraging sector-specific investments allows CINDE to target the promotion of SEZs to specific lead firms and smaller ones producing related inputs, and to capitalize on local comparative and competitive advantages. For established corporations, the focus of the organization is unequivocally talent. CINDE representatives meet periodically with heads of the human resources department to meet the skill sets they require to expand production or business activity in their Costa Rican subsidiaries.

Improving Local Firms' Access to Business Support Services

City-level LED offices can improve the offer and access to business support services. As mentioned in the previous section, successful economic development strategies at the national level combine proactive investment promotion with the continued provision of a comprehensive range of business support services.

In growing their businesses, firms and entrepreneurs in Central America may seek assistance from private and institutional service providers, from up-to-date information on export markets to advisory services on compliance issues, quality certification, or access to finance.

Business support mechanisms tend to be scattered across multiple agencies and departments of national government. Today, the portfolio of competitiveness support programs available to firms is not usually consolidated under one roof so businesses must navigate an often bureaucratic public structure to do so, and the specifics needs from firms must adjust to the parameters of a given program to be supported, not the other way around. However, there are ongoing efforts in streamlining and consolidating national competitiveness support. Costa Rica passed a law in October 2015 for the rationalization of a support portfolio for micro, small, and medium enterprises through the creation of FOMPRODUCE.[11] With an initial budget of US$34 million, FOMPRODUCE integrates six different bodies (DIGEPYME, INAPYME, PRONAMYPE, FODEMIPYME, PROPYME, and CONICIT[12]) and brings together four ministries (MEIC, MICITT, MAG, and COMEX). Its governing board will have permanent private sector representatives, including chambers of commerce and UCCAEP, a guild grouping business associations.

The rationalization of the provision of business services at the national level should be accompanied by the development of similar integrated windows at the local level. Doing so would not only simplify things from the perspective of beneficiary, but it would also allow public officials to gain a more complete understanding of the competitive challenges faced by the private sector, giving them the opportunity to inform their intervention decisions accordingly.

How to Do It? Priorities for Developing LED Policies in Central America

The review of experiences in terms of developing and implementing LED policies in Central America reveals several limitations. LED strategies which have been developed in the region often suffer from a lack of rigorous analysis of the local situation in terms of economic activity, employment, and economic development potential. There is a limited systematic engagement of the private sector in the processes of definition of development strategies at the local level. Finally, cities lack the capacity to facilitate the dialogue between local actors and deliver the key services that are critical to the definition and implementation of LED strategies.

Based on the experience of Central American countries and lessons from global case studies, key priorities to develop improved LED policies in Central America are:

- Understanding their local economy through benchmarking and analysis
- Facilitating a long-term vision for the city or region and a stronger PPD to prepare competitiveness agendas aimed at reaching that vision
- Translating strategies into action through gaining subnational capabilities and fostering intragovernment coordination

Understanding the Local Economy through Benchmarking and Analysis

Any discussion on LED policy priorities must be informed by an accurate understanding of the local or regional economic reality.[13] Local authorities must capture the distinct nature of their local economies to understand potential sources of comparative and competitive advantage. Some initiatives, like the Municipal Competitiveness Index in El Salvador and similar attempts to assess subnational investment climate conditions, are important steps toward gathering accurate benchmarking economic indicators in local settings. In this context, firm-level surveys and investment climate indicators can tell us about the perceived constraints to PSD in each country and the region as a whole. Thanks to a 2010 survey[14] we know that the most binding constraint in day-to-day operations in El Salvador and Guatemala is perceived to be crime, while electricity is a top constraint in Nicaragua, access to finance in Costa Rica, and corruption in Honduras and Panama. We also know that when country-level results are averaged, registered businesses rank competition from informal firms as a top binding constraint in day-to-day operations.[15] However, these must be coupled with a refined understanding of qualitative issues and trends affecting the city's economic structure.

The analysis must account for rapid changes in the industry mix, as exemplified by Central American capital cities. As costs of production rise in cities, manufacturing jobs are replaced by service-oriented activities. The emergence of the call center industry illustrates this trend, as multiplexing and cloud-based technologies are creating the conditions for a boom in the contact center outsourcing (CCO) and BPO industries. In Guatemala City, 80,000 manufacturing jobs have been lost in the last 15 years, but job creation in call centers for BPO is growing very fast. Quetzaltenango, a mid-size city with limited trade infrastructure, expects to create 70,000 in the near future. This sector employed 9,000 people in 2008 in Guatemala, but in 2014, 75 firms already employed 35,000 and this figure is expected to increase to 55,000 by the end of 2016. Recent predictions (Frost & Sullivan 2014) situate future employment at 150,000. Similarly, the call center industry in Costa Rica created 45,000 jobs in the last 15 years, spread among 28 contact centers and 18 major companies offering BPO services.

The rest of Central American economies are catching up at an impressive speed. Panama's industry emerged in 2010 and, averaging a 25 percent annual growth since then, now accounts for 40 centers and 13,000 jobs. El Salvador's grew by 19 percent to create 17,500 jobs, and Nicaragua has 25 centers in operation as of today. The call center industry in Honduras has been the fastest-growing economic sector in the last three years. It employs roughly 27,000 people, but 10,000 of those jobs were created in 2014 alone. San Pedro Sula, the industrial capital, is becoming a hotspot for call centers and has developed a dedicated industrial park to attract key global players. Honduras is home to 30 contact centers and 12 BPOs from international investors.

Facilitating a Long-Term Vision and a Competitiveness Agenda through Action-Oriented Public-Private Dialogue

LED in Central America can improve the impact of past attempts to develop nationwide economic development agendas. By facilitating bottom-up processes, LED policies can overcome a certain degree of political gridlock that has negatively affected the implementation of national priorities in competitiveness. In 1994, countries in the region created the Central American Alliance for Sustainable Development aimed at improving regional cooperation in the field of economic development. A team of international experts[16] recommended policy strategies to strengthen the global competitiveness position of the region and prompted the emergence of national competitiveness councils, or *Consejos Nacionales de Competitividad*.[17] These *consejos* recognized the virtues of a closer interaction between the private and the public sector supporting competitiveness, updated the analysis of economic challenges, and set national priorities to address them. However, they were unable to sustain a renewed interface with the private sector and were seldom coupled with a corresponding allocation of resources for implementation.

Effective local governance prioritizes policy actions that align with a long-term economic vision. A city's vision for sustained prosperity must be established through a participatory process and informed by an assessment of the economy and its comparative advantages. Central American municipalities that have strategic roadmaps seldom have an economic development component and, when they do, these are not supported by thorough analysis. A shared vision is essential when it comes to building consensus on the strategies necessary to reach it, so the selection of actors in a city-wide PPD process should reflect the real geographic scale of the city economy.[18] Facilitators in Central American capital cities, by way of example, must determine what metropolitan administrative boundaries will be better suited to tackle key economic development challenges. It is imperative to think long term and encourage public and private sector buy-in so that they are able to take ownership of the overall process.

In defining strategies to support this vision, the group of public and private participants in PPD efforts can be narrower in scope. LED actors can maximize the impact of the resulting interventions given that they have a better knowledge of the market trends in the industry where local firms compete. In regions with an ample cluster of companies and a diverse economic structure, the role of convening stakeholders in the local economy may reside in a permanent LED team or unit to facilitate periodical updates of the economic vision based on economic performance indicators. Successful projects require a business-centric philosophy that recognizes strategic analysis as the means to avoid intuitive top-down recipes for growth. As demonstrated by the global analysis of competitive cities, when LED staff conduct the proper analysis and understand business strategy concepts, they can perform a similar role to that of strategy consultants, combining process facilitation and strategic analysis with participants that result in LED action plans. Effective PPD often starts with raising strategic evidence–based questions about an issue at hand supported by supply and demand-based analysis.

When the overall development of strategies takes place in one specific economic sector or value chain, the resulting LED actions tend to be more advanced. The path to competitiveness is not the same for all firms in an economy. Those that belong to the same value chain or business segment will be influenced by similar success factors to compete, which are increasingly influenced by global trends. LED teams can therefore facilitate a more specific discussion on the strategic challenges they face by engaging sector stakeholders in demand-driven analysis. Traditionally, MNCs concentrated productive processes in one location, so developing countries were left with very few options to diversify their economy: to attract a lead firm in that sector, to develop new sectors from scratch, or to keep a low-wage specialization in the agriculture sector. The intense globalization pattern seen during the last decades caused the fragmentation of productive activities, opening up a whole new set opportunities for firms to participate in GVCs[19] by progressively capturing more value-added activities.

Translating Strategies into Action through Subnational Capabilities and Intragovernment Coordination

Leadership in LED implementation comes from various combinations of stakeholders in a city's economy. Notwithstanding the intrinsic difficulties in defining a long-term economic vision, it is during the implementation phase when most LED policies tend to fail. Common bottlenecks surface when actions are poorly formulated, when funding is dependent on a sole actor, or if the initiative is promoted in large part by a single public figure. Interviews conducted across Central America revealed that several success stories in LED have built on the influence of "personal leaders," be it mayors, well-known businesspeople, or industry experts. While their involvement may trigger action to solve specific issues, it also indicates the lack of a systematic and action-oriented dialogue with other relevant stakeholders, jeopardizing the overall sustainability of LED processes. Since economic challenges are dynamic and problems change over time, the structure of PPD should be capable of supporting long-term initiatives, adapt to them, and, more important, survive political shocks across different electoral cycles. City managers must explore performance-based formulas binding LED structures to impact metrics.

Coordination with regional stakeholders and other tiers of administration is essential. Competitive cities use their leverage to join forces with those sharing similar interests, given that the most transformational initiatives often require interjurisdictional cooperation with neighboring communities in lobbying for funding. At a smaller scale, and as previously discussed, LED actors will also need to coordinate with national government to assist local businesses in navigating the portfolio of multifaceted instruments to support competitiveness. The collaboration between subnational and national economic development officials goes both ways. Nationwide reforms can permeate more easily to firms when the outreach of local and regional actors represents an active and efficient conduit to communicate particularly with micro, small, and medium enterprises.

The allocation of LED capabilities must be preceded by a discussion on the appropriate scale to engage in LED policies, which can be progressively expanded according to results. Expanding LED capabilities in institutional structure, financial resources, and human capital can happen gradually. Considering that even large cities in the region do not have an LED unit, and those that do are primarily involved in the regulation of nontraded sectors like commerce and retail, upgrading LED policies may not necessarily require the initial setup of new institutional structures. Prior to expanding LED staff structures and allocating other capabilities, a discussion must take place to determine what scale is the best to engage in LED. El Salvador, the smallest country in Central America and one of the most densely populated in the world, has encouraged alliances among its 292 municipalities and is now pushing for regional economic development policies with a more manageable group of 24 municipal associations, or *mancomunidades*. Once the unit of administration to engage in subnational economic development has been properly defined, LED teams can find inexpensive ways to facilitate quick wins in different policy levers while learning in the process.

This "learning by doing" approach can allow city officials to design an LED structure more reflective of the local economy dynamics. What's more, these field-based experiences and early wins tend to act as the proof-of-concepts to ignite the participation of a wider spectrum of local stakeholders. A prospective LED unit will need the adequate set of skills to perform its role as facilitator of regional and sector strategies and its performance should be measured by indicators, such as evidenced impact on local competitiveness or the traction generated with the private sector.

Notes

1. The "demographic dividend" refers to opportunities derived from changes in age structure as a country's economy gradually develops. When average life expectancy increases and the size of families is progressively reduced, there's a period of time in which a large pool of young educated people enter the labor market.

2. Progressively during the early and mid-1990s, Central American countries ended long periods of civil conflict and political unrest, including major civil wars, a regional war between Guatemala and Honduras, and the involvement of the region in the Cold War. Remarkably, being center stage in Cold War disputes boosted inflows of international aid, which each government used very differently. While Honduras expanded military capacity, Costa Rica prioritized education, health, and housing investments.

3. Unlike the rest of Latin America and the Caribbean (LAC), Central America is a net importer of oil and therefore overly dependent on hydrocarbon prices as 40 percent of electricity production relies on fossil fuels.

4. Forty-four percent of the population still lives on less than US$4 a day, only a 9 percent reduction since 2000 compared to a decline of 40 percent in the LAC region for the same period.

5. Costa Rica and Panama went from being the least unequal countries in LAC in 2000 to being around the median by 2012.

6. *Underemployed* workers are either (i) highly skilled employees working in low-pay low-skilled jobs or (ii) part-time workers who would prefer to work full-time. In the Northern Triangle this figure is 30–40 percent.

7. *Better Jobs in Central America: The Role of Human Capital* is a flagship 2012 report prepared by the Human Development Department for the LAC region at the Word Bank.

8. The quality of primary education is poor, as evidenced by low reading scores and performance levels. Guatemala, Honduras, and Nicaragua have a labor force with an average of less than six years of schooling, while Costa Rica and Panama have 8.4 and 9.4 respectively. These levels stand in contrast to the U.S. level of 13 years of schooling. Worryingly, the region as a whole has shown little improvement in the last 10 years. As per the share of the labor force with some years of postsecondary schooling, Costa Rica tops the list in the region, with 18.6 percent. Guatemala, Honduras, and Nicaragua have levels that are significantly below 10 percent, whereas El Salvador reaches 10.6 percent. These levels compare to the U.S. figure of 50.1 percent. Public expenditure on education in the region is low, and only Costa Rica and Panama are slightly above LAC average. LAC average for the 2000–09 period was 4.14 percent of GDP, only surpassed by Costa Rica (4.98) and Panama (4.31). This is still a third of the average in Organisation for Economic Co-operation and Development countries.

9. The reduction of human capital in Central American migrant-sending countries generally takes place in the educated segments of society, as those leaving the country tend to be better prepared than those staying behind. Emigration rates of population with tertiary education in El Salvador, Guatemala, Honduras, and Nicaragua are within a staggering 25–30 percent band. These emigrants generally end up in low-paying jobs in the United States, destination for roughly 70 percent of total migrants from Central America. Bashir, Gindling, and Oviedo 2012; *World Bank Migration and Remittances Factbook 2011.*

10. Industrial zoning categories include six types: (i) free trade zone, (ii) export processing zone, (iii) enterprise zone, (iv) single factories, (v) free port, and (vi) specialized zone. In Colombia, the Barranquilla zone was opened in 1964; in the Dominican Republic, 1965. El Salvador, Guatemala, and Honduras followed in the early 1970s. After this came Nicaragua in 1976, Jamaica in 1976, and Costa Rica in 1981.

11. Agency for Productive Development, Innovation and Value-Added.

12. In that same order, these acronyms stand for: Directorate-General for Support to Small and Medium Enterprises; Small and Medium Enterprises Development Unit; National Program for Microenterprise Support and Social Mobility; Fund for the Development and Micro, Small and Medium Enterprises; Program to Support Small and Medium Enterprises; and National Council for Scientific and Technological Research.

13. In small countries like those in Central America, the boundaries of this economic reality may be local or regional in scope, calling for a corresponding administrative setting of the LED initiative accordingly.

14. The IFC Enterprise Survey (World Bank 2014) included 12,855 interviews with enterprises with more than five employees in 30 LAC countries belonging to

nonagricultural sectors (manufacturing, construction, services, transport, storage, and communications, and information technology). Respondents in Central America were predominantly from the capital cities.

15. Informality has traditionally been high in the LAC region, only second to Sub-Saharan Africa in global terms. The real share of employment in the informal sector is estimated at 71 percent in El Salvador, 81 percent in Guatemala, and 84 percent in Honduras. The multiple ramifications of informality on the economy are not confined to competition environment. The fact that almost 9 out of 10 firms in LAC start formal and remain formal reinforces the pivotal role local authorities play in addressing entrepreneurship because simplifying procedures required to start a business and new firm registration fosters the expansion of the formal economy.

16. Harvard Business School and INCAE facilitated a set of working sessions with public officials from five countries.

17. These initiatives followed the success of similar public-private institutions in pushing for productive transformation in some Asian and European countries, Colombia, and the Dominican Republic.

18. Companion paper. Framework for Public-Private Dialogue in Cities.

19. Every economic sector, traditional or nontraditional, is influenced by GVCs one way or another. Thanks to trade facilitation reform undergone over the last decades and the proximity to large markets, Central America has clearly managed to excel at providing supply chain solutions. However, supply chain and value chain are not exactly the same concept. Value chains revolve around the concept of value and what processes can add more of it, while a supply chain has to do with the efficient moving of inputs for the manufacturing and distribution of a product. Trade facilitation is about making supply chains more effective, and the success of GVCs depends on the efficiency of supply chains.

Bibliography

Bashir, S., Gindling, T. H., and Oviedo, A. M. 2012. *Better Jobs in Central America: The Role of Human Capital*. Washington, DC: World Bank.

Cunha, Barbara, and C. Felipe Jaramillo, C. Felipe. 2013. *Trade and Logistics in Central America*. Washington DC: World Bank.

Fernández -Arias, E. 2010. *Multilateral Safety Nets for Financial Crises*. Washington DC: Inter-American Development Bank.

Fernandez Arias, Eduardo, Manuel Agosin, and Charles Sabel. 2010. "Phantom or Phoenix? Industrial Policies in Latin America Today." In *The Age of Productivity: Transforming Economies from the Bottom Up*, edited by Carmen Pages. Development in the Americas Series. Washington, DC: IDB.

Frost & Sullivan. 2014. *Latin American Contact Center Systems Market 2014 Report*. Frost & Sullivan.

Guillén, R. 2011. "The Effects of the Global Economic Crisis in Latin America." *Revista de Economia Política* 31 (2): 187–202.

IMF (International Monetary Fund). 2012. "Central America, Panama, and the Dominican Republic: Trade Integration and Economic Performance." IMF working paper N. 12/234.

ITC (International Trade Centre). 2014. *Panama Country Report*. ITC.

Lederman, Daniel, Julián Messina, Samuel Pienknagura, and Jamele Rigolini. 2014. *Latin American Entrepreneurs: Many Firms but Little Innovation.* Washington, DC: World Bank.

MPI (Migration Policy Institute). 2013. "Tabulation of Data from the U.S. Census Bureau."

Porter, Michael E. 2013. "Economic and Social Development: The New Learning. Americas Competitiveness Forum." Presentation, Panama City, Panama.

World Bank. 2012a. *Logistics in Central America. The Path to Competitiveness.* Washington, DC: World Bank.

———. 2012b. *World Development Report 2013: Jobs.* Washington, DC: World Bank.

———. 2013a. *Unlocking Central America's Export Potential Knowledge Platform Summary Document.* Washington, DC: World Bank.

———. 2013b. *Shifting Gears to Accelerate Shared Prosperity in Latin America and Caribbean.* Latin America and the Caribbean Poverty and Labor Brief. Washington DC: World Bank.

———. 2014. *Mapping Enterprises in Latin America and the Caribbean.* Enterprise surveys Latin America and the Caribbean series: Note num. 1. Washington, DC: World Bank.

———. 2015a. *Competitive Cities for Jobs and Growth: What, Who and How.* Washington, DC: World Bank.

———. 2015b. *Doing Business in Central America and the Dominican Republic 2015.* Washington, DC: World Bank.

Environmental Benefits Statement

The World Bank Group is committed to reducing its environmental footprint. In support of this commitment, we leverage electronic publishing options and print-on-demand technology, which is located in regional hubs worldwide. Together, these initiatives enable print runs to be lowered and shipping distances decreased, resulting in reduced paper consumption, chemical use, greenhouse gas emissions, and waste.

We follow the recommended standards for paper use set by the Green Press Initiative. The majority of our books are printed on Forest Stewardship Council (FSC)–certified paper, with nearly all containing 50–100 percent recycled content. The recycled fiber in our book paper is either unbleached or bleached using totally chlorine-free (TCF), processed chlorine–free (PCF), or enhanced elemental chlorine–free (EECF) processes.

More information about the Bank's environmental philosophy can be found at http://www.worldbank.org/corporateresponsibility.

green press
INITIATIVE